STO

ACPL
DISCARDED

P9-BHR-637

3 1833 0

10·18·78

Evangelizing the American Jew

by
DAVID MAX EICHHORN

JONATHAN DAVID PUBLISHERS
MIDDLE VILLAGE, N. Y. 11379

EVANGELIZING THE AMERICAN JEW

Copyright © 1978

by

David Max Eichhorn

No part of this book may be used in any manner
without written permission from the publishers.
Address all inquiries to:

Jonathan David Publishers, Inc.
68-22 Eliot Avenue
Middle Village, New York 11379

Library of Congress Cataloging in Publication Data

Eichhorn, David Max.
    Evangelizing the American Jew.

    Bibliography: p.
    Includes index.
    1. Missions to Jews—United States—History.
I. Title.
BV2620.E42   266'.022   77-28975
ISBN 0-8246-0225-0

Printed in the United States of America

2033422

INTRODUCTION

This is an account of Christian attempts to convert the Jews of the United States and Canada. It does not include within its scope an analysis of those conversions that have come about as a direct result of inter-marriage or because of a desire to gain social or economic advantage. It does not deal with those American Jews who have quietly passed into Christianity without outwardly displaying symptoms of a genuine change in their religious convictions. Nor does this study concern itself with Jews who, after being converted to Christianity in other parts of the world, came to the United States or Canada, lived normal Christian lives, and made no attempt to convert Jews to Christianity.

In short, this study is limited to a consideration of the activities of those non-Jewish and born-Jewish Christians who have made definite efforts to draw into the Christian fold the Jews of the United States and Canada—and the tangible results of those efforts.

Fully aware of the delicate nature of his task, the author has endeavored not only to remain within the clearly defined limits of his field of study, but also to write in a manner thoroughly critical yet as objective as his rabbinic convictions and the frailties of human nature permit.

Table of Contents

Chapter One

The Missionary Urge

The ranks of present-day Christianity are cleaved sharply asunder. Two giant armies, known technically as fundamentalists and modernists, are locked in theological combat. One is spurred on by traditions built around an ancient drama. The other fights for principles enunciated nearly two thousand years ago by a man.

The man, a Jew among Jews, born in poverty, reared in the rugged hills of the Galil, moved by love for his people, challenged the authority of his people's oppressors and died a martyr's death.

The drama centers around a god-man, born of a virgin, a miracle worker, faith healer, and caster out of devils, who, scorned and betrayed by the Jews, crucified by the Romans, rose on the third day after his death, ascended into heaven, sits at the right hand of God, and brings eternal salvation to all who believe in the wondrous power of his saving grace.

The man was born about four years before the beginning of the Common Era and died about thirty-three years later. The drama, composed of elements taken from various non-Jewish religions of that time, was the brain child of a Hellenistic Jew, Saul of Tarsus, better known as St. Paul, and was first publicized about the fiftieth year of the Common Era.

The intelligent religious Jew has often manifested a keen interest in and a fond affection for Jesus the man. No genuinely intelligent re-

1

ligious Jew has ever believed that the Paulinian drama is "for real" and, in consequence, has become a follower of its teachings.

Those modern Christians who are disciples of Jesus the man have, to a large degree, in their theology and ethics, "Judaized," without actually converting to Judaism. Those Christians of the past and present who have believed or who still believe fervently in Jesus the god-man never have, do not now, and probably never will comprehend the inner disdain with which the intelligent religious Jew regards their irrational dogmas. Obsessed by a crusading zeal to conquer the world for their Christ, they have never ceased to pound on the doors of the synagogue in the vain hope that the Jews will accept this fantastic story put together by Saul of Tarsus.

It is easy to understand why Pauline Christians have made such desperate efforts to convert the Jews, despite the constant failure of such efforts. The Jew is a continual reminder of the basic weakness of the Pauline position. If the Jews, among whom this god-man lived, taught, and did his magic tricks, refuse to acknowledge the wondrous power of his saving grace, why should those who have not had the benefit of such a close relationship with him acknowledge that he is "the way and the life"? The Jew has been and remains a key figure in the mind and heart of the Christian evangelist. The conversion of the Jews is a logical and emotional necessity if all humanity is ever to be persuaded "to accept Christ."

Another theological factor which makes the conversion of the Jew so important is the fundamentalist belief with regard to "the second coming." For most fundamentalists, the return of the Jews to their ancient homeland, the reestablishment of Jewish rule there, and the conversion of all the Jews are indispensable prerequisites to the Christian millennium. There are considerable differences of opinion about the manner, time, and place of the Jewish acceptance of Christianity. Some believe that only when all Jews have returned to the Holy Land will the mass conversion take place. Others maintain that such a return by all Jews is not necessary. Some say that the Jews will be converted singly and others assert that the entire "Jewish nation" will be converted miraculously and simultaneously. Most Christian fundamentalists look upon the establishment of the State of Israel as an act of direct divine intervention in the affairs of humanity and as a clear indication that the second coming is close at hand. There is a considerable group of fundamental theologians who now oppose missionary efforts to the Jews, not out of consideration for Jewish sensitivities, but because they deem such efforts to be contrary to the Scriptures and the will of God. God, they say, will convert the Jews in His own time and without human aid. It is undoubtedly true that many of these scholarly divines have been helped to reach this conclusion by their knowledge that every organized effort to evangelize the Jews has failed miserably.

The long, shameful story of the Church's treatment of the Jew need not be repeated here. For the Jew, it has been a horrible nightmare of torture, robbery, murder, and exile, a nightmare which is not yet completely over. Large numbers of fundamentalist Christians are still being taught that the modern Jew bears part of the guilt for the murder of their "Christ." Large numbers of fundamentalist Christians are still being told that the Jews will continue to suffer for their "rejection of Christ" until they accept him as their divine redeemer and savior. To this day, Fundamental Christendom, Catholic and Protestant, has not properly repented, apologized, nor atoned for its desperate, ofttimes fiendish, efforts to "persuade" the Jew to renounce and denounce his religion.

Changing Jews into Christians, by fair means or foul, became a major activity of the Church after it was declared the official religion of the Roman Empire in 325 C.E. But it was not until the latter half of the seventeenth century that Christian missionary societies specifically designed to win Jewish souls came into being, a type of approach to the Jew that was regarded in fundamentalist circles, until quite recently, as the best way to handle "the Jewish problem."

The first such organized effort was born in the city of Hamburg, Germany. In 1658, the Reverend Esdras Edzard, a disciple of John Buxdorf, began to try to convert the Jews of Hamburg. He labored toward that end for about fifty years. In 1667 he founded the Esdras Edzard Institute for the conversion of the Jews, the first missionary society formed for the specific purpose of reaching Jews. The Institute lasted for more than two hundred years. It ceased to function about 1888.

The next major effort was made by the Moravian Brethren in the eighteenth century. It established the Institutum Judaicum in Halle, Germany, in 1728 under the leadership of Professor John Henry Callenberg, 1699-1760. Much literature was printed and distributed and many missionaries were trained. The most famed of these was Stephen Schultz, 1714-1776, who traveled all over Europe and Asia in search of Jews who would listen to his gospel message. On one of his journeys, his activities were observed and analyzed by the German poet-dramatist-philosopher, Johann Wolfgang von Goethe, who expressed his reactions with these words:

Mr. Schultz is one of the worst missionaries who have ever disturbed
the nations. The conversion of the Jews is his purpose, and the talent
which directs him to that end is his ability to speak Hebrew and
what belongs to that. . . . He runs through the world, barks at the
Jews, who, at least, are cleverer than he, occupies himself with them,
accomplishes nothing, and gratifies the good people who refresh
him with eating, drinking, etc.

The rationalist spirit, which played much havoc with traditional religion
toward the end of the eighteenth century, was responsible for the demise
of the Institutum Judaicum in 1792.

The high watermark of organized Christian efforts aimed directly at
the Jews was reached in the nineteenth century. During this century
hundreds of societies were founded and labored all over the world to
make the children of Abraham Christians. Only a small number of these
organizations outlived their founders. Most flourished for a few years,
some for a few decades. Fewer than twenty reached their fiftieth birth-
days. Five are still alive: The London Society for Promoting Christianity
amongst the Jews, organized by J.S.C.F. Frey in 1809 and now known
as the Church's Ministry among the Jews; the British Society for the
Propagation of the Gospel among the Jews, 1842, now known as the
International Society for the Evangelization of the Jews and recently
merged with the Barbican Mission to the Jews; the Messianic Testimony,
a British missionary entity which emerged, in 1973, from a combining of
the Mildmay Mission to the Jews (1876) and the Hebrew Christian
Testimony to Israel (1893); the Chicago Hebrew Mission, 1887, founded
by William E. Blackstone and now know as the American Messianic
Fellowship; and the Williamsburg (N.Y.) Mission to the Jews, 1894,
founded by Itsak Leib Joszovics, alias Leopold Cohn, and known since
1924 as the American Board of Missions to the Jews.

The twentieth century has been marked by an ever decreasing interest
in separate missions to the Jews and an ever increasing tendency among
evangelical Christians to regard the conversion of the Jew as an interest-
ing aspect of the general scheme of worldwide evangelization. Most
Christians who cling to "the old time religion" still think of the Jew
as somebody special but, if he is to be won over, it will be through
missionary efforts directed toward unbelievers of all peoples and all non-
Christian religions.

One of the best proofs of the downgrading of evangelism in the
modern Christian world is what happened to Key 73, a mammoth 1973
evangelistic effort participated in by practically every major Christian

denomination. It had no lasting effect on either the Christian or Jewish communities. The average American Christian now looks on a revival as a kind of religious circus to which he and his family may go, if they so desire, to have some good, clean fun, hear some stirring Bible preaching and sing some rousing, old-fashioned, religious songs. American Jewish public relations "experts" and some highly emotional rabbis give Key 73 and similar ventures an importance they do not have by finding in them a threat to Jewish survival which is also not there. The unwise zeal of these Jewish spokesmen gives evangelists some welcome publicity and helps them to draw additional dimes, quarters, and dollar bills from the pockets of naïve Christian peasants, whose sympathies they arouse by tales of how they are being persecuted by Jewish leaders because of their devotion to the gospel message.

With this brief general survey of the past history and present status of Christian efforts to convert Jews, we take leave of the larger scene and turn our attention to the major purpose of this particular book, which is to present an account of Christian attempts to convert the Jews of the United States and Canada.

Chapter Two

The Colonial Period (1607-1800)

THE MATHERS

In 1667, seven years before the first Jew is known to have settled in Boston, the Reverend Increase Mather, 1639-1723, minister of the Second Church of Boston, eminent son of an eminent father and eminent father of an eminent son, preached a series of sermons entitled "The Mystery of Israel's Salvation, Explained and Applyed," published in London in 1669. Why this interest in Jews and Jewish conversion in a colony totally devoid of Jewish inhabitants?

The Massachusetts Puritans were imbued with a deep reverence for Hebraic culture. They were ardent advocates of the theory that the American Indians were the Lost Ten Tribes. More importantly, they were staunch premillennialists. They taught that the Jews were to be dispersed to every part of the world, that this dispersion, once accomplished, would speedily effect the conversion of the Jews and their restoration to Palestine, which restoration would be followed quickly by the second coming. In consequence, they followed with intense interest the excitement created in Jewish circles by the pseudo-Messiah, Sabbatai Zevi, 1626-1676, and the successful effort of Manasseh ben Israel, 1604-1657, to persuade Cromwell to readmit the Jews to England in 1655. They knew that Jews were already living in other colonies in the New

6

World. Now, they believed, the dispersion is almost complete and the time for the conversion of the Jews is at hand. This was the theological conviction that made Puritan Massachusetts the most lively center of Jewish conversionist activity in pre-Revolutionary America.

However, the handfuls of Jews in the other colonies were not entirely neglected by enterprising zealots. They, too, were subjected to lengthy explanations of the sterling attributes of sundry varieties of Christian doctrine. As late as 1816, there were only three thousand Jews in the entire United States. Wherever the American Jew went, before that date and after, he was singled out and told ad nauseum that the Kingdom of God would not become a reality for all mankind until he embraced the dominant faith.

Many of the Jews of this period intermarried. A few converted. But the majority lived and died in the faith of their ancestors. For them the well-meant but futile efforts of their Christian neighbors to induce them to forsake Judaism was a minor discomfort that had to be endured. The problem was not new. Fifteen hundred years of contact with European Christianity and Christians had left a permanent scar upon the memories of the Jewish people that neither kindness nor threat would erase.

The arrival of Jewish settlers in Boston in 1674 and the years following was a great stimulus to the millenarian preachments of the Puritan divines. Judge Samuel Sewall noted in his diary, February 7, 1685 or 1686, that, at the service at the First Church "Mr Moodey preached from Isaiah 12:1 . . . shewing that 'twas chiefly a Directory of Thanks for the Conversion of the Jews; and should get our Praises ready before hand."[1]

The earliest recorded attempt to convert an American Jew dates from about 1692. During a revival meeting that year in Boston's North Church, a young woman went into a trance and predicted that "that Jew whom Mather the Elder has taken great Pains to Convert to the Xn Faith, shall be converted . . . which . . . never was verified . . . for the Jew went over to Jamaica and dyed a hardned wrech."[2]

The second recorded effort was even more disastrous. This time it was Increase Mather's son, Cotton Mather, "Mather the Younger," 1663-1728, who tried his hand at the intriguing game of soul snatching. Sometime during the 1690's, Cotton tried to convert a Boston Jew named "Frazier" by means of trickery. Again it is Judge Sewall's diary which records the episode. Sometime after its unsuccessful conclusion, Sewall wrote:

I find him [Cotton Mather] in Spirituals as failable as in Politicks, or he would not have attempted, by a *Pretended Vision*, to have converted Mr. Frazier a Jew, who had before conceived some good Notions of Xnity: The Consequence was, the *Forgery* was so plainly detected that Mr. C. M. confest it; after which Mr. Frazier would never be perswaded to hear any more of Christianity.[3]

The Jew referred to was probably one of the Frazon brothers, who were merchants in Boston at that time.

But Cotton Mather did not give up. Day after day, month after month, year after year, he hoped and prayed for the time when the Lord would give him the privilege of converting at least one Jew. His diary is full of references to this ambition.[4]

For example, under the date of July 18, 1696, he wrote:

> This day, from the dust, where I lay prostrate before the Lord, I lifted up my cries: For the conversion of the Jewish Nation, and for my own having the happiness, at some time or other, to baptize a Jew, that should by my ministry bee brought home unto the Lord.

His prayers failed to produce the desired result. So Mather, being practical as well as spiritual, determined to wage an active literary campaign against those who were delaying the millennium. His never idle pen did his bidding. Mather's *Faith of the Fathers*, a book designed to attract Jews to Christianity, appeared on April 6, 1699.

Mather busily distributed this volume among his Jewish acquaintances. His diary records, April 28, 1699:

> I have now, for divers years, employ'd much prayer for, and some discourse with, an infidel Jew in this Town; thro' the Desire to glorify my Lord Jesus Christ in the Conversion of that Infidel, if Hee be pleased to accept mee in that Service. I this day renewed my Request unto Heaven for it. And writing a short letter to the Jew, wherein I enclosed my "Faith of the Fathers" and "La Fedei Christiano," I sent it unto him.

The erudite Cotton had written and published the latter work in Spanish, for the purpose, perhaps, of reaching those American Sephardic Jews who were unable to read English.

The hope Cotton nourished of converting at least one Jew seems to have taken on new life. This, on May 21, 1699:

> I had advice from Heaven—Yea, more than that; That I shall shortly see some Harvest of my Prayers and Pains, and the Jewish Nation also.

The heavenly news was verified on September 2, 1699:

> This Day, I understand by letters from Carolina, a thing that exceedingly refreshes me, a Jew there embracing the Christian faith, and my little book, *Faith of the Fathers*, therein a special instrument of good unto him.

In October, 1700, Cotton Mather published another tract especially for Jews, *American Tears upon the Ruines of the Greek Churches*. Also in this year, Samuel Willard, 1639/40-1707, pastor of Boston's Old South Church, published a 210-page book *The Fountain Opened: or, the Great Gospel Privilege of Having Christ Exhibited to Sinful Man, wherein is also proved that there shall be a national calling of the Jews, from Zechariah 13:1*. About the same time, Samuel Stow, c. 1622-1704, a clergyman of Middletown, Conn., wrote *Ten Essays for the Conversion of the Jews*. It seems that these essays were never published. All three works were purely theological and made little or no impression upon the Jews of their time and place.

The first definitely documented conversion of an American Jew to Christianity occurred on Sunday, September 13, 1702, on which day Simon Barnes, also known as Simon the Jew, was baptized in the First Church of Charlestown, Mass., by the Reverend Mr. Bradstreet.[5] From the records of this church and the pages of the invaluable Sewall diary, we learn that Simon was known before his conversion as Simon Judeus, or Simon the Jew, that he was a young man, that he was converted through the efforts of Bradstreet, and that, after his baptism, he assumed the name of Simon Barnes. Nothing more is known concerning the prior or later history of this pioneer American Hebrew Christian. The chroniclers of his generation ignored his existence. This absence of mention speaks louder than printed words. Had he been a worthy man, his every deed would have been extolled as proof of the moral excellence acceptance of Christianity implants in a converted Jew. The best evidence that Barnes was not a worthy man or that he may have reverted to Judaism is furnished by Increase Mather who wrote that Judah Monis was the first Jew "that ever I knew converted in New England."[6] Monis was baptized in 1722.

JUDAH MONIS

Much material is available about the second Jew known to have been converted in colonial New England, much more than may be reproduced here.

Judah Monis was born in Italy on February 4, 1683. He came from a Portuguese Marrano family which migrated to Italy in the sixteenth century and returned to Judaism. He was educated in the *yeshivot* of Leghorn, Italy, and Amsterdam, Holland. There is no documented proof that he received ordination at either of these schools or that he ever officiated as rabbi in any European or American Jewish community. He has been referred to often, in his time and since, as "Rabbi" Monis. So he may be considered the *adam ha-rishon* in the long line of American Hebrew Christian "ex-rabbis" who have taken unto themselves an honorable title to which they have had no rightful claim. Very few validly ordained rabbis have been converted from Judaism to Christianity. Nevertheless a sizable number of the American Hebrew Christians who have made it their business to seek to convert their ex-coreligionists have fraudulently dubbed themselves "ex-rabbi."

It seems that Monis migrated from Italy or Holland to Jamaica and from Jamaica to New York. He became a citizen of New York City on February 28, 1715/16. In his deposition, he described himself as a merchant.

Sometime during the next five years he moved to Boston. On June 29, 1720, he presented to the overseers of Harvard College a copy of a Hebrew grammar he had written. In recognition of this scholarly achievement, Harvard awarded him an M.A. degree the same year, the only degree conferred on a Jew by Harvard prior to the nineteenth century.

Several ministers, and especially the aged Increase Mather, took a deep interest in Monis and, within two years, persuaded him to become a Christian. One "theological" argument that Monis found very convincing was that only bona fide Christians could serve on the faculty of Harvard College; and Monis was eager to become a member of that faculty. There is no mention of Cotton Mather in any of the Monis documents. The two must have known one another; yet their names are never linked together. Cotton Mather published his last "Jewish" tract, *Faith Encouraged*, in 1718.

Monis was publicly baptized in the Common Hall at Harvard College on March 27, 1722. Increase Mather, an eighty-three-year-old semi-invalid, was scheduled to preside but he was not well enough to attend. His place was taken by the Reverend Benjamin Colman, 1643-1747, a prominent Boston clergyman and a Harvard fellow. Both Increase Mather and Colman seem to have had some doubts about Monis' sincerity. In Colman's charge to Monis, delivered before the formal baptismal rite was performed, he said,

It is easy for you to receive a place in the visible Church and the Kingdom of the Messiah, but within it there is an Invisible State of Grace and Salvation; Are you *in That?* . . . Be sure that You have no By-ends, no sinister and corrupt *Views,* no *worldly* Advantages, in what you do this day. GOD forbid, that *these* should act you. We hope, *we believe* they don't; You have *solemnly professed* that they do not.

This is an exact reproduction of the way in which these remarks were later printed. The purport of Colman's statement is unmistakable.

Following the baptismal ceremony, Monis entertained the large gathering, "as numerous an Assembly as the place would admit,"

with a learned Discourse, answering (from holy Scripture and their own Approved Authors) Nine of the chief Arguments brought by modern Jews to prove that the Messiah is not yet come. He introduced His Discourse with those Words, Psalm 116.10; and concluded with a solemn Profession of Faith in the Messiah already come.

Soon afterwards, Monis' remarks were published in three parts, titled "The Truth," "The Whole Truth," and "Nothing but the Truth." Increase Mather wrote the introduction to this series of essays, which were bound at first in one volume and later issued as individual tracts. They were widely and eagerly read by the Christian clergy. In his introduction, Mather dwells at some length on the fact that several Jews, who became Christians in order to secure positions on the faculties of European Protestant universities, later recanted and returned to Judaism. Lest his remarks become too pointed, Mather added, reassuringly:

"There is no cause to fear that Mr. Monis will renounce his Christianity, since he did embrace it voluntarily and gradually, and with much consideration, and from the Scriptures in the Old Testament."

There is no evidence that, following his conversion, Monis ever attempted to induce any Jews to become Christians. From 1722 until his death forty-two years later, he appears to have lived an exemplary Christian life. The one concession made to his Jewish background was that, to the end of his life, he observed the Sabbath on Saturday.

Five weeks after baptism, Monis was elected instructor in Hebrew at Harvard at a salary of fifty pounds a year. A year later his salary was raised to eighty pounds. In 1724 he married Abigail Marret. They had no children. His salary grew until, by 1748, he was making almost as much as a Harvard head tutor. He published his grammar in 1735 and

used it as a textbook in his classes. After 1748, the size of his salary and
the number of his students began to decline. Hebrew was not a popular
subject at Harvard. By 1753, his instructor's income had sunk so low that
he was compelled to supplement it by again going into business. In 1760
his wife died and, in that same year, Monis resigned from the Harvard
faculty. In November he sold his library and went to live with his
wife's sister's husband, the Reverend John Martyn of Northborough,
Mass. He died on April 25, 1764. He is buried in the cemetery of
Northborough's Second Church. The inscription on his tombstone concludes as follows:

> A native branch of Jacob see,
> Which once from off its olive broke,
> Regrafted from the living tree,
> Of the reviving cup partook;
> From teeming Zion's fertile womb,
> As dewy drops in early morn,
> Or rising bodies from the tomb,
> At once be Israel's nation born.

RELIGION IN EIGHTEENTH-CENTURY AMERICA

There were two conflicting religious philosophies in seventeenth-cen-
tury America: the Puritan belief that the Church should control the State
and the Anglican principle that the State should control the Church. The
chief stronghold of the first was, of course, New England, and of the
second, the colony of Virginia. The type of colonist who began to arrive
in America at the end of the seventeenth and the beginning of the eighteenth centuries did not favor either of these philosophies. Puritanism was
too rigorous and too cold. Anglicanism was not sufficiently democratic.

The American religious mood which dominated the eighteenth century
favored a spiritual way of life that would be warmer and more humane
than either Puritanism or Anglicanism and would lead to a complete
separation of Church and State. This mood created a breach between
the old and the new that finally resulted in the War of the Revolution.
The Loyalists or Tories were chiefly Puritans of the old school and
Anglicans. Those who followed the lead of the Continental Congress
were, for the most part, liberal Puritans, Methodists, and Deists.

Deism, a system of beliefs which contributed greatly to the downfall
of clericalism in eighteenth-century America, had its roots in primitive
Christianity and was revived by the spirit of scientific realism that followed the Renaissance. The principal effects of Deistic thought upon

American religious life were that it led to a schism within the Puritan church which split that denomination into Congregationalists and Unitarians; and that it influenced the thinking and actions of many of those who established the American republic and embodied the principles of freedom and justice in the American constitution. The best known of this splendid group of liberal and enlightened men are John Adams, Benjamin Franklin, Thomas Jefferson, Thomas Paine, and George Washington. These blessed rebels initiated a brief period of political and intellectual sanity that may well be called "the golden age" of American liberalism.

These revolutionary heroes had no interest whatever in converting Jews to Christianity. Their only desire was that people of all faiths should live under the American flag in harmony with one another and at peace with the world.

Tom Paine wrote the only piece with an anticonversionist theme that has been discovered in the literature of pre-Revolutionary America. It is a satirical poem, "A Bigot's Immersion," printed in 1775 in the *Pennsylvania Magazine* of Philadelphia:

> An unbelieving Jew one day
> Was skating o'er the icy way,
> Which, being brittle, let him in
> Just deep enough to catch his chin,
> And in that woful plight he hung,
> With only power to move his tongue.
>
> A brother skater near at hand,
> A Papist born in foreign land,
> With hasty steps directly flew
> To save poor Mordecai the Jew;
> "But first," quoth he, "I must enjoin
> That you renounce your faith for mine,
> There's no entreaties else will do,
> 'Tis heresy to help a Jew."
>
> "Forswear mine fait—no! Got forbit!
> Dat would be ferry base indeed;
> Come, never mind such dings as deese,
> Tink, tink, how ferry hart it freeze;
> More coot you do, more coot you be,
> Vat signifies your fait to me,
> Come tink agen how cold and vet,
> And help me out von little bet."
>
> "By holy mass! 'tis hard, I own,
> To see a man both hang and drown,

Yet can't relieve him from his plight,
Because he is an Israelite;
The church refuses all assistance,
Beyond a certain pale and distance,
So, all the service I can lend
Is praying for your soul, my friend."

"Pray for mine soul! ha, ha, you make me laugh;
You petter help me out py half.
Mine soul, I varrant, vill take care
To pray for her own self, mine tear;
So tink a little now for me,
'Tis I am in the hole—not she."

"The church forbids it, friend, and saith
That all shall die who have no faith."

"Vell, if I must pelieve, I must,
But help me out vun little first."

"No, not an inch without amen,—
That seals the whole."

"Vell, hear me den:
I hear renounce for coot and all,
De race of Jews both great and small;
'Tis de vurst trade peneath de sun;
Or vurst religion, dat's all vun.
Dey cheat and get deir living py it
And lie and swear de lie is right.
I'll go to mass as soon as ever
I get to toder side de river;
So help me out now, Christian friend,
Dat I may do as I intend."

"Perhaps you do intend to cheat,
If once you get upon your feet."

"No, no; I do intend to be
A Christian—such a one as dee."

For, thought the Jew, he is as much
A Christian man as I am such.
The bigot Papist, joyful-hearted,
To hear the heretic converted,
Replied to the designing Jew—
"This was a happy fall for you;
You'd better die a Christian now,
For if you live you'll break your vow."
Then said no more, but in a trice
Popped Mordecai beneath the ice.

The majority of Revolutionary-period Americans were not Deists and did not share the Deistic disdain for narrow sectarianism. However, even the most conservative preachers were so engrossed in the political turmoil of the latter half of the eighteenth century that they paid scant attention to the leisure-time sport of Jewish evangelizing.

EZRA STILES

During this time of national gestation, there was one famous Christian minister and educator who made some earnest though ineffectual efforts to make Christians out of his Jewish friends.

He was Ezra Stiles, 1727-1795, Congregationalist clergyman, friend of Benjamin Franklin, fine Hebrew student, most learned man of his generation in New England, one of the founders of Rhode Island College, now Brown University, pastor in Newport, R. I., 1755-1778, active patriot in the Revolutionary War, and president of Yale College, 1778-1795.

Stiles' interest in Hebrew culture was a lifelong passion. He read Hebrew fluently and intelligently and taught his children to do likewise. He frequently attended the Newport synagogue services. His diary contains extensive references to the Jews of Newport, their rabbis, religious holidays, customs, and traditions. One rabbi, Haym Isaac Karigal, was an especially close and dear friend. In 1781, sometime after Karigal's death, Stiles persuaded Aaron Lopez, a prominent Jewish citizen of Newport, to present a portrait of Karigal to the library of Yale College.

Despite his admiration for Hebrew language and literature and his affection for Rabbi Karigal, Stiles' Christianity prevented him from looking with favor upon the theological teachings of Judaism. Once, having just returned from a synagogue service, he wrote in his diary: "How melancholy to behold an Assembly of Worshippers of Jehovah, Open and professed Enemies to a crucified Jesus!"

When Aaron Lopez died in 1782, Stiles praised him highly. Lopez was a paragon of virtue,

> without a single Enemy & the most universally beloved by an extensive acquaintance of any man I ever knew. His Beneficence to his Family Connexions, to his Nation, & to all the world is almost without a Parallel. He was my intimate Friend & Acquaintance.

But—

Oh! how often have I wished that sincere pious & candid mind could have perceived the Evidences of Xty, perceived the Truth as it is in Jesus Christ, known that Jesus was the Messiah predicted by Moses & the Prophets! The amiable and excellent Characters of a Lopez, of a Menasseh ben Israel, of a Socrates, & a Gangenelli, would almost persuade us to hope that their Excellency was infused by Heaven, and that the virtuous & good of all Nations & Religions, notwithstanding their Delusions, may be brought together in Paradise on the Xtian System.

Whenever and wherever possible, Stiles expounded the doctrines of Christianity to the Newport Jews. He made a careful study of the essays of "Rabbi" Monis, hoping to discover therein arguments with which to combat Jewish disbelief. His diary mentions a number of times that he discussed theological matters in his home with young Jews. He often attempted to convert Rabbi Karigal who turned aside such attempts courteously and good-naturedly. Once, after Karigal had expressed a desire to attend his service, "I sent my son," wrote Stiles, "to wait upon him to his house before Meeting and he came accompanied with two Jews." The sermonic notes of Stiles' sermon on that occasion indicate that his remarks were directed primarily at his Jewish listeners.

Beginning with the premise that "The Seed of Jacob are a chosen and favorite people of the Most High, and the subjects of the peculiar care of Heaven, and of most marvellous Dispensations," he goes on to hold out hope for their future salvation, if they but recognize their Messiah.[7]

Stiles' efforts to convert Newport Jewry were completely unsuccessful. His diary does record one conversion which allegedly took place in Philadelphia.

I was told last week that Mr. Hays, a Jew of Philadelphia, was lately converted to Christianity, was baptized by Reverend Morgan Edwards & Become a member of the Baptist Church at Philadelphia. Mr. Hays Brother lives here in Newport. Two days ago I asked him about it. He said he knew nothing of it, & did not believe it; and added, if his Brother had become a Christian, it was only to answer his Ends, he was not sincere, for he never knew one sincere in changing his Religion and becoming a Christian. . . . But I suppose the Thing is true; for Mr. Edwards is now here at the Commencement at Providence [of Rhode Island College], and told this story in Town last week. It is said that another of Mr. Hays Family, who lived in N. York, once became a Christian but afterwards renounced Christianity for Judaism.

Morgan Edwards was a prominent Baptist minister in Philadelphia from 1761 to 1771. His fondness for strong drink resulted in his being forced to give up the ministry. The citation from Stiles' diary is dated September 8, 1771. Coming so close to the end of Mr. Edwards' involuntarily terminated ministerial career, the conversion of Mr. Hays may possibly have been a product of Mr. Edwards' alcoholically stimulated imagination.

* * * *

According to George A. Kohut, "intermarriage with Christians about this time was not uncommon in New York and proselytes were made in goodly numbers."[8] Kohut then qualifies this statement by quoting N. Taylor Phillips:

> Among the Jewish community in New York, though a man were even to publicly renounce Judaism, nevertheless he could not become a Christian in the full sense . . . for he was, notwithstanding, always regarded as a Jew . . . something in the nature of a "dead-wall between the church and the synagogue, or like blank leaves between the Old and New Testaments," being to Jews always a Christian and to Christians always a Jew.[9]

CANADA

During the French occupation of Canada, neither Protestant nor Jew was allowed to dwell in that country. After the English took possession of Canada in 1759, a few Jewish families settled in the conquered territory.

A certain J. Bicheno of Providence, R. I., wrote a tract titled *A Friendly Address to the Jews* in 1795. According to Louis Meyer, Bicheno "took an especial interest in the Spanish-Portuguese Jews in Montreal."[10] This is the only reference found which indicates any overt attempt was ever made to convert Canadian Jews prior to the nineteenth century.

Chapter Three

Joseph Samuel Christian Frederick Frey

We now take temporary leave of the American scene in order to consider the European phase of the career of the American missionary pioneer whose long name stands at the head of this chapter.

Joseph Samuel Christian Frederick Frey was born in Maynstockheim, near Wuerzburg, in the province of Franconia, Germany, on September 21, 1771. His father was a Hebrew teacher named Levy. The infant was initiated into the covenant of Abraham as Joseph Samuel Levy. He was given a traditional Jewish education and rearing. At the age of six, he contracted smallpox, which permanently injured the sight of his left eye and gave him a speech impediment he was never able to overcome. When he was eighteen years old, he was sent to the province of Hesse to serve as a *melamed* (Hebrew teacher). Three years later, he was granted rabbinic permission to act as a *chazan* (synagogue cantor). One year after that he passed an examination before the rabbi of Hesse Cassel which permitted him to be a *shochet* (ritual slaughterer) also.

Having a wandering disposition, he soon tired of the duties of his multiple religious offices. He used some money he had saved to travel about western Germany. In Hamburg, with his funds almost exhausted, Levy accepted an offer to become a Hebrew tutor for a Jewish family in Schwerin, a community three-days' journey from Hamburg by stagecoach. On the stagecoach Levy made the acquaintance of a young Christian, an agent for a Hamburg tobacco company, en route to Rostock, a city northeast of Schwerin. As they traveled, this gentleman attempted to convince Levy that, on the matter of the Messiah, the Christians were right and the Jews were wrong. When Levy got off the coach at Schwerin, he was grievously discomfited to discover that the teaching position promised him did not exist. Very much in need of financial help, he journeyed on to Rostock to enlist the aid of his recent traveling companion. But, alas, the tobacco salesman-evangelist was nowhere to be found. The Rostock inns refused to accept Levy as a guest because of a local law that forbade Jews to remain in the city overnight without special magisterial permission. Levy finally gained the sympathy of an innkeeper by stating that he had come to Rostock "to inquire into the truth of the Christian religion, and was resolved to embrace it in case I should become convinced of its veracity."[1]

The innkeeper took Levy to a clergyman, who examined the young man and, discovering that he knew very little about Christianity, suspected that he was moved by worldly motives. Levy was then taken before a magistrate, subjected to further questioning, and finally was given permission to remain in Rostock as long as he showed signs of attempting to become a sincere follower of the Christian way of life.

> I was told that there had been many Jews who had embraced Christianity only for secular advantages, and lived afterwards as heathens, which made them very cautious of receiving any before they were thoroughly convinced of their sincerity.[2]

In order to prove his sincerity, Levy was forbidden to accept any monetary gifts and was ordered to work for a living. He was not regarded as very desirable Rostock citizen material for, three weeks later, he was told "to apply to ministers in three neighboring towns, and, if none of them were willing to instruct me, I should return, and they would take me under their patronage."[3]

He then went to Wismar, where he apprenticed himself to a shoemaker for a period of three years and found a clergyman who consented to give him Christian instruction twice a week. He was not well treated and was accused frequently of being a hypocrite. After he had worked in Wismar for one and a half years, his employer went out of business. Levy then found similar employment in the city of New Brandenburg. After another one and a half years of apprenticeship, he became a fully qualified journeyman shoemaker.

A few months before his apprenticeship expired, he was baptized publicly, "or, more correctly speaking, 'sprinkled.' " Twenty-nine years later, Levy came to the conclusion that the correct method of baptism is not sprinkling but immersion, and so he was re-baptized by immersion in 1827. In that year, a Baptist church in New York City invited Frey to become its pastor, with the proviso that he first become a Baptist. It was after receiving this invitation that Frey arrived at the aforementioned conclusion.

The initial baptismal ceremony took place in the Lutheran church at New Brandenburg on May 8, 1798. The minister who presided gave Levy three new names, Christian Frederick Frey.

> The first is expressive of the religion I embraced; the second, which signified "rich in peace," to express his good wishes; and the last, as my surname, to remind me of the text from which he preached on this occasion, viz., John 8:32 and 8:36, "And ye shall know the truth and the truth shall make you *free*. . . . If the Son therefore shall make you *free*, ye shall be *free* indeed." *Free* in English signifies the same as Frey in the German language, but is pronounced Fry, and should be pronounced in English the same as the pronoun *they;* but most of the people, while I was in England, attending more to the origin and signification than to the spelling of my name, pronounced it generally as if written *free:* and I myself got into the habit of doing the same.

So the Jew, Joseph Samuel Levy, was metamorphosed into the Christian, Joseph Samuel Christian Frederick Frey. In all his writings, he employed his full Christian name.

Late in 1798, he secured employment in Prentzlow, Prussia. While in Prentzlow, he left the Lutherans and joined the United Brethren. Six months later he went to Berlin to continue to work as a shoemaker. This occupation was too strenuous for him. He was ill frequently. He decided to abandon shoemaking and become a schoolteacher. Just as he was about to implement this decision, he had a vision in which Jesus ordered him to become a missionary. Obedient to the summons, Frey enrolled, in February, 1800, in the Berlin Missionary Seminary. This was a non-denominational school supervised by the Reverend Mr. Jaenicke of the Berlin Bohemian Church.

In June, 1801, Jaenicke informed his students that three missionaries were wanted by the London Missionary Society to go to Africa. Frey and two others volunteered. They left Berlin on July 11. They arrived in England on September 15. They waited in London for more than two months for a ship to take them to Africa. Impatient with the long delay, Frey had another vision in which he was instructed to give up his African intentions and to remain in England to preach to its Jews.

Again Frey quickly obeyed the dream message by writing a letter, on November 24, to the London Missionary Society, asking to be permitted to stay in London for at least one year to work among the Jews.

One unsuccessful effort had already been made in London to do missionary work among the Jews. On August 28, 1796, the Reverend William Cooper, a twenty-year-old clergyman, had commenced preaching to the Jews but his preachments had produced no new Christians. After about a month's deliberation, the London Missionary Society decided to renew the experiment.

On December 21, 1801, Frey was informed that he would be kept in England, for a trial period of one year, as a Jewish missionary. In February, 1802, Frey enrolled in the Gosport Missionary Seminary in order to learn the English language and improve his missionary technique. He preached his first sermon to London Jewry at the Zion Chapel in May, 1802. His employers were so pleased with his initial effort that they decided to keep him in England indefinitely and to train him for his chosen field of work.

He remained at Gosport Seminary until May, 1805, and thereafter devoted himself full time to missionary work. At first he was not provided with a chapel and had to conduct his meetings in his home. On July 6, he began to give weekly lectures to the Jews at the Reverend Mr. Ball's chapel in Jewry Street, Aldgate. This continued for about a year. Then he moved to Zion Chapel for a year and then back to Ball's chapel. Three months of each year were spent traveling about collecting funds for the Society.

His first missionary lectures were well attended by Jews; but their curiosity was rapidly satisfied. His audiences kept dwindling until, finally, very few came to hear him. He did manage to baptize three Jews in 1806. One of them was his future wife, Hannah Cohen, whom he baptized September 18, 1806, and must have married shortly thereafter, since their first-born, John, arrived on September 6, 1807.[4] Three other children were born to this Hebrew Christian couple during their years in England. A fifth and last child was born in New York City in June, 1827, when Frey was fifty-five years old. This indicates that Mrs. Frey was considerably younger than her husband.

At last, attendance at Frey's lectures ceased entirely and he was forced to abandon this method of attracting prospective converts. In January,

1807, he opened a school for Jewish children, in the hope that this would provide a new and better means of winning Jewish souls. The rabbis of the neighborhood denounced him so vigorously that he was able to obtain only twelve pupils. The London Missionary Society began to realize that their Jewish work was not yielding a very large return. Frey, too, was very discouraged by his lack of success. In October, 1807, he submitted a memorandum to the Society's board of directors stating that his lectures had failed to produce conversions because no provision had been made for the support and protection of those poor Jews who might be converted. He stated further that the Free School had been unsucessful because the children who attended were not boarded or clothed. He was certain that if "some kind of workhouse or small manufactory might be established, where many Jews of both sexes and different ages might be employed" and if arrangements were made to "board, clothe, and educate the children till a certain age, and then bring them forward into suitable situations among Christians," the Jewish work of the Society would prosper exceedingly.

Much to Frey's chagrin, the board refused to adopt his recommendations and directed him to continue his work in the same manner as heretofore. Determined to have his own way, Frey set about gathering a group of people who shared his point of view. On August 4, 1808, this group established a formal organization, the London Society, "for visiting and relieving the sick and distressed, and instructing the ignorant, especially such as were of the Jewish nation."[5] Frey was elected president.

At first the London Society declared that it wished to be considered a subsidiary of the London Missionary Society, provided that the latter would agree to certain conditions. These, presented by Frey, were as follows: The mission to the Jews was to be separated completely from the other activities of the Society; it was to have an independent board; Frey was to be a member of this board; and Frey's salary was to be increased. These bold demands were indignantly rejected. Frey was told that "his wants were more liberally supplied than those of three-fourths of the Dissenting ministers in England." The directors also reminded him that they had furnished his house and had, at times, given him money in addition to his regular salary.

When Frey carried word of his rebuff back to his friends, they decided that the time had come to break away completely from the London Missionary Society. On March 1, 1809, they issued a declaration of independence and announced the assumption of a new name, the London Society for Promoting Christianity amongst the Jews. This society has continued to exist to the present day, being now known as the Church's Ministry to the Jews. It is the oldest of all contemporary missionary efforts organized for the specific purpose of converting Jews. The founders of the new society declared that a major weakness of the London Missionary Society was that it was composed entirely of Dissenters. The London Society for Promoting Christianity amongst the Jews would welcome into its ranks not only Dissenters but members of the Established Church and all other Protestant denominations. On March 24, Frey informed the London Missionary Society that he was leaving its employ to direct the program of the organization he had helped establish. He condemned the London Missionary Society for having rejected his suggestions. He declared his work with them had failed because of their lack of understanding and appreciation. He revealed that

> notwithstanding the Gospel has been preached three years, and is now preached four times a week professedly to the Jews, yet there are not five of them that attend regularly; and, though a free school has been opened for nearly two years, there are only six children that receive instruction.

The new society now proceeded to carry into operation the plans which Frey had advocated so strongly. Unlike the London Missionary Society, the London Jews Society, the name by which the LSPCJ was best known for many years, was composed chiefly of members of the Church of England, although its membership also included some from other denominations, mostly Dissenters and Quakers. A place of worship was purchased in Spitalfields, a church formerly occupied by Huguenots. It was renamed the Jews Chapel and Frey was installed as minister.

The membership of the London Jews Society increased rapidly. It was soon recognized as one of London's outstanding philanthropies. Within a few years, it had established three schools for Jewish children and a cotton spinning plant and printing office for the employment of Jewish converts. The printing office was used mainly for the publication of tracts for the Jews and for the members and friends of the Society. These tracts were distributed profusely in Great Britain, Europe, Asia, and North America. They were directly responsible for the formation of the fiirst missionary society to the Jews in the United States, the society founded in Boston in 1816 by Miss Hannah Adams.

In 1813 the London Jews Society decided to erect a second chapel in Bethnel Green, to be known as the Episcopal Chapel, in which only Anglican doctrines would be taught to the Jews. The cornerstone of the new edifice was laid on April 7, with impressive ceremonies. The Society president and presiding officer was no less a personage than His Royal Highness, the Duke of Kent. The Duke's leadership of the Society gave it a temporary importance that far exceeded its merit.

The Society's magazine[6] describes the imposing occasion:

> His Royal Highness and train passed through a line formed by the militia with presented arms, the band playing "God Save the King," in the following order:

COMMITTEE

STEWARDS

CLERGY

The Rev. J. S. C. F. Frey
Schoolmaster

JEWISH BOYS—two and two
Schoolmistress

JEWISH GIRLS—two and two
Converted Jews

VICE PRESIDENTS
Master Builder, with a Mallet, Silver Trowel, and Coins,
placed upon a Crimson Velvet Cushion.
Architects

HIS ROYAL HIGHNESS THE DUKE OF KENT
Right Honourable the Lord Mayor
Sheriffs, and Aldermen,
Nobility, Clergy,
and Gentry.

> The Committee and Stewards filed off right and left, to receive His Royal Highness and train upon a platform erected for the purpose, in front of a semicircular theatre filled with about 1000 ladies—the stone and materials being arranged in the area between.

What a day of triumph that was for the Reverend Joseph Samuel Christian Frederick Frey, who had once been merely Melamed-Chazan-Shochet Joseph Samuel Levy!

This display of power won the Society the admiration and support of Lewis Way, a wealthy philanthropist, who, from this time on, played a prominent role in its activities.

The year 1813 is also important in the history of Jewish missions because it marks the first effort of converted Jews to organize themselves into some sort of mutual aid society. On September 9, 1813, forty-one Hebrew Christians assembled in the Jews Chapel and formed the "Beni Abraham," "for prayer and other purposes relating to the spiritual welfare of their brethren."[7] Frey was, of course, elected Chairman. The "Children of Abraham" published their rules and regulations on page 86 of the Society's sixth report and concluded their pronouncement with the following postcript: "N. B. Donations and Subscriptions will be thankfully received by the Treasurer, at the Jews Chapel, Church street, Spitalfields." Thus began the first of the many Hebrew Christian Associations, Brotherhoods, and Alliances that have solicited Christian contributions and Jewish toleration in the nineteenth and twentieth centuries.

The London Jews Society did not long enjoy national acceptance and acclaim. Little more than a year after the cornerstone laying, the Society had lost not only its high standing in philanthropic circles but was involved in serious financial difficulties. Mismanagement of funds and continual quarreling between the Anglican and Dissenting factions were chiefly responsible for the Society's plight. Its ambitious missionary program was in danger of complete collapse. It owed more than than twelve thousand pounds. The Duke of Kent resigned his presidency late in 1814 and withdrew his patronage. The end of the London Jews Society seemed imminent.

At this critical point, Lewis Way offered to assume full responsibility for the debts of the organization, provided that it would become completely subject to the beliefs and practices of the Church of England. The offer was accepted. Within a few months, the Society was completely reorganized and Anglicized. All non-Anglican officers and workers were dropped except the Reverend J. S. C. F. Frey. In March, 1815, the Jews Chapel was closed and its approximately fifty Hebrew Christian members and their activities were transferred to the Episcopal Jews Chapel in Bethnal Green. Frey was to continue as missionary and fund raiser but not as preacher. Because he was not an ordained Anglican priest, the sermonizing to the Jews was to be done by Anglican clergy connected with the society.

The sphere of usefulness in which Mr. Frey may hereafter be called to act, with the greatest benefit to the cause of his Jewish brethren, is a point which as yet the Committee do not feel themselves competent to determine; but they are of the opinion that, under all the circumstances of his peculiar case, the prosecution of his studies, with a view to ordination, and his presence in London, for the purpose of assisting the operations of the Society, are highly expedient.[8]

In the eighth report of the Society, page 24, it is stated that "a door not being at present opened for Mr. Frey's ordination in the Established Church, the Committee judged it expedient to give him the designation of Superintendent" and to place under his care the printing office and the schools. The cotton spinning factory had proved costly and unprofitable and had been closed.

So matters stood in June, 1816. Frey was busily engaged in raising funds for the London Jews Society. He was in charge of its conversionist activities. Eventually he might have been given Anglican ordination.

He never received that distinction. In June, 1816, Frey's connection with the London Jews Society ended quickly and permanently. He was accused by a Mrs. Josephson, the wife of a convert, of having seduced her. Although before marriage this woman had been a prostitute and had had a number of illegitimate children, the charge was investigated. It was learned, from Frey's housemaids, from the girls in a house of ill fame in Ipswich, and from other sources that Mrs. Josephson had not been the only recipient of Frey's amorous attentions.

When the evidence was presented, Frey admitted his guilt.

> The result of which was, lest the disgraceful occurrence should injure the reputation of the London Society, perhaps for ever, that he was, in as quiet a way as possible (for no expositor, no friend of Israel noticed the event) sent out, at the expence of the London Society, to New York, America.[9]

The London Jews Society did everything it could to protect Frey by concealing the cause of his dismissal. To all who inquired, it would only say that he had not been dismissed because of any financial irregularities.

For many years after Frey came to America, his friends and his enemies tried without success to get the truth out of the London Jews Society. His friends said he had been discarded because he was not an Anglican. His enemies alleged that he had stolen money from the Society and had fled to America with a woman not his wife. In the ninth edition of his *Narrative*, published in New York City in 1832, Frey writes that he was forced out of the English missionary society because he was not a member of the Established Church. All these explanations are inaccurate. The London Jews Society discharged Frey because it disapproved of his extramarital activities and it sent him to the United States to avoid a public scandal.

Accompanied by his wife and children, Frey left London for the United States on July 23, 1816. His ship arrived off Sandy Hook on September 8. One week later, September 15, 1816, the Reverend Joseph Samuel Christian Frederick Frey landed in New York City.

Chapter Four

The Earliest Organized Efforts (1800 - 1820)

The decline of theocratic sentiment and the growth in democratic thought in eighteenth-century America have already been noted. While a large percentage of American churchgoers continued to adhere to principles rooted in strict Puritanism or stern Calvinism or stately Anglicanism, the number of adherents to these religio-political philosophies steadily decreased. The religious spirit of the age was more truly represented by the rapidly growing Methodist and Baptist churches, the emphasis placed on individual salvation through faith, the development of the revivalist type of evangelism, the desire of the intellectuals to square theology with scientific thought, the ever increasing number of denominations, and the waning power of the clergy.

The orthodox mood continued strong in the Presbyterian and Congregationalist churches. It is not surprising, therefore, that the urge to convert the heathen was more frequently manifested in these two denominations than by the Methodists and the Baptists during the first half of the nineteenth century. The Methodists and the Baptists were too busy winning members from the older groups and consolidating their organizational gains to put much emphasis on winning the souls of unbelievers. Much lip worship was paid to the necessity of winning the world for the Methodist and Baptist Christ; but most of the actual missionary work was done by the Presbyterians and the Congregationalists and that staunchly Calvinistic sect, the Dutch Reformed Church.

No formal effort was made to convert the Jews of the United States prior to 1816. This does not mean that the spirit of the Mathers was completely dead. Their dreams, their hopes lived on and needed but the magic touch of some devoted and dynamic personalities to be translated into concrete plans of action. A quartet of such personalities was very much alive during the first quarter of the nineteenth century. They gave the Jewish missionary movement in North America its initial push. Their names: Hannah Adams, the Reverend Philip Milledoler, Peter Wilson, and the Reverend J. S. C. F. Frey.

HANNAH ADAMS

On April 3, 1804, the Reverend John Henry Livingston, 1746-1825, eminent Dutch Reformed theologian, first professor of the first Dutch Reformed theological seminary in the United States, delivered a lecture before the New York Missionary Society on the subject of Jewish conversion.

At about the same time an intense interest in Jewish history and literature and a passionate devotion to the cause of Jewish evangelization began in the life of a frail, middle-aged, bookish spinster of Boston, Hannah Adams. Hannah was no ordinary woman. In a period when education was considered an exclusively male prerogative, she dared to write books for a living and to publish them under her own name. Her first volume antedated the initial work of "Miss" George Eliot by more than sixty years. She was, so far as is known, the first American female professional litterateur.

Hannah Adams was born in Medfield, Mass., on October 2, 1755. She was one of "the" Massachusetts Adamses, a lineal descendant of Henry Adams of Braintree and a distant cousin of President John Adams. Her father was such an omnivorous reader that he was known as "Book Adams." His daughter inherited his desire for learning. In her *Memoirs* she wrote, "My first idea of the happiness of Heaven was of a place where we should find our thirst for knowledge fully gratified." She was such a sickly child that she was unable to go to school. Instead, the theological students who boarded with her father taught her such unwomanly subjects as Latin, Greek, and logic. She became interested in religion at an early age and read widely and deeply in works of religious lore.

As a result of her studies she wrote her first book in 1784, *An Alphabetical Compendium of the Various Sects Which Have Appeared from the Beginning of the Christian Era to the Present Day.* Despite its unwieldy title, the book enjoyed a large sale. Although the publisher got most of the profits, Miss Adams won recognition as a writer of ability and she determined to devote her life to the profession of literature. A second edition of the *Compendium*, published in 1791, had an even greater sale than the first and was of greater financial benefit to the author. In 1799 she wrote *A Summary History of New England* and, in 1805, an abridged version of the same for use in elementary schools. She was never in good health and was handicapped by poor eyesight. A number of prominent New Englanders, including Josiah Quincy and Stephen Higginson, recognizing her unusual literary talent, settled a life annuity on her shortly after 1800 which, in her later years, relieved her of financial worry. In 1804 she gave further evidence of her religious interest and knowledge by writing *The Truth and Excellence of the Christian Religion.*

She maintained a correspondence with the famous French liberal, Abbé Gregoire, who sent her his writings on the subject of granting citizenship to the Jews. His views interested her greatly. She determined to make a thorough study of Jewish history. She began in 1804 and labored diligently for eight years. The result was her best known work, *The History of the Jews,* published in the United States in 1812 and by the London Jews Society in England in 1818.

After her death, a close friend, discussing the period of her life that began in 1804, wrote:

> Many said, "If you want to know Miss Adams, you must talk to her about the Jews." And this was indeed, a subject that always called forth the energy of her mind. She had faithfully studied their history, and she venerated the antiquity of their origin. Her inquiring mind was deeply interested by their "wonderful destination, peculiar habits, and religious rites." She felt for them as a suffering and persecuted people; and she felt yet more, when she considered them as a standing monument of that religion, which she regarded as the first and best of God's gifts to man. It was the long contemplation of this chosen race that induced her, amidst all the obstacles that were in her way, to write their history. It was an arduous labor.[1]

Miss Adams was very eager to engage actively in the task of Christianizing the Jew; but no society existed for this purpose in the United States. Prior to 1811, she does not seem to have been aware of the Jewish work of the London Missionary Society. In that year she learned about this when Frey's *Narrative*, first published in England in 1809, was re-published in the United States and widely circulated. Her longing to help save the Jews was given a welcome means of concrete expression when, in 1815, the London Jews Society came under the control of the Church of England.

THE BOSTON FEMALE SOCIETY

Hannah Adams was an Episcopalian. She quickly associated herself with the Anglican effort to convert British Jewry. In July, 1815, only a few months after the Dissenter officers and workers were purged from the LJS, she persuaded a group of Boston ladies to send a contribution of fifty dollars to the English conversionist organization.

Encouraged by this display of female interest, Hannah Adams determined to set up an American branch of the London Jews Society. On June 5, 1816, the Female Society of Boston and Vicinity for Promoting Christianity amongst the Jews was born. It was the first society on the North American continent organized for the sole purpose of converting Jews to Christianity.

With characteristic Yankee shrewdness, Miss Adams declined the First Directorship of the Society and accepted the less prominent but more important post of Corresponding Secretary. She held this position until her death more than sixteen years later. Mrs. Elizabeth E. Winthrop of "the" Massachusetts Winthrops was elected First Directress. The Society soon boasted a membership of over four hundred of Boston's leading ladies. The minimum dues were fixed at one cent a week. Payment of ten dollars in a lump sum entitled any Christian female to life membership.

In August, 1816, to arouse public interest in the work of the Boston Female Society, Miss Adams published a tract, "A Concise Account of the London Society for Promoting Christianity amongst the Jews." In November, she organized a branch of the Society in her birthplace, Medfield, Mass. Early in 1817, another branch was established in Portland, Maine.

The first annual report of the Society, August, 1817, shows that, during its first year, $1263.50 was collected. Of this amount only 100 pounds or $444.44 was sent to London. The rest was invested in stock. Why had the Society, ostensibly organized as a branch of the London Jews Society, kept almost two-thirds of its income for its own use? The report explains this clearly. It states that the scope of Miss Adam's ambitions had now enlarged considerably. She had decided not only to aid the work of the LJS but also to become a missionary in her own right. She had kept the major portion of the Society's funds in Boston in order to spread the gospel among the Jews of America.

She knew, of course, that the number of Jews then in the United States was very small. In the 1812 edition of her *History of the Jews,* she had cited the estimates of Rabbi Gershom M. Seixas that there were about 400 Jews in New York City, between 80 and 100 families in Pennsylvania, 30 families in Richmond, Va., and 1,000 Jews in the Carolinas, mostly around Charleston. The entire American Jewish population in 1812 was about 2,000.

The second annual report, July, 1818, is decidedly less optimistic in tone. It confesses that the "field of exertion" of the Society is "very limited" and that it has been unable to put the income from the trust fund to any use. Miss Adams, it appears, was already convinced that it was useless to attempt to convert Jewish adults, for she now announced that the Society's new policy would be to try "to obtain Jewish children, whom they may take under their protection, and educate in the principles of Christianity." Enough funds were available to take care of two children, but, alas, the Society had searched vainly for two Jewish youngsters who were willing to be nurtured in the bosom of the would-be converters.[2]

During its third year, the Society's income was $725. It sent $444.44 to the London Jews Society for its New Testament distribution fund, $100 to Bombay, India, to a mission school for Jewish children, and it spent $40 on the board and tuition of one N. Myers.[3] Nothing more is known about the last named recipient of the Society's bounty. Presumably he or she was an American Jewish child whom Hannah Adams had been able to persuade to accept an education "in the principles of Christianity." The available records of the Society make no mention of the success or failure of this experiment in child training. So, unless and until further evidence is uncovered, the juvenile career of N. Myers will remain a childish mystery.

We turn now to an account of the conception, birth, and christening of another American missionary scheme involving the Jews which, for the nineteenth century, deserves first prize for imagination, size and importance.

MILLEDOLER AND WILSON

"In 1813, a venerable Professor of Columbia College and a minister had a conversation in which they decided that something must be done for American Jews."[4]

With these modest words, the minister in question began his account, more than thirty years later, of the circumstances that led to the creation of the American Society for Meliorating the Condition of the Jews.

The minister was Philip Milledoler and the "venerable Professor," Peter Wilson.

Milledoler was born in 1775 in Rhinebeck, N.Y. His parents, of Swiss descent, were members of the German Reformed Church. He was graduated from Columbia College in 1793 and became a German Reformed minister in 1794. His early pastorates were in Philadelphia and New York City. In 1800 he switched to the Presbyterian Church and served in 1808 as moderator of the New York Presbyterian General Assembly. In 1813 he went over to the Dutch Reformed Church and became pastor of the Collegiate Dutch Reformed Church of New York. Milledoler was a good preacher, evangelical, learned, and dogmatic.

Peter Wilson was born in Scotland in 1746 and educated at the University of Aberdeen. He came to New York in 1763 and soon won recognition as a learned and efficient pedagogue. Until 1789 he was principal of the Academy in Hackensack, N.J. During this time he served a number of years in the New Jersey legislature. From 1789 to 1792 he was professor of Greek and Latin at Columbia College. He resigned to become principal of Erasmus Hall Academy on Long Island. In 1797 he resumed his professorship at Columbia and continued to teach there until he was pensioned in 1820. He was an unusually gifted student of the classics.

> His portrait, which hangs in Faculty House, Columbia University, shows a man of noble presence, with fine eyes and patrician features, the face of a scholar and a gentleman.[5]

He was one of the leading laymen of the Dutch Reformed Church. "In fact, he was so eloquent a speaker that he was urged to enter the ministry."[6]

From early colonial times, the Dutch Reformed denomination was involved in missionary activities. It made strenuous but unsuccessful efforts to convert the Mohawk Indians. That its members should pray and work for the salvation of the Jews was to be expected. That its American endeavor in this direction was initiated by the minister of its leading church and one of its most outstanding laymen clearly indicates the high place the conversion of the Jews held in the Dutch Reformed program of world redemption.

As a result of the aforesaid conversation, Milledoler organized, in August, 1813, the Hebrew Christian Prayer Union, a monthly prayer meeting for the conversion of Israel. It consisted of Milledoler, Wilson, and three converted female Jews. The most ardent of these was Mrs. Emma Rosenbaum Kingate, about whom nothing more is known.

The Prayer Union did not merely address its petitions to the Almighty. It asked the consistory of the Collegiate Church to begin a Jewish missionary program. In December the consistory passed on the request to the New York classis, the citywide Dutch Reformed organization, with the recommendation

> to take the subject into their serious consideration, and by the appointment of monthly Lectures, or in such other mode as to them may seem meet, endeavour to promote the conversion of the Jews, provided the measure appears to be proper, seasonable, or in any degree attainable.[7]

In October, 1814, a committee of the classis was appointed to study the possibility of sponsoring such a project.

The committee must have been either extremely careful or extremely dilatory in its deliberations because it did not present a report to the classis until September 18, 1816. It recommended that an interdenominational society be organized in New York City for the purpose of converting the Jews. The minutes of the classis meeting also contains the following entry:

> Mr. Joseph S. C. F. Frey, who had lately been connected with the Society for the Conversion of the Jews in London and had recently and unexpectedly arrived in this country, was providentially present at the meeting.[8]

Mr. Frey had arrived in New York City only three days earlier. He too, must have regarded the Dutch Reformed interest in the Jews and its September 18 classis meetings as "providential" windfalls.

THE AMERICAN SOCIETY FOR EVANGELIZING THE JEWS

Accepting its committee's recommendation, the classis convened a meeting of representatives of all the Christian denominations in New York City on November 6, 1816, to consider the question, "Is a Mission to the Jews Necessary?" After lengthy discussion, those in attendance decided unanimously that it was. A committee was chosen to draft a constitution for an interdenominational Jewish missionary society.

The committee presented its report on December 30. The society was formally organized as the American Society for Evangelizing the Jews and a constitution was adopted. This was the first missionary society formed in the United States for the primary purpose of converting *American* Jews. Milledoler was elected president and Wilson vice president. The Society's first and only missionary was appointed, who was, of course, the "providentially present" Reverend Joseph Samuel Christian Frederick Frey.

In the three and a half months since his arrival, Frey had created quite a sensation. He was a curiosity of curiosities, a character most American Christians had envisioned but never seen in the flesh, a Jew who not only practiced Christianity but preached it as well. For the orthodox Christians, Frey was a modern Elijah, a Messianic harbinger. For the liberal Christians, freethinkers, and Jews, Frey was a worthless turncoat and an impudent humbug. Both his well-wishers and his detractors did not hesitate to express their feelings. The presence of the ex-melamed-chazan-shochet was well publicized in New York's newspapers and magazines.

Frey preached his first American sermon exactly one week after arriving in New York City. Appropriately enough, that occasion happened to coincide with the eve of the Jewish New Year. It was, indeed, the beginning of a new stage in the life of the changeling. He spoke on September 22 in the Cedar Street Presbyterian Church before a capacity audience. The weekly *Christian Herald* reported on September 28:

> To hear the unsearchable riches of Christ proclaimed by a converted Jew was too interesting a circumstance not to excite a very extensive desire in Christians of all denominations among us to attend the worship. It accordingly drew many more than the Church could contain. . . . It was a subject of much regret that very few Jews were present that evening, owing to its being the commencement of a great feast day among them, the first of the year.

Frey's initial effort was such an outstanding success that he was deluged with invitations to speak in churches throughout the city. Wherever he spoke, the auditoriums were crowded. Not all his listeners were sympathetic to the cause he represented. Many were attracted by curiosity and not a few were either openly or secretly hostile.

"TOBIT'S LETTERS TO LEVI"

The first attack on Frey's integrity and ability came from a non-Jew. It was a series of letters, written in October, 1816, signed pseudonymously by "Tobit," whose identity remains undetermined. The entire collection, including an introduction and six letters, was published a short time later under the long and self-explanatory title *Tobit's Letters to Levi, or a Reply to the Narrative of Joseph Samuel C. F. Frey, Submitted to the Consideration of Christians of Every Denomination, Whether He Is What He Describes Himself to Be, A Converter of Jews.* The arguments and facts contained in the forty-six-page tract are based on Frey's early New York sermons plus the 1811 American edition of his *Narrative*.

The letters are addressed to "Joseph Samuel Levi, alias Christian Frederick Frey." The beginning of the first letter is a good sample of the biting satiric quality that permeates the tract:

> I have seen you, I have heard you preach, and I have read your book, three things which you must think of considerable importance. I cannot flatter you, however, by saying that I am pleased with your physiognomy, although you certainly must be its devoted admirer, by placing it as the frontispiece to the 108 pages of the narrative you have given of your life and adventures; neither do I admire your delivery, which is downright Jewish; or your doctrine, which is an incomprehensible jargon, not even intelligible to yourself. But as regards your book, if I express my opinion fairly and candidly, I pronounce it the *ne plus ultra* of contradiction and inanity; and I should be tempted to return it to the shelf that robbed me of five shillings, if it did not afford me the means of chastising an impudence which would, on these shores of the Atlantic, pretend to impose on the understanding of men of free habits and a generous method of thinking. If by principle or persuasion, I considered that you had thrown off the cloak of your ancestors, and put on your now more fashionable tunic, far would it be from me to invade your sanctuary. The thoughts, beliefs, and doctrinal tenets of a man are his own; and I should no more pretend to interfere with them than I would with the common concerns of his household; but when I behold a man at once converted from one belief to another, and then become a demagogue and the mouthpiece of that persuasion, and deliver discourses from a pulpit for the express purpose of what he terms conversion, I am naturally led to inquire whether something more than religious zeal may not actuate him in his career.

2033422

"Tobit"'s third letter contains this important observation:

> On inquiry I have found but very few stragglers from the Jewish faith throughout the United States; as regards this city the number is very small indeed, and those who have seceded have felt more contumely and shame from their desertion than peace of mind. . . . I am induced to speak of these as stragglers, in order to discountenance the

opinion which might get abroad that they were converts of Mr. Levi. Perhaps a dozen in union might swell his volume of converts and pride also—but should he meet with them, let it be known that they were stray sheep before his shepherd-like countenance visited our shores.

"Tobit" concludes his letters to "Levi" with the assurance that he would continue to harass him as time and circumstance permitted, but no further products of his pen have been discovered. The only effect of his castigation was to make Frey's sermons more popular than ever. He sorrowfully admitted, in his fourth letter, that Frey's pulpit lectures "are attended with crowds unparalleled in this city—the effect of curiosity and folly." The Christian Herald of November 9 also proclaims that "Mr. Frey still continues to preach with great acceptance and edification to crowded assemblies."

Toward the end of 1816, another anti-Frey publication appeared. This was *Koul Jacob in Defence of the Jewish Religion; containing the Arguments of the Rev. C. F. Frey, of the Committee of the London Society for the Conversion of the Jews, and the Answers thereto,* which had been written by Jacob Nikelsburgher, while Frey was still in England, and printed in Liverpool. It was reprinted in New York and distributed to all who would read it. Like the letters of "Tobit," its only effect was to give Frey additional publicity.

Despite the efforts of liberal Christians and exasperated Jews, Frey's fame continued to spread, his audiences increased, and the cause which he advocated won additional adherents. This public adulation and approval reached its logical culmination on December 30, when Frey was appointed by the newborn American Society for Evangelizing the Jews to be its missionary messenger to New York City's somewhat less than one thousand Jews.

America's first all-American society to the Jews lasted less than six months. It took just that long for Frey's real value as a religious box office attraction to assert itself. He began a series of "Lectures to the Jews" at the North Dutch Church in the middle of January, 1817. The lectures were a total failure. The Jews paid them no heed. He then decided to go on a "missionary tour" of New England on behalf of the Society. This was a bit more profitable. In Dorchester, Mass., he collected $102.30. Boston's famed Park Street Congregational Church gave him $220.15,

and also a box containing a few gold rings, bracelets, and other trinkets, which were doubtless contributed by pious females, under similar impressions with those which induced the good Hebrew women of old to make a willing offering to the Lord of their valuable ornaments and Jewels, for the service of the sanctuary.[9]

Discouraged by their unsuccessful attempt to attract New York Jews to Frey's lectures, the backers of the American Society for Evangelizing the Jews speedily lost interest in the project. The society quietly folded up shortly after Frey's return from Boston.

Frey had to look about for some other means of supporting his family and himself. In June, 1817, he began to preach on Sundays in a schoolhouse on Mulberry Street. Each week more and more Christians from the neighborhood came to listen to the Christian Jew. Finally the group became large enough to form an independent church with Frey as the minister.

Frey had now been preaching the gospel for twelve years and yet had never received formal ordination from any Christian denomination. To fill this void, Frey decided to join the Presbyterian Church and become a Presbyterian minister. He applied for ordination to the presbytery made up of New Jersey's Morris County and New York's Westchester County. His application was approved. He was ordained on April 15, 1818. His good friend, the Reverend Stephen Grover of Caldwell, N.J., preached the ordination sermon. Frey thus became the first Jewish convert to be ordained into the Christian ministry in North America. In 1820, Frey's church was admitted into the New York presbytery.

THE BIRTH OF THE ASMCJ

For a time, a very short time, Frey settled down to the regular routine of a normal clergyman. But this was not to his liking. The desire to be in the limelight and to preach to great crowds was very strong within him. Frey seized the first opportunity to put his name back on the front pages of the newspapers.

In March, 1817, a twenty-nine-year-old Jew, David Donatty, was publicly baptized in the Episcopal Jews Chapel in London. Donatty, a native of Glogau, Silesia, had been a melamed in Frankfurt, Germany, before coming to London. At his baptism, his name was changed to John David Marc. Immediately thereafter he was sent back to Frankfurt by the London Jews Society to work among the Jews of that city. He was supported by the Moravian Brethren. One of his staunchest friends in that sect was an idealistic young nobleman, Count Adalbert von der Recke.

Early in 1819, Marc wrote a letter from Frankfurt to his "dear brother in Christ," Frey. This letter played such an important role in nineteenth-century American Jewish missionary history that it will be quoted *in extenso:*

From the time it has pleased God to call me from darkness into his marvelous light, next to the care of the salvation of my own soul was the salvation of my people and kindred. By mature consideration, I soon saw that we cannot reasonably expect an extensive spread of Christianity amongst the Jews, at least not a great number of true converts, until the Christians establish, or form, a Christian Jewish settlement.

There are many difficulties in the way of the Jew, by which the very first idea in favour of Christianity is arrested in its progress. Some of these difficulties are:

1. The ungodly lives of nominal Christians.
2. The want of kindness among many who are true and sincere Christians, but whose heart the Lord has not yet stirred up to compassion towards this afflicted nation.
3. The dreadful idea to separate from a nation, whose distinct and lasting existence, as a peculiar people, God had so clearly promised. . . .
4. That brotherly love which he enjoys amongst his own people, but which he nowhere else observes in such degree.
5. The mere idea of going amongst Christians excites in him a timidity indescribable.
6. The greatest difficulty lies in the way of the poor. Where is he to seek for help and assistance in time of need? He stands alone in the world; he is forsaken by his Jewish brethren; and to apply to the Christians—the very thought is painful to his feelings, and from their past conduct to the Jews, he is apprehensive to be looked upon, nay, even treated, as a self-interested hypocrite.

All these difficulties might be removed by forming a Christian Jewish settlement. Such a colony ought to be established upon plans well matured, with all possible precaution and Christian prudence. The advantages of such an institution are many:

1. It would excite the attention of Jews in every part of the world.
2. It would be most suitable to carry on friendly correspondence with Jews on the subject of Christianity, especially if it should contain a number of pious and learned men.
3. It would be of great use to those Jews amongst Roman Catholics, Mahometans, and Heathens, who through the multitude of superstitions and errors, mixed with truth, and the numerous sects among the Christians, are at a loss both how to judge of the truth of Christianity and which sect or denomination they are to join.

In Germany, and in most places in Europe, the nature of the government, and especially the prejudice of the people, is very unfavorable to the formation of such a colony, whilst America possesses every advantage for such an institution.

In that extensive country, there must yet be much ground uncultivated and uninhabited. There, where every year colonies of poor people meet with assistance and encouragement, might not a similar favour be shown to Abraham's seed, everywhere else oppressed and persecuted? I ask, now, whether you would be willing to form a society of the proper persons to assist in this undertaking? The assistance necessary would be,

1. To select and procure the proper place for settlement for 200 families.
2. To facilitate, as much as possible, their passage from Europe in American vessels.
3. To assist them in case of necessity during the first years.

The conversion of the Jews must be a matter of the highest importance to every enlightened Christian. To convert the Jew, it is his first and indispensable duty. This you have felt, and therefore have laboured to promote the spiritual welfare of our nation with a noble spirit such, to my knowledge, as no converted Jew has done since the days of the apostles; and although it has pleased the Lord, by heavy trials, to hinder your labours, yet I hope not for ever. O! He is too good to hurt and too wise to err! He may have made you more fit for a glorious work; he may have placed you into a country where, contrary to human expectations, you may yet be more useful. . . .

. . . The zeal of the [American] patriot might be excited [in favor of the settlement idea] by many arguments. To him it might be suggested:

1. As America is the only republic in the world, it ought to be well prepared for attack from the united monarchs, to whom the very existence of a free people can not be very pleasing.
2. That it, therefore, ought to increase its internal strength, i.e., its population.
3. That its sanction and encouragement to the importance of Jews promises a great increase of population.
4. That they are peaceable and obedient subjects; for, during the long series of centuries, not one single example can be produced of their rebellion, even in those parts where they were most numerous and most oppressed.
5. That they are good and faithful soldiers when called upon has been manifested during the late war in their conduct to Bonaparte and others.
6. That America could not find better guardians of its borders against Spain than the Jews would be, nor could the late acquisition of Spanish territory be better secured than by Jewish inhabitants.

7. That Jews, after so long and bitter experience of oppression and persecution, would doubtless be most faithful and zealous adherents to a country of so liberal a constitution.
8. That by the peculiar character and genius of the Jews, they are most likely to promote friendship between the uncivilized tribes and Americans. Lastly, it would not a little promote American trade if it should be favourable to a people scattered over the whole world, and everywhere engaged in traffic.
   [When Frey published his translation of this letter from the German, he added the following comment at this point: "The translator takes leave to add to the above advantages the invaluable benefits of such an institution, as a pleasant and faithful nursery of Jewish missionaries to every nation under heaven; and a means of recognizing many of the Indians as descendants of the ancient Israelites."]

This subject needs no farther recommendation to the true Christian; nor will any be required by the philanthropist, who considers the barbarity and cruelty with which Jews are oppressed in most parts of the world. . . .

Assistance may be expected from the London Society, as well as from other Christian countries, especially Germany, where many true Christians and persons of great influence, are ready to assist, with all their power, to promote this object.[10]

Frey maintained that at first he was not greatly interested in Marc's proposal.

Having already met with so many difficulties and discouragements in my former labours among my dear Jewish brethren in London, and my time being taken up with my congregation, I refused for a long while to do anything in the matter.[11]

Marc wrote him again and insisted that he must become involved.

The closing paragraph [of Marc's later letter], viz., "The blood of the Jews will be found in the skirt of your garment if you do not make the attempt," had such an effect upon my mind that I could no longer resist.[12]

Now convinced that Marc's idea was worth pursuing, Frey searched for some way to bring the project before the public. He decided to read Marc's letter before a group of his New Jersey friends, who had organized the Morris County Society for Promoting Learning and Religion. The letter, read by Frey to the Society in April, 1819, was received enthusiastically. In August the Society wrote to Marc requesting him to come to this country at its expense to try to put his plan into operation. Marc, for reasons not specifically spelled out in his response, refused the invitation but offered to assist in every way possible from his post in Europe. Frey and the Reverend Stephen Grover were then designated by the Society to devise the most practical ways of arousing public interest in the proposed Christian Jewish settlement.

In November, Frey and Grover organized a Prayer Union for Israel in New York City as the first step to win support for the project. It will be remembered that Milledoler and Wilson used the same method to bring a similar matter to the attention of the Dutch Reformed Church. That first Union lasted from August, 1813, until early in 1817. It dissolved for a rather peculiar reason. When Frey was appointed missionary for the American Society for Evangelizing the Jews in December, 1816, he naturally took a great interest in the meetings of the prayer union. Influenced probably by his orthodox Jewish background, he refused to permit the three Hebrew Christian female members to assist in conducting the prayer services. This ban angered the ladies and they ceased to attend the meetings. Their withdrawal reduced the active membership to three gentlemen: Milledoler, Wilson, and Frey. These three, feeling no deep personal need for their Hebrew-Christian Prayer Union, disbanded it. The second Prayer Union was composed entirely of born non-Jews except for Frey and a Reverend Mr. Phillips, concerning whom no further mention is made.

Toward the end of November, Frey convened a meeting in Princeton, N.J., of four very prominent ministers: Archibald Alexander, 1772-1851, and Samuel Miller, 1769-1850, professors at Princeton Theological Seminary; Ashbel Green, 1762-1848, president of the College of New Jersey, now Princeton University; and John H. Livingston, 1746-1825, president of Queen's College, now Rutgers University. The first three were Presbyterians. Livingston was the acknowledged national leader of the Dutch Reformed denomination.

The four listened with great earnestness and sympathy to Frey's presentation and then signed the following statement:

> Having understood by a letter from Mr. Marc, a Christian Jew, as well as by letters from James Miller, Esq., of London, that an ardent wish prevails among some Christian Jews in Germany to emigrate to the United States for the express purpose of forming a settlement, to obtain, without interruption, instruction for themselves, and to promote more effectually the Christian religion among the Jews: We, whose names are underwrit, do hereby certify, that as far as the

object is at present comprehended by us, we most cordially approve of the same.

Fortified with this document, Frey moved on to Burlington, N.J., where on the evening of November 25, he explained the plan to the aged and beloved Elias Boudinot, 1740-1821, statesman, author, and a man of saintly character.

Elias Boudinot was born in Philadelphia of French ancestry. He was baptized by the famous evangelist George Whitefield. He became a lawyer in 1760 and soon acquired a reputation for legal learning and forensic skill. He achieved national fame and high honors during and after the Revolution. A close friend and advisor of George Washington, he was a member of the Continental Congress from 1777 to 1784 and its president, 1782-1784. He was one of the commissioners who negotiated the treaty of peace with Great Britain. He served in the first three sessions of the federal Congress and left that body in 1795 when President Washington appointed him Director of the Mint. He resigned from this position on July 1, 1805, to devote the remainder of his life to Bible study. In 1815 he was elected the first president of the American Bible Society. His religious writings include *The Age of Revelation*, 1801; *Memoirs of Rev. William Tennent*, 1807; *The Second Advent*, 1815; and *The Star in the West*, 1816. The last is an attempt to prove that the American Indians are directly descended from the Ten Lost Tribes. Obviously Boudinot's approval would be a great asset to Frey.

That Frey's visit to Burlington was successful is shown by the letter which Boudinot wrote him the day after their meeting:

> I have carefully attended to the important subject of our last evening's conversation. It is only to part of your plan, that is of minor consequence, to which I have at present any objection. As I have but a few minutes to express my opinion in writing, your own memory will serve you with the particulars. My present design is to express, in as short a manner as possible, my cordial acquiescence in the whole of your designs, if pursued with caution in detail. My wish would be to revive, as soon as convenient, the late Society for Evangelizing the Jews, established in New York a few years since, that they should apply, without further explanation, for a charter of incorporation to the legislature at their next session; afterwards, a plan for further proceedings and appointment of the proper officers may then take place, and every proper measure pursued, for effecting so useful and essential a business to the church of Christ; and may he bless you, in all you do, agreeable to his rich promises in the Gospels.

On December 15, Frey announced these good tidings to his New York Prayer Union. On January 25, 1820, the Union resolved unanimously to organize a society for the purpose of establishing a colony of foreign Christian Jews in the United States. On February 8, 1820, the Society was formally founded; it was named the American Society for Colonizing and Evangelizing the Jews. A constitution was adopted. Milledoler was named temporary chairman and R. Havens, Esq., was chosen temporary secretary. Frey was instructed to go to Albany to secure an act of incorporation from the New York state legislature.

To this point the Jews of New York City had shown no interest in the proposed scheme; but, when the name of the new Society was announced, the Jewish community reacted promptly and hostilely. The Jews had no objection to any attempt to "colonize" their brethren; but they were determined not to permit the incorporation of any society which also wanted to "evangelize" American Jews. Therefore they requested the legislature to dismiss Frey's petition. The legislature did so on the ground that "proselyting of citizens is prohibited by the constitution." Dismayed by this rebuff, Frey appeared before a committee of the legislature and explained that the Society did not intend to proselytize American Jews, but wanted to organize a colony of foreign Jews who had become Christians prior to coming to America. The committee promised to try to persuade the legislature to reconsider its action, provided that the name of the Society was changed to accord with Frey's explanation.

Frey returned to New York and discussed the situation with his coworkers. They decided to revive the unincorporated American Society for Evangelizing the Jews and, through this agency, to endeavor to convert American Jews; and to change the name of their incorporated branch to the American Society for Meliorating the Condition of the Jews. The incorporated body was to have only one function, i.e., to found and maintain a settlement of foreign Christian Jews somewhere in the United States. Article two of the amended constitution stated explicitly:

> The object of this Society shall be to invite and receive from any part of the world such Jews as do already profess the Christian Religion, or are desirous to receive Christian Instruction, to form them into a settlement, and to furnish them with the ordinances of the Gospel, and with such employment in the settlement as shall be assigned them; but no one shall be received, unless he comes well recommended for morals and industry, and without charge to this Society, and both his reception and continuance in the settlement shall be at all times at the discretion of the Directors.

Having made its purpose clear and having changed its name, the Society again applied to the New York legislature for articles of incorporation. This time the request was granted. The American Society for Meliorating the Condition of the Jews was born, legally and officially, on April 14, 1820.

Chapter Five

The ASMCJ "Foreign" Period (1820-1839)

During the first twenty years of its existence, the American Society for Meliorating the Condition of the Jews made no overt attempts to convert American Jewry. Its efforts were directed solely toward "meliorating the condition" of Jews in foreign lands. Yet there are good reasons for including the early history of the Society in our account. In the first place, its supporters hoped that, through their efforts, missionaries would be trained to Christianize America's Jews. In the second place, the "domestic" phase of the Society's history, 1840-1870, can be comprehended adequately only through a knowledge of the happenings of the first two decades.

The ASMCJ held its first annual meeting on Friday, May 12, 1820, in the auditorium of the New York City Hall. Boudinot presided. The amended constitution was adopted and officers were elected: Elias Boudinot, President; Alexander McLeod, Secretary for Foreign Correspondence; John Knox, Secretary for Domestic Correspondence; and Peter A. Jay, Treasurer. The first three maintained their connection with and interest in the Society for the rest of their lives. Jay seems to have become inactive about 1826.

The Reverend Alexander McLeod, 1774-1833, was minister of the First

Reformed Presbyterian Church of New York City, one of the best orators and foremost leaders of his denomination. The Reverend John Knox was one of the organizers in 1816 of the American Society for Evangelizing the Jews. Peter A. Jay, 1776-1843, a prominent lawyer and Episcopalian, was the eldest son of the eminent statesman, John Jay.

The Society remained inactive for almost two years. Frey wrote that

> for nearly two years, the Board met regularly, but few attended; and, having charge of a large church and congregation, I could not travel much to make the Society known, and consequently no progress was made.

It may also be noted that the projected revival of the American Society for Evangelizing the Jews never materialized. The six-month-old infant died in the middle of 1817 and never came back to life.

"ISRAEL VINDICATED"

Although the Society did not achieve nationwide attention until late in 1822, one Jewish citizen of New York City made a determined effort to give the organization some very unfavorable publicity. George Houston, disturbed by the program of the meliorators, wrote a 110-page brochure titled *Israel Vindicated: being a refutation of the Calumnies propagated respecting the Jewish Nation: in which the objects and views of the American Society for Meliorating the Condition of the Jews are investigated by an Israelite*, and published his remonstrance anonymously in December, 1820.

Israel Vindicated consists of a series of thirty-two letters, supposedly written by "Nathan Joseph" of New York to his friend, "Jacob Isaacs" of Philadelphia. In the preface, Houston discusses the refusal of the New York legislature to grant the organization a charter when it wanted to convert American Jews and he states that the ultimate aim of the ASMCJ is to set up an establishment with the same goal in mind. He says that the Society has deliberately limited its membership to Presbyterians and Episcopalians.[2]

He ridicules the idea that humanitarian motives have prompted the formation of the ASMCJ:

> If these Nazarenes, dear Isaacs, are really desirous of doing service to the poor of our nation, thousands of whom at this moment feel distress in Europe; if they wish to imitate the example of the good Samaritan, whose charity was not regulated by the cold calculating

rules of sectarianism; if they are truly what they profess to be— philanthropists desirous only of the happiness of their species; let them lay aside, in the outset at least, all attempts to interfere with our religious principles; let them consider our needy brethren only in the light of men suffering under the pressure of a common calamity, and, as such, entitled to their compassion; let them unite their efforts with the more wealthy of our nation, in endeavoring to procure an allotment of land for them in this widely extended country; and, having succeeded in obtaining this, let them, as with one heart and one voice, invite them to take possession of it, by holding out suitable inducements, and proffering them pecuniary aid. . . . But when they commence, as they do, with telling a people, devoted, more than any other, to the worship of their fathers, that, before they will contribute a single cent to enable them to escape from their present calamities, they must renounce that worship, bring with them sufficient testimonials of character, and, without means of stirring a single inch from the spot, convey themselves, many of them thousands of miles, into their presence, "without charge to this Society":—When I reflect, dear Isaacs, on a representation of so extraordinary a nature, sent forth to our nation, under so many respectable names, I stand amazed at the stupidity of those who could conceive that it would be listened to by any one possessing his right senses. If this is what nowadays is called the proper way of "ameliorating" the condition of a people, how far indeed must we have retrograded in our notions of true policy. I question if the whole history of society-making could furnish an example of a "Constitution" so fraught with absurdity as the one now published to the world by the American Society for Meliorating the Condition of the Jews.

BOUDINOT'S BEQUEST

Weakened by its own inertia and the barbs of a hostile press, the Society would probably have died a lingering but painless death if two events, late in 1821, had not rescued it from the slough of public indifference. The first was the death on October 24 of Elias Boudinot, and the second was the departure for America of David Christian Bernhard Jadownicky, Hebrew Christian emissary of the noble Adalbert, Count von der Recke und Volmarstein.

The fourth item in Boudinot's long and charitable will, dated July 3, 1821, read:

Whereas I have given some encouragement, that I would aid and assist in promoting the settlement of a body of Jews, who have been represented to me as desirous of removing from the Continent of Europe to some asylum of safety, if any should offer, where they may be able to examine and judge for themselves, into the great things of our divine religion, without fear or terror; therefore, in order to accomplish what I conveniently can in this important business, . . . in case if any number of Jews to the number of fifteen families or upward, should migrate to this country and put themselves under the care, management and protection of the Society for Meliorating the Condition of the Jews, incorporated and established in the State of New York, whereof I am President, and that within seven years after my death, shall voluntarily apply to the Society, and obtain their consent, my trustees shall convey to the said society such lands as they may want from time to time so as to supply each family with fifty acres to be taken out of the tract of 4000 acres, part of my land left to my trustees, situate in Warren County in the State of Pennsylvania which I direct to be held by them separate from my other lands and which shall be selected and appropriated to this use, by my trustees or their agent, which society shall or may give to each immigrant or his family in case of his death, a lot within same, who shall be willing and shall actually become a settler by being on such lot so assigned to him which he shall enjoy for seven years, by clearing at least fifteen acres thereof, building a dwelling house, planting fifteen apple trees, and paying all the taxes thereon. And if at the end of seven years, if the said immigrant or his family in case of his death, shall continue to remain thereon, he shall receive a deed in fee simple to him or to his assigns forever from my trustees or the majority of them. But if the said society shall think most for the advantage of said immigrants or if they prefer it as a body to settle in the states of New Jersey, New York, or any other place, and shall certify this to my said trustees, through the said society, then I revoke the whole of this devise and make it entirely void, and instead thereof give and bequeath to the said society or its assigns, the sum of one thousand dollars to be paid within two years after my death for the use of the said institution.[3]

Three months after the foregoing was written, this good man died; and the Society faced its first major decision: Should it accept four thousand acres of land in the wilds of northwestern Pennsylvania, more than three hundred miles from New York City, or should it take one thousand dollars in cash? A committee was appointed to consider the matter.

DUESSELTHAL

Meanwhile, the originator of the settlement scheme, J. D. Marc of Frankfurt, Germany, had not been idle. Having learned of the establishment of the American society, he convinced his wealthy young friend, Count von der Recke, that a similar institution must be set up in Europe where prospective America Jewish Christian colonists could receive their initial agricultural and manual training. With the characteristic zeal of an idealist who is both young and rich, von der Recke agreed to create such a preparatory establishment. He expended, in fulfillment of that agreement, a large portion of his inherited fortune and seven years of his life. Early in 1821, the Count began to use his estate at Duesselthal, a small community in the Rhine valley between Duesseldorf and Elberfeld, as the agricultural training school for the Jewish converts.

The first future farmer sent by Marc to Duesselthal was Bernhard Jadownicky, about twenty years of age, converted by Marc. Jadownicky, a Pole, had served for about two years before his baptism as melamed in Solingen, a town a few miles southeast of Duesseldorf. Typically, ex-melamed Jadownicky was metamorphosed by his Christian associates into "converted rabbi" Jadownicky and "David Christian" was prefixed to the name his parents had given him.

A few months later, von der Recke, dissatisfied with the lack of ardor displayed by his American confreres, decided to send Jadownicky to America to give the American society firsthand information about his plans and to urge them to labor more actively on behalf of the settlement project. En route to America, Jadownicky visited Erasmus H. Simon, a Hebrew Christian missionary in Amsterdam, and interested him in the Duesselthal experiment.

Jadownicky arrived in New York City in January, 1822. He presented his credentials and was welcomed warmly. He delivered to the ASMCJ Board the message given him by Count von der Recke. Having completed this task, Jadownicky, aided by the ASMCJ, enrolled in Princeton Academy to complete his college requirements. Later he studied at Princeton Theological Seminary and was preparing himself for graduation from that institution when his American career was terminated abruptly in July, 1825, by circumstances to be narrated in their appropriate time sequence.

FREY'S FIRST ASMCJ TOUR

The ASMCJ now began to awaken from its lethargy and to go to work with great enthusiasm. Rumors soon began to spread throughout religiously Christian America that a Hebrew Christian settlement would soon be established somewhere in the United States.

In September, 1822, Frey resigned his pastorate to devote himself full time to the task of raising money for the ASMCJ and organizing auxiliaries throughout the land.

He began his first Society journey in December 1822. He returned to

New York City early in June, 1823. He had visited 8 states, preached 197 times, formed 51 auxiliaries, and collected nearly five thousand dollars.

> He has been greatly favored both by the Jews and the Christians; and even the slanderous paragraphs that aimed, in a few of the news-papers, to injure the cause in which he was engaged, seem to have been overruled to give it greater success. The restoration of the Jews is now contemplated as an *immediate* concern by thousands who be-fore had scarcely thought of the subject, and the liberal collections for the society afford an earnest that greater things will yet be done by the numerous auxiliaries he has been instrumental in forming.[4]

Frey's successful tour elated the ASMCJ Board. In January, 1823, the Society began to publish a monthly magazine, *Israel's Advocate,* which appeared regularly until the end of 1826.

THE FIRST REPORT

Although the ASMCJ had been in existence almost three years, it had never issued a formal report to the public. This void was filled on May 9, 1823, when it held its fourth annual meeting and gave out its first report.

The meeting was held at the City Hotel. In the absence of ailing Peter Wilson, who had succeeded Boudinot as president, vice president Mil-ledoler presided. The treasury balance was $4,198. Requests for informa-tion about the Society were being received from all over the country. The committee on the Boudinot bequest reported that the Pennsylvania land was unfit for colonization. It was too wild, would require too much time, effort, and money to prepare for cultivation. The committee recom-mended that the Society take the one thousand dollars instead of the land and that the proposed colony be established in the state of New York. The committee's recommendations were approved.

Sixteen of the fifty-two men elected to the Board of Directors at that 1823 meeting are in the select group deemed worthy of inclusion in the *Dictionary of American Biography.* Their names, the offices they held on the ASMCJ Board, and their public positions in 1823 are: President, Peter Wilson, emeritus professor, Columbia College; Vice Presidents, John Quincy Adams, 1767-1848, Secretary of State of U.S. President James Monroe; Jeremiah Day, 1773-1867, president of Yale College; Ashbel Green, 1762-1848, editor, Philadelphia *Christian Advocate;* John H. Livingston, president of Queen's College, now Rutgers University; Philip Milledoler, minister of New York's Collegiate Dutch Reformed Church;

Colonel Robert Troup, 1757-1832, Revolutionary hero and judge of U.S. district court in New York City; General Stephen Van Rensselaer, 1764-1839, eighth patroon and U.S. congressman; James Wadsworth, 1768-1844, capitalist and philanthropist; Treasurer, Richard M. Blatchford, 1798-1875, just beginning a distinguished career in law, politics, and philanthropy; Secretary for Foreign Correspondence, Alexander McLeod, minister of New York's First Reformed Presbyterian Church; Secretary for Domestic Correspondence, Samuel H. Cox, 1793-1880, pastor of New York's Spring Street Presbyterian Church; and the following directors, John Adams, 1735-1826, ex-President of the United States; John McComb, 1763-1853, eminent architect; Ebenezer Burrill, prominent businessman; and Peter A. Jay, prosperous attorney.

One might think that the names of these celebrities were used merely as window dressing, that they took no active interest in the affairs of the Society, and that, perhaps, some of their names were used without permission. This does not seem to have been the case, with one exception. This exception was the Honorable John Adams. That grand old American liberal, who had a decided antipathy for "frigid John Calvin" and whose religious beliefs were conspicuously Deistic and Unitarian, must have felt that he was in very strange company, for this is the one and only time that his name appears on the ASMCJ Board roster. The other fifteen continued their directorships for a number of years, so it may be assumed that they were well aware of the purpose and doings of the ASMCJ and quite willing to have their names associated with it. All were active in local and national religious organizations, such as the American Bible Society and the American Tract Society, founded in 1825, and various missionary enterprises.

JOHN ADAMS AND SON

John Adams was probably included on the ASMCJ Board because of a mistaken belief that he shared the religious point of view of his son, John Quincy Adams. Although John Quincy Adams is usually referred to as a Unitarian, he was much more conservative religiously than his father. This is clearly shown in *The Letters of John Quincy Adams to His Son, on the Bible and Its Teachings,* written in 1811-1812 and published in 1850.

John Quincy Adam's interest in the conversion of the Jews was long and deep. After he became U.S. President in 1825, he continued his membership in the ASMCJ. Shortly thereafter he became convinced that it is virtually impossible to convert Jews. After 1827 his name does not appear on the rolls of the Society. He recorded in his diary, on January 6, 1839, that it is useless to send missionaries to the Jews because "their hatred of all Christians is rancorous beyond description."[5] But his interest in the matter never ceased. An ASMCJ missionary reported, in February, 1846, that a lecture he delivered in Washington had been attended by the aged ex-president as well as by many other senators and congressmen.[6]

THE OPPOSITION

The opponents of the ASMCJ did not watch its growth in scornful silence. Wherever Frey appeared, his speeches were followed by an outpouring of letters of protest, written to local newspapers and magazines by Jews, Unitarians, and freethinkers. Unlike the Jews and freethinkers, most Unitarians were not opposed to the conversion of Jews to Christianity. They believed that, at some future time, the Jews would be restored to Palestine and would be converted there by the grace of God and without human assistance. They opposed all missionary work on the premise that it was a violation of the principle of religious freedom.

The ASMCJ was directly responsible for the appearance of the first Jewish magazine published in the United States. It was named simply *The Jew*, "being a Defense of Judaism against all Adversaries, and particularly against the insidious attacks of 'Israel's Advocate.'" The editor and publisher was Solomon H. Jackson, a Jew of New York City. The first number appeared in March, 1823, and it was published monthly through March, 1825. The magazine consisted, in the main, of articles defending the theology of Judaism and of attacks on Frey and the ASMCJ, attacks which seems to have been motivated more by sheer hatred than by literary ability or common sense. In November, 1823, the magazine made a unique and ridiculous contribution to ASMCJ folklore. It printed a letter which asserted that the real purpose of the ASMCJ was not to convert Jews but to make Presbyterianism the established religion of the United States.

The ASMCJ and *Israel's Advocate* paid no attention to Jackson and his magazine until December, 1824, when the *Advocate* published a brief statement that it had no desire to engage in controversy with *The Jew* and was interested only in serving as a source of information for those who wanted to know more about the ASMCJ. After two years of attempting vainly to arouse the antagonism of the ASMCJ and the support of New York Jewry, *The Jew* ceased publication. In its final number,

Jackson repeated the baseless charge that the ASMCJ was plotting to make Presbyterianism the American state religion.

Criticism of the colony project was not limited to those whose theologies differed from that of the ASMCJ. At least one founder and outstanding member of the Society changed his mind and voiced his disapproval as early as 1823. The Reverend John H. Livingston, who had sanctioned the project in November, 1819, wrote a long letter to ASMCJ President Peter Wilson on July 24, 1823, saying he now considered the scheme unwise and doomed to fail. His gloomy forecast fell on deaf ears. The Society went ahead with its plans for a permanent settlement. Although Livingston's name continued to appear on the list of the Society's officers, his interest in it ceased. He died on January 20, 1825.

ERASMUS H. SIMON AND COMPANY

Simon and his wife joined the Duesselthal group in May, 1822. In April, 1823, von der Recke wrote the Society that Simon

> is now gone to see his old father, a Rabbi in Sloppa, near Posen, in Poland, and to preach the gospel to him; and intends to embark for America next year, together with twelve young Jews.[7]

Also in 1823 the London Jews Society sent two of its staff to Duesselthal to determine whether that undertaking was worthy of the Society's support. Their report was so negative that the London Society decided not to support the German venture. The report stated:

> Count von der Recke's plan is perhaps somewhat too enlarged and complex, and has so little connection with the special object of our Society, that we could not recommend it to the Board for their support. . . . There were, when we visited Duesselthal, five Jewish children and three adults there, and the Count was daily in expectation of a Jewish family, which would be added to their number.[8]

Erasmus H. Simon did not wait until 1824 to come to America. He, his wife, and Frederick Gustavus Primker, a young Hebrew Christian, took ship at Rotterdam on August 22 and landed at Boston on September 8. They and all who came later traveled to the United States at their own expense, in accordance with Article Two of the ASMCJ constitution. Neither they nor the later arrivals informed the ASMCJ that they were coming nor sought to secure permission from the Society to make the ocean crossing. They just paid their way across the Atlantic and, on reaching our shores, demanded that the Society support them, which it did to the best of its ability.

Late in November, John Edward Zadig arrived from London. A native of Breslau, Prussia, he was converted by Marc and baptized in June.

Primker was sent to Elizabethtown, N. J., to the home of a local Presbyterian minister. Zadig was quartered with the young principal of the Princeton Academy. They studied English with these excellent tutors and, in turn, gave instruction in foreign languages to other students.

This little group of Hebrew Christians organized themselves into a "Jewish Converts Society." Its charter members were Frey, Jadownicky, Primker, Zadig, Simon, and Mrs. Simon, even though the latter was a non-Jew. The Hebrew Christians who arrived later also joined the organization. Its life was brief and unimportant. It ceased to exist about 1826.

In December, 1823, Simon was appointed ASMCJ agent to collect funds and organize auxiliaries. He held this position until he parted company with the Society in June, 1825. He was quite successful as a field representative. Wherever he went, he told his audience that the ASMCJ Jewish Christians would eventually be the nucleus of a Hebrew Christian Church

> which shall try and divide between Christians and sectarians—while, as a bond of union, it will assimilate those Christians of all denominations who are only separated by names and opinions of human invention.[9]

His announcement, made without the authorization of the Society, was enthusiastically received by those who heard it. "Prayers are already offered up in many pulpits in New England for the prosperity of *literal Zion*, to which let us respond, Amen."[10]

The officials of the Society refused to respond "Amen." In April, 1824, the editor of *Israel's Advocate* wrote:

> The Board has not yet determined that the settlement shall be called a "Hebrew Christian Church." It will of course not be called after either of the existing *sects* of Christians; and it may hereafter be known by the name Mr. Simon has given it, but as yet the Board has not deliberated on the subject.[11]

Simon convinced Jadownicky of the wisdom of his idea and the latter, too, whenever he addressed any gathering on behalf of the Society, advocated the formation of a Hebrew Christian Church. This manifestation of independence of thought displeased the Board greatly. It was a major contributing cause to the upheaval in the spring and summer of 1825 that shook Simon and Jadownicky loose from the ASMCJ.

THE WHEELS START TO TURN

In January, 1824, the committee appointed to find a suitable site for the proposed settlement presented its report. It had not yet discovered such a site; but it had drawn up a basic plan for the operation of the settlement. The converts were to be employed principally as farmers and artisans. The general superintendent must be a minister. A schoolmaster would teach the children. Such young people as possessed the requisite piety and aptitudes were to be trained as clergymen and missionaries. An experienced farmer would supervise the maintenance of the farm.

The original plan for an extensive colony in the interior of New York State had been abandoned as too expensive. The committee recommended that a tract of four thousand to six thousand acres, located not too far from New York City, be purchased. Until such a tract was acquired, it recommended that a house be secured near New York City to serve as a temporary residence of the future American Jewish Christian farmer-missionaries. In February, the Society announced it had rented such a place.

> The Committee appointed . . . to procure such a place . . . reported . . . that a large mansion together with three acres of land, at a distance of three miles from the city, and in a commanding and healthy situation, could be obtained at the rate of $300 per annum. The house being admirably adapted for the temporary purposes for which it is intended, having fifteen commodious rooms; and the rent being considered low for the accommodations afforded, the board did not hesitate but accepted the report of the committee and hired the house.[12]

There is no indication that any of the ASMCJ Jews ever lived in this house. At the time it was rented, it certainly was not needed. Frey and Simon were traveling almost continuously. Jadownicky, Primker, and Zadig were studying in New Jersey. When the one-year lease expired, the Society relinquished the property and rented a tenement house on Murray Hill in New York City.

In April, 1824, another prominent Society member "saw the light." The Reverend Gardiner Spring, 1785-1873, pastor of New York's Brick Street Presbyterian Church, wrote an open letter in *Israel's Advocate* in which he expressed strong opposition to the settlement scheme.

I feel the fullest assurance that there will be funds sufficient to meet all the necessities of the Foreign christian Jews that will ever land in America. And when they are here amongst us, we can much better determine how we can best serve their interest, than now, before they do come; and especially as we know not whether many, if any considerable number, will ever come.[13]

His bold and frank words had no effect whatsoever. Despite his adverse feelings, Spring continued his membership in the Society until 1827.

The fifth annual meeting was held May 14, 1824. Members of the Board had gone on "exploring tours" of proposed settlement sites but had found all unsuitable. Frey was elected a Director for Life. The Board expressed a desire to send missionaries to the Jews of Europe and also to establish fund collecting agencies in England and Germany, foreign offices which would weed out unworthy converts and help secure transatlantic passage for poor, worthy, ASMCJ missionary-farmer-type Christian Jews. *Israel's Advocate* now had two thousand subscribers. The treasury balance was $7,886.43½.

The Treasurer has also in his possession . . . eight gold finger rings, three pair of gold earrings, one silver freemason's medal, two strings of gold beads, and one pair of gold bracelets.[14]

Addresses were delivered by Christian clergymen and also by Zadig and Primker. This is the last time that the names of Zadig and Primker appear in the Society's records. It may be that they became discouraged by the many delays in the settlement planning and returned to Europe.

Soon thereafter, there were indications that the Society was facing increasing public opposition. In the forty-five years that were yet to elapse before the Society's demise, its history was to be an unending succession of disappointments and failures.

Ill-natured reports and barefaced falsehoods have been industriously handed about, concerning the parent Society, its agents, its objects, and its aims. . . . The indefatigable and worthy agent of the Parent Society, Rev. Mr. Frey, has received his share, and all who know anything of the reproach he has been called to suffer will doubtless be ready to say his portion has been a very bountiful one. To their shame, be it said, that, almost from Georgia to Maine, editors have been found, willing to lend their columns to the most unfounded aspersions, and to the most unworthy abuse of a man whose praise is in all the churches. . . . Another cause . . . was the necessary delay which has attended the final determination . . . of the location of the colony. . . . Another cause . . . is to be found in our not furnishing ourselves with proper information upon this subject. . . . We make up our minds quite too soon, and condemn what we know little about.[15]

In June, 1824, another Marc convert, Dr. Christian Sebastian Elias Wolf, M.D., arrived. During the next seven or eight months, letters were received indicating that the Duesselthal project was on the verge of collapse. A letter from Marc to Dr. Wolf, January 3, 1825, said:

Many of the converts at Duesselthal, if they do not soon realize their hope and expectation of going to America, will be scattered; nothing but this hope hath kept them together so long. Several mechanics have made application, but they cannot continue long in one place; and, notwithstanding their love and zeal for the cause, yet hope deferred maketh the heart faint. Two have been so discouraged that in greatest misery they have cast themselves on the wide world. One of the converts, who for a year worked diligently at Duesselthal, but could make no improvement, went to Amsterdam and offered to work his passage as a sailor for New York, but could not get such a situation; and, not being able to raise the expense of his passage, he engaged himself as a sailor for five years to an East India captain. Another who had no prospect at Duesselthal, joined the Roman Catholics, where he has devoted himself to the study of Theology. Two others had done the same, but have since returned, one of which is Mr. Jacobi, who hath since gone to America, by way of England.[16]

The Mr. Jacobi referred to is John Christian Gottlieb Adolph Jacobi, 1800-1874, who will be mentioned quite frequently in later chapters. Jacobi was born in Gnewkowo, province of Posen, German Poland, as the son of a wool merchant. After receiving a yeshiva training, he got a job, in 1819, as chazan-shochet-melamed in a small town near Giessen, Germany. He was converted by Marc and baptized in July, 1821. For a time he was employed by the London Jews Society as interpreter in Poland for missionary Alexander McCaul. In 1823, he went to Duesselthal.

After having applied myself there for some time to agriculture, and having no prospect of accomplishing my wish of going to America, I was in danger of being seduced by the suggestions of the papists, but, God be thanked, who soon delivered me from them, and brought me to Frankfurt, whence I went, by Christian assistance, through Amsterdam, London and Liverpool, to this blessed country.[17]

Jacobi arrived in the United States in March, 1825.

In April, 1825, the Board finally located a satisfactory site on which to begin its settlement. It rented a four hundred-acre farm near Harrison, in Westchester Country, about fifty-five miles northeast of New York City. The farm was leased for seven years at an annual rental of seven hundred dollars. It contained "a gristmill, sawmill, a spacious mansion, and convenient outhouses."[18]

The sixth annual meeting was held in Washington Hall, New York City, on May 13, 1825. Almost two thousand people crowded into the hall to hear the annual report. *Israel's Advocate* now had 2,750 subscribers. The treasury balance was $14,320.98. Peter A. Jay was elected president, replacing the very sick Peter Wilson, who died less than three months later.

THE CRISIS OF 1825

Four days before the sixth annual meeting the Board drew up the rules by which the Harrison farm was to be governed. Rule #5 stated: "All officials of the settlement must be born Christians. All profits resulting from the labor of the colonists are to become the property of the Society."

On May 19, duplicate letters were sent to the four Jewish Christians who were in the care of the Society: Simon, Jacobi, Jadownicky, and Wolf. Each was furnished a copy of the rules and was asked to state in writing, before May 24, whether he intended to go out to the farm.

On May 21, the four converts gathered at their tenement house on Murray Hill, composed a spirited but dignified reply to the Board's communication and sent it to the Board. Here are some of the key sentences in their communication:

> After mature consideration, we are unanimously brought to the painful but urgent duty of remonstrating against the conditions prescribed in some of your rules. We assure you, gentlemen, that we are actuated by no sinister motive in desiring to have our Hebrew Christian church and community free. . . .
>
> Our wishes relative to this important subject have long been before you and the public. . . . They are simply to establish a free community and church among ourselves, where we may unite in the name of Christ to labour for our support, and worship God according to his revealed will and the dictates of our own conscience.
>
> . . . Hebrew Christians, desirous of being in amity with all denominations, but called by none, require that their spiritual concerns should be conducted by their own brethren, in order that the Hebrew

Christian church may not become a sectarian institution; but this would inevitably be the case, or at least be considered so, should you appoint a clergyman of any denomination as the spiritual superintendent. . . .

With regard to your rules for the management of our temporal concerns, we request you to reconsider them, and then tell us whether they do not belong rather to the regulations of an almshouse or an asylum than to a free community. For what well educated and enlightened Hebrew would wish to join the settlement under such an aspect?

We think it the duty of every true Christian to deny himself, seeking not his own but his neighbor's weal. We are willing to act on this principle. Can we do more? But you seem to exact a degree of self-denial above what the gospel enjoins, in requiring that, as babes in their nonage, we should put the earnings which some of our brethren shall acquire by the sweat of their brow, and others by the talents and attainments they possess, into your hands for your disposal, thus leaving ourselves dependent on your discretion for our very clothing.

We are providentially here not alone for ourselves, but in some degree as representatives of those of our brethren whom the Lord may send to partake with us of the dearest blessing of a free country, *liberty of conscience*. We are sufficiently acquainted with their sentiments to anticipate their agreement with our determination, never willingly to submit either to temporal or spiritual bondage.[15]

A special committee of the Board was appointed to meet with the converts to try to persuade them to change their minds. At this meeting, Jacobi and Wolf withdrew their objections, submitted meekly to the ASMCJ power structure and went to live on the farm. Jacobi worked as a fieldhand and Dr. Wolf acted as physician to the farmers in the neighborhood.

The controversy boiled down to a quarrel between the Board and Simon and Jadownicky. About July 1, rumors began to circulate that the two intended to leave the ASMCJ and organize a settlement project of their own. The Reverend Stephen N. Rowan, pastor of New York's Eight Presbyterian Church and secretary of the Board, wrote to Jadownicky, asking him if the rumors were true. Jadownicky replied that this was the situation and he intended to leave for Europe shortly to seek funds for the new settlement. The Board met on July 11 and dismissed Jadownicky from its care and employ. Simon was present at the Board meeting and was asked if he was associated with Jadownicky in this matter. "Mr. Simon replied . . . that 'he was acquainted with the plans of Jadownicky, associated with him, and the principle actor in the business.' "20 Jadownicky left for Europe on July 12 and Simon remained behind to do battle with the ASMCJ Board.

The war between the ASMCJ and the two Hebrew Christians ended in complete victory for the ASMCJ. The effort of Jadownicky and Simon to collect funds for another settlement was a failure. But the prestige of the Society was weakened considerably by this happening. Many members, disgusted by the bickering, lost their enthusiasm for the colonizing venture. Simon returned to England, where he and Jadownicky continued their careers as missionaries. The 1827 report of the London Jews Society shows that Jadownicky was then employed by them as a missionary in Jerusalem.

Simon's later missionary activities seem to have been confined entirely to England. In 1828-1829 he caused the ASMCJ further trouble, as we shall learn presently. Years later he came back to this country and again became interested in the affairs of the ASMCJ, because the Society's twenty-third report, issued in 1846, lists Erasmus H. Simon "of Long Island" as "a member for life." When he returned to America, why, what he did and how long he stayed are not known.

Where was the Reverend J. S. C. F. Frey during all this hubbub and turmoil? He stayed on the sideline, rooting for the eventual winner. The August, 1825, *Israel's Advocate* states that, when the settlement rules were adopted by the Board, "Mr. Frey . . . was present and voted for them all." This is the only time he is mentioned during the entire controversy. During 1825 he continued to journey to and fro on behalf of the Society.

The Harrison farm project collapsed in less than a year. No more converts arrived from Europe. The Board decided it was useless to keep the farm going for only two Hebrew Christians. Dr. Wolf, disheartened and disillusioned, departed for parts unknown. Jacobi returned to New York and began to learn a trade. The Society approached its sixth birthday with exactly one Christian Jew in its employ and under its care, the Reverend Joseph Samuel Christian Frederick Frey.

THE CRISIS OF 1826

On April 22, 1826, the ASMCJ Board made two important decisions: 1. The settlement idea would be abandoned; 2. The ASMCJ would direct its missionary efforts toward the six thousand Jews now living in America. The following article would be substituted for the second article of its present constitution:

Article II. The object of this Society shall be, to extend to the Jews the Gospel of our Lord and Saviour Jesus Christ; and, if necessary, to communicate temporal assistance in procuring employment to those from among them, who are either converts to Christianity, or appear to be sincere inquirers after the way of life and salvation through Christ our Redeemer.[21]

These decisions were presented to the annual meeting of the Society in May, 1826, together with the following facts: In six years, the ASMCJ had received $31,560.06 and had expended $15,587.29; and yet had nothing to show for its efforts beyond the balance in the treasury and the headaches it had experienced trying to assist seven Christian Jews. The Christians of New York City had furnished only a very small part of the funds. Most of the money had come from small collections in towns and villages along the eastern seaboard.

The incoming Board was directed to take the necessary legal steps to have the ASMCJ changed from a colonization to a missionary society. Jay resigned as president and was succeeded by Jonas Platt. This is the last time that Jay's name appears as an active ASMCJ worker.

On July 25, Platt, as chairman of the Legal Committee, reported to the Board that the Society had no legal right to change Article Two of its constitution or to use the funds of the Society for any other purpose except that for which they had been collected. The Board decided to request the New York legislature to permit it to change its constitution.

In August a communication was received, signed by a number of members, informing the Board that the signers would resist strenuously any attempt to alter the original charter. Unnerved by this unexpected opposition, the Board rescinded its decision to seek legislative approval for a change "lest other great Christian charities, as well as this one, should be injured by a public exposure of our difficulties."

Jewish settlement or missionary society? A mood of confusion and helplessness settled over the Board. It knew not what to do. No activities were being carried on, no money collected. *Israel's Advocate* suspended publication at the end of 1826. The Reverend Stephen Rowan was relieved of his duties and salary as Editor and Agent.

The individual most deeply affected by this cessation of activity was the Reverend J. S. C. F. Frey. He could not continue to earn his living by acting as "travelling beggar for the Jewish Nation," a title conferred upon him by an unfriendly contemporary. He and his family were in great financial distress. He appealed to the Board for help. The Board responded that "while they maintain a high regard for Mr. Frey, and sympathize with him in his pecuniary embarrassments," giving him financial help in the existing circumstances would be a misuse of the funds of the Society. They advised him to seek regular employment as a clergyman.

In the ninth edition of his *Narrative*, published in 1832, Frey did not choose to reveal the exact manner in which the Society dispensed with his services in 1826. He describes the circumstances of his leaving the ASMCJ employ as follows:

> In 1826, finding that there was more than $16,000 in the treasury, and nothing done for meliorating the condition of the Jews, I could neither see the necessity nor justice of my continuing any longer as agent and eating the bread of idleness. I therefore resigned my agency and returned to my ministerial labors.

At its December meeting, the Board arrived at another important decision. Since there were so many obstacles in the way of engaging in missionary activities in the United States, the ASMCJ would continue its effort to establish a Jewish Christian settlement. Once more a committee was appointed to select a suitable location for the colony.

THE CRISIS OF 1827

The committee appointed by President Platt was composed entirely of friends and supporters of Frey. Perhaps Platt hoped that the committee would not only find a site that would please the Board but also furnish a means of relieving Frey's difficulties. In the meantime, Frey had moved to Yorkville, a community in the suburbs of New York City, to a section then known as Harlem Commons, and had commenced to hold services there.

At the January, 1827, meeting the committee presented a report which indicated that it had tried valiantly to please the Reverend Mr. Frey. It recommended the purchase of several lots in, of all places, Yorkville! The majority of the Board frustrated the good intentions of Platt and the committee and the hopes of Frey by rejecting the committee's recommendation. So Platt had to instruct the committee to seek some other settlement site.

On February 13, the Board met again. This time Frey and his friends made sure that the Board would vote as they wanted it to vote. Twelve persons, never before members of or interested in the ASMCJ, attended the meeting, paid five dollars each to become directors, and voted as Frey wanted them to vote. Ten of these newcomers were from Yorkville.

At this meeting a committee headed by the Reverend Gardiner Spring, a committee which had been assigned the task of drawing up plans for the proposed settlement, brought in two resolutions:

> First, that a committee be appointed to look out for a suitable Agent to proceed to Europe, for the purpose of ascertaining the condition of the Jews, and satisfying the Board as to the best plan of operations in forming and conducting a Jewish settlement in this country, agreeable to the Constitution; and that, in the meantime, a committee be appointed to inquire for a suitable location for the settlement and to report to the Board.
>
> Second, that, in the event of the rejection of this resolution, a committee be appointed to report on the most expedient and prompt course to be pursued in order to refund the monies now in the treasury to their original donors. This last resolution, the committee beg leave to say, is the plan of their choice.[22]

The resolutions were defeated by a vote of 24 to 15. Immediately thereafter, the Reverend Mr. Spring and a majority of his committee resigned as directors of the Society.

Another Board meeting was held two weeks later. The resignation of Jonas Platt as ASMCJ president was received and accepted. The Board voted to continue the settlement project. The location committee recommended that six lots of ground in Yorkville be leased at a yearly rental of $250. The recommendation was adopted by a vote of 13 to 9.

More Board meetings were held on March 27 and May 4. At the latter meeting, Frey was again taken under the wing of the Society. He was given permission to live in a dwelling on the ground leased in Yorkville and was voted a donation of $200.

The annual meeting was held on May 11. The Board reported that "it had to confess and deplore a year of fruitlessness." At least thirty members of the Board of Directors resigned from the Society at this meeting. Most were young and liberal enthusiasts, whose affiliation with the ASMCJ had been prompted by humanitarian as well as theological considerations. Their withdrawal was due mainly to a realization that little hope of rendering any useful service to the Jewish people was embodied in the program of the ASMCJ. Frey reported that only five of the Society's four hundred auxiliaries were currently active. John Savage, Chief Justice of the New York Court of Appeals, succeeded Platt as president. Platt continued to serve as a member of the Board.

Those who remained loyal to the ASMCJ at this critical juncture did so not only because of their Christian duty toward the Jews but also

because of their Christian interest in the almost sixteen thousand dollars
that remained in the Society's treasury. There is little doubt that, if the
Society's finances had been as low as its spirit, it would have collapsed
completely in 1827.

During the next year, the inactivity of the Society was as marked as
the public disfavor in which the Society now found itself. The group
of directors who had resigned published the story of what had been happening within the Society during the early months of 1827. This helped
to increase the volume of the criticism heaped upon the ASMCJ from
every quarter, Christian as well as Jewish, conservative as well as liberal.

Once more the Society ceased to function. Frey's financial resources
were again exhausted. His efforts to organize a Presbyterian church in
Yorkville failed. The Society had no work for him to do. He was unable
to obtain a Presbyterian pastorate anywhere. Beset by these personal
problems, he again experienced one of those theological changes of heart
which always seem to have coincided with the demands of economic
necessity. He left the Presbyterians and became a Baptist. He was baptized
by immersion at New York's Mulberry Street Baptist Church on Sunday,
August 28, 1827. As a reward for taking the plunge, he was called to
serve a Baptist church in Newark, N. J. Although his name continued to
appear on the ASMCJ directors' list, his active connection with the organization ceased for nearly nine years. Not until January, 1836, did he
again attempt to obtain financial sustenance from the Society.

THE NEW PALTZ VENTURE

In April, 1828, the Society was aroused from its quiescent state by a
report of the settlement committee that a suitable site had finally been
located, a five-hundred-acre farm at New Paltz, Ulster Country, about
seventy miles north of New York City and eight miles west of the Hudson
River. The Board approved the purchase of the farm for $6,500. Because
no converts were then within reach, the farm was rented to the farmer
resident upon it for one year for $100.

At the ninth annual meeting in May, the Board noted that, since the
last annual meeting, two prominent vice presidents of the Society, the
Reverend Samuel Blatchford and DeWitt Clinton, had died. DeWitt
Clinton, 1769-1828, served as Mayor of New York City, Governor of
New York State, and U.S. Senator. He was chiefly responsible for the
building of the Erie Canal.

After reporting the purchase of the New Paltz farm, the Board recommended that an agent be sent to Europe to visit the United Kingdom, Poland, and Germany to obtain the cooperation of European Christians and "to ascertain the state of the Jews." The recommendation was adopted. The Reverend Stephen Rowan was designated as the agent. He was to obtain a year's leave of absence from his church. He was given $1,500 to support his family during this period and $2,000 for traveling expenses.

Rowan left for Europe on September 8 and arrived in London about a month later. He was greeted by the news that Count von der Recke's Duesselthal operation was no more. Just as it was beginning to achieve prominence and success, it was closed by order of the government. Rowan informed his colleagues that "its dissolution is owing to causes which render the establishment of a similar institution *indispensable*." A short time later he reported that two of the former Jewish residents of Duesselthal were on their way to America and many more were planning to make the same journey. Rowan also learned that Erasmus H. Simon had neither forgotten nor forgiven.

> Actuated by a strong malice against that Society which had done him no wrong, but had detected and exposed his unprincipled conduct while here, and had expelled him from the Board, he gained over another individual or two, and made an attack on Dr. Rowan which for violence, pertinacity, and falsehood, has seldom been equalled in a Christian land. Our good cause sustained some little injury. But our Agent vindicated the Society in every point assailed, and gained even more friends than ever. It so happened that Mr. Simon is too well known in London and in Edinburgh to effect much injury in this matter.[23]

Rowan then traveled through Great Britain, Ireland, Holland, Germany, and Poland, organizing Society auxiliaries and refuting various charges made by Simon and others against the ASMCJ. He sailed from Liverpool on July 24 and arrived in New York on August 24. He informed the Board that his traveling expenses had amounted to $500 more than the allotted $2,000. The Board voted him the additional sum.

This transatlantic journey cost the Society more than $4,000 and accomplished practically nothing. The European auxiliaries never helped the Society in any way and quickly ceased to exist. Nor did Rowan succeed in inducing any great number of Christian Jews to migrate to the United States. Only three converts took advantage of the golden opportunity and journeyed to the American ASMCJ haven.

When the year's lease on the New Paltz farm expired in April, 1829, the Board took over the farm and began to make preparations for its early occupancy, because of Rowan's claim that many of the former Jewish inhabitants of Duesselthal would arrive very soon.

The tenth annual meeting was held on May 15, 1829. No funds had been collected during the year. Cash on hand was $5,178 and value of the property $7,250, making the total assets of the Society $12,428. Speeches were delivered by two Hebrew Christians, Jacobi and the Reverend Judah Isaac Abraham.

Abraham was an English Jew of Dutch descent, born in 1802, who became a Christian at age fifteen. He landed in Boston in 1822 destitute. He was helped by the American Board of Commissioners for Foreign Missions, a Congregationalist society. He is said to have been learned in English, French, Spanish, Italian, Latin, Greek, and Hebrew and also knew some Portuguese and German. In March, 1823, he was sent to the ABCFM school at Cornwall, Conn., where he both studied and taught. In 1826, he entered Andover Theological Seminary and was graduated from there in 1829. For the next year he lived in and about New York City and was supported by the ASMCJ.

Shortly after the 1829 annual meeting, the New Paltz Christian Jewish settlement got under way. It was inhabited by four Christian Jews, Jacobi, Abraham, and two of the three converts that Rowan had succeeded in finding in Europe. The third, for some unknown reason, did not satisfy the Board and was soon cast adrift. The four proselytes lived on the farm during most of the following year. They worked six days a week and, on Sundays, conducted a Sunday School for the children of the neighboring farmers. The farm failed to meet expenses and the Board was forced to contribute a large sum of money to its upkeep.

The agricultural venture soon became so expensive that the Board decided to bring the converts back to New York City and support them there. Abraham was given permission to prepare for ordination as a Presbyterian minister and the others were apprenticed to mechanical tradesmen. One was taught to be a saddler, another to make locks. The occupation of the third is not recorded. None ever went back to the farm. By October, 1831, all had severed their connection with the Society.

Discouraging indeed were the facts placed before the Society by its Board at the eleventh annual meeting in May, 1830. The treasurer reported cash on hand, $955.81 and value of farm $8,250, or total assets of $9,305.81. The Board announced that since its charter forbade it to do missionary work in the United States, it had decided to send missionaries to the Jews of Europe. The first would be the Reverend Judah

Isaac Abraham, who would be located in Thessalonica, Greece. Rowan was about to give up his pulpit to occupy the combined positions of Clerical Superintendent of the New Paltz settlement and Traveling Agent for the ASMCJ. He was to receive use of the house, farm, and sawmill at New Paltz, rent free, "and firewood and all produce, if he cultivates it himself, and $800 per annum in money, in equal quarterly payments."[24]

Abraham received Presbyterian ordination at about this time. Two months later he left for Europe. His passage money was raised through special collections taken in Presbyterian churches in New York and Philadelphia. Much to the disappointment of the ASMCJ, he never reached Thessalonica, Greece. He was offered a position by the London Jews Society, accepted it, and was employed by the LJS as a missionary to the Jews of England. Thus began and ended the only attempt of the ASMCJ to send missionaries to Jews of foreign lands.

The activities, if any, of the Reverend Dr. Stephen N. Rowan as Clerical Superintendent and Traveling Agent are shrouded in mystery. They are not recorded in the annals of the Society. All mention of Rowan ceases after 1830, except that, on several occasions, his European trip is referred to as having been a stupid and fruitless waste of money.

From the end of 1830 until the beginning of 1836, the ASMCJ did absolutely nothing except try to get rid of the New Paltz farm. It made no attempt to found settlements or support missionaries. This period of its history witnessed a shift in the nature of the leadership of the Society. From 1820 to 1830, all the presidents were outstanding laymen. From 1830 until the Society expired in 1870, all the presidents were outstanding clergymen. From 1830 to 1835, no reports were issued. No annual meetings seem to have been held. It appears that during these years the Reverend William C. Brownlee was president.

The heyday of the Society, replete with grandiose schemes and nationally known officers and hundreds of auxiliaries and thousands of members and tens of thousands of speeches, came to an end in 1830. The Society did not really come of age, figuratively as well as literally, until about 1841. Its most rational efforts, even though they accomplished very little, are found in the years from 1841 to 1855. These later years are marked by fewer and less prominent officers and members; but the aims and ideals of these years sound a note that is less ethereal and more realistic. From 1820 to 1830 the ASMCJ was primarily a layman's spiritual plaything. Following 1835, its affairs were handled by hardheaded, practical preachers.

The expenses incurred in the maintenance of the New Paltz farm were so heavy that, in October, 1831, the Society was compelled to mortgage the property. It remained unoccupied for a number of years, during which the neighboring farmers, regarding it as lawful plunder, cut down its most valuable timber, carried away its fences, built roads through it and stole everything on the premises that was movable. Perhaps, in the interest of absolute truth, the word "everything" should be changed to "almost everything." A committee, sent by the Society to collect the farm implements and the tools, reported that "we could not find said property, in whole or in part, except one cart, one old workbench and one small grindstone." In 1835, the Society decided to sell the farm. To the Board's great surprise and delight, it brought the very good price of $8,400, a fine increase over the $6,500 paid for it. When all bills were settled, the Society had a favorable balance of $6,079. Happy days were here again! The Board, freed of its financial worries, could concentrate once more upon its task of bringing the glorious gospel to the Jews.

But how was this to be done? It had no settlement, no missionaries, no converts, nothing but $6,079. In that critical hour, when the Board yearned for proper guidance, a noble, unselfish, consecrated man appeared before it and said, "I've got the answer you seek!" Who was this man? None other than the Reverend Joseph Samuel Christian Frederick Frey.

FREY'S EUROPEAN TOUR

In the years since 1827, Frey had experienced his habitual ups and downs, although during these years and those yet to come, the downs far outnumbered the ups. He remained in Newark until April, 1830, and then became pastor of a Baptist church in New York City. After two years in this pulpit, he resigned to devote his energies to the lecture platform. For the next few years, he traveled about, delivering speeches in hundreds of Christian churches. Wherever he went, large audiences gathered to see and hear this religious oddity. The novelty finally wore off and Frey was compelled to find some other means of earning a livelihood. In December, 1835, he began to preach in a schoolhouse in Jamaica, Long Island. As had happened in 1817, a number of people soon began to attend Frey's services regularly and he was able to establish a new Baptist congregation. In March, 1836, Frey's congregation built a church.

Evil rumors concerning Frey's character continued to circulate. On March 12, 1829, Frey found it necessary to secure the following statement from the recording secretary of the ASMCJ:

It is hereby certified that the accounts of the Rev. C. F. Frey as an agent of the American Society for Meliorating the Condition of the Jews were audited and settled to the entire satisfaction of the board, on his ceasing to be their agent.[25]

Some unscrupulous persons spread the report that Frey had fled to the United States after fleecing three thousand pounds from the London Society, that he had embezzled a considerable sum of money from the ASMCJ, and, in consequence, had been excommunicated by the New York presbytery and forced to become a Baptist. In December, 1831, the N.Y. *Baptist Register* published a statement, signed by four Baptist ministers, saying that these charges had been investigated thoroughly in England and America and were absolutely untrue. These false rumors reached their most absurd height a few years later when the N.Y. *Transcript* printed a story, copied by many other papers, that

> Mr. Frey, the converted Jew, has absconded with $100,000 collected for converting the Jews, and is now living in a splendid palace in Italy, where he is enjoying otium cum dignitate.[26]

During his spare time, Frey wrote and published a missionary tract, "Joseph and Benjamin." It is a polemic which defames Judaism and exalts Christianity. Frey declares he wrote this work to effect the conversion of some American Jews. He admits that, until now, his following has been entirely non-Jewish.

> During my twenty years residence in this country, I had but little opportunity of preaching to my Jewish brethren, there being but comparatively few of them here; still I never lost sight of their precious and never-dying souls. . . . As I could not preach to my brethren, I resolved to write to them.[27]

In January, 1836, Frey attended an ASMCJ Board meeting and suggested it publish his tract and distribute it among the Jews of the United States, England, and Germany. The Board assented and implemented the action by passing the following resolution:

> Whereas, this Society was established for the twofold purpose of *colonizing* and *evangelizing* the Jews, and
>
> Whereas, the attempt to colonize them has been unsuccessful;
>
> Resolved, that this Board will take early measures to carry into effect the other equally important object of the Society, to evangelize the Jews.[28]

The Society's legal advisors raised an objection almost immediately. Once more the Society was informed that it could not use its funds for missionary purposes, since its charter stated that its money must be used for the specific purpose of establishing a Jewish Christian settlement and for no other purpose. Undaunted, the Board voted to raise a separate fund to carry out the tract project. Notices were placed in a number of religious papers soliciting contributions. Letters were sent to those considered "friends of Israel," asking for financial support. The results were disappointing. Little money was raised. The ASMCJ reputation was so bad that even the most orthodox Christians refused to aid its latest venture. It became clear that not enough money would be raised in the United States to finance Frey's tract. So, on November 22, the Board decided to send Frey to Great Britain and Ireland to try to raise the necessary funds in those countries. Frey was very willing to go. And, of course, in addition to his financial mission, Frey was given another task, i.e., to ascertain whether there were any European Christians, especially those of Jewish birth, who were still interested in the settlement idea.

Frey resigned from his church, left his business affairs in the hands of his son John and, at age sixty-five, embarked upon his second European adventure. Accompanied by his wife and youngest child, he sailed for England in February, 1837, and arrived in London on March 8. He brought with him a large number of letters of recommendation from American clergymen. A "respectable meeting" was held in London at which Frey was authorized to solicit funds in Great Britain for the publication of his writings. Shortly thereafter Frey found himself in serious difficulty. Those who disliked him and the cause he represented did much to make trouble for him.

Three obstacles stood in his way. The first was

> the great prejudice excited against this Society, both in England and in Germany by the former agency [i.e., Rowan's 1828-1829 trip]. I succeeded, however, in removing this difficulty by assuring our friends that the affairs of the Society are now better managed.[29]

The second was a report spread by a Reverend Dr. Reed that Frey was not highly regarded in the United States. The third was a rumor that Frey, in 1816, had stolen three thousand pounds from the London Jews Society.

Frey's supporters in England and American rallied to his defense. Sir Thomas Baring, who had been president of the LJS in 1816 and was still president, issued a statement in which he absolved Frey from the charge of having misused any of the London Society's funds. He carefully refrained from mentioning the real reason for Frey's dismissal. When a committee requested him to serve as treasurer of the funds being collected, he told them

> I have retired from business some years ago and have refused several offers; but, knowing how Mr. Frey has been slandered and persecuted, I will not only accept the office of Treasurer but also commence the subscription with a donation of twenty pounds.[30]

The ASMCJ Board sent Frey a resolution on August 1 expressing complete confidence in his integrity and ability.

Frey spent the rest of 1837 and the first few months of 1838 supervising the publication of a second tract, "Judah and Israel," and traveling about England making speeches and collecting money.

He attempted to sail for Germany in January but was turned back by a severe winter storm. In May he journeyed to Hamburg without mishap. On June 1, the Berlin Society for Promoting Christianity among the Jews endorsed the settlement proposition and offered to distribute five thousand copies of "Joseph and Benjamin" among German Jewry if Frey would make a German translation and raise the funds for the printing and binding. This Frey promised to do.

Frey made the translation and returned to Great Britain to raise the money needed to have the German edition published. He journeyed all over England and Ireland gathering funds and explaining the settlement idea. By May 31, 1838, his labors were completed. He had collected 1,119 pounds, 4 shillings, 5½ pence, and he had spent 1,252 pounds, 1 shilling 2 pence. The expenses included the cost of printing the five thousand German copies of "Joseph and Benjamin" and Frey's traveling expenses. So there was a balance due Frey of 132 pounds, 16 shillings, 8½ pence, plus the cost of returning to the United States. Frey had no money with which to pay the unfavorable balance or to buy passage tickets. Again Sir Thomas Baring came to his rescue. Baring contributed ten pounds to help make up the deficit and also assisted Frey to secure the needed passage money.

Frey returned to the United States early in October, 1839, to learn that, during his absence, his American financial state had gone from bad to worse. To pay for the eastern leg of his Atlantic crossing, he had sold his library to the New York Conference of Baptist Ministers for "the trifling sum of $300, in hopes of still having the use of same on my return. . . . The Conference, not being able to repay the money they had borrowed to pay me for the library, sold it at auction." He owed the printer of the *Jewish Intelligencer*, a magazine Frey had published from June, 1836, to January, 1837, a considerable amount of money. Of $1,700 due for unpaid subscriptions, only $30 had been retrieved. In addition, he had lost three-years' salary as pastor, his income as editor of his magazine, and had brought back with him nearly a thousand-dollars' worth of unpaid bills.

Frey also now learned, to his great dismay, that the ASMCJ Board was of the opinion that it had not pledged to pay any part of his trip expenses but had merely *loaned* him $700 to help him get started. Frey was expected to support himself and to pay for his trip from the profits which would accrue from the sale of his tracts.

A special Board committee was appointed to consider Frey's plight. On October 28, it recommended that the Board adopt the following resolutions:

> Resolved, That the thanks of this Board are due to Mr. Frey for his exertions to carry into effect, during his late mission, the objectives of the Board in the publication and distribution of the work entitled "Joseph and Benjamin."

> Resolved, That this Board are pained to learn that the pecuniary circumstances of Mr. Frey are in such an embarrassed condition as he describes; but inasmuch as he has already received from this Society the full amount which he agreed to accept for his services at the time of his appointment, this Board is not bound to grant him any aid, nor has he any claim whatever upon this Society.

The Board approved these resolutions. Frey protested vigorously. He pointed out that the Rowan agency had cost the ASMCJ more than $4,000. When Rowan announced, on his return, that he was in debt, the Board not only failed to reprove him for his extravagance or to say that it felt "pained," but it had granted him an additional $500 and the use of the New Paltz farm rent free. Frey concluded by asking the Board to appoint him its missionary to the Jews of New York City.

The Board decided to reconsider and turned the matter back to the committee. On December 2 the committee reported again. Its recommendations remained as before with one addition—that the Society refuse Frey's request to serve as its New York missionary. This time the Board accepted the report completely and irrevocably.

This action angered and hurt Frey deeply. For a number of years he maintained a hostile attitude toward the ASMCJ. A few days after the the final Board decision, Frey printed and distributed a twenty-four·page pamphlet titled "The Report of the Late Agency of the Rev. J. S. C. F. Frey, presented to the Board of Managers of the ASMCJ." The pamphlet described the entire matter in great detail.

Later Frey charged that the Board had refused to employ him as a missionary because it was predominantly Presbyterian and he was a Baptist. In February, 1846, the ASMCJ magazine, the *Jewish Chronicle*, heatedly denied this accusation.

> We solemnly assert . . . not only that there is no foundation for the insinuation that (Frey's) "being a Baptist was an insurmountable objection," or any objection at all, in the way of his appointment, but that the Board is not aware of the existence of any circumstances which could possibly be so far perverted as to justify even the remotest suspicion of such a thing. Nay, if the whole truth may be told, his being a Baptist rather weighed in his favor; but there were other considerations connected with the case which exercised a controlling influence on the decision of the Board.[31]

After being cast adrift by the ASMCJ, Frey attempted to go into the missionary business on his own. He started a mission to the Jews in a room of the South Baptist Church on Nassau Street, New York City, on December 29, 1839. The pioneer effort soon collapsed.

Frey finally landed a job as pastor of the Bethel Baptist Church in Williamsburgh, Long Island, at a salary of four dollars a week.

Chapter Six

Other Efforts: Organized and
Disorganized (1820-1839)

The other attempts to convert American Jews during this period were puny and feeble.

The Female Jews Society of Boston and Vicinity continued to do what it could to advance the cause of Jewish evangelization. In 1822 it reported a contribution of $50 toward the support of Jadownicky at Princeton and a treasury balance of $435. In 1824 the annual contribution was sent to the London Jews Society and assistance was given to the mission which Pliny Fisk and Levi Parsons established in Palestine in 1819 for the Congregationalist American Board of Commissioners for Foreign Missions. From 1826 until the Society ceased to function in early 1844, it was practically a one-man organization, i.e., it did little except aid the efforts of a well-known missionary to the Jews of Constantinople, William Gottlieb Schauffler, 1798-1883.

Schauffler, a German non-Jew, was converted from Lutheranism to Anglicanism by the Hebrew Christian missionary, Joseph Wolff. (There are erroneous accounts that Wolff was in the United States for a time between 1831 and 1836 and was converted to Christianity and ordained as an Episcopal clergyman while in this country. The facts are that Wolff, born in Bavaria in 1796, was converted to Roman Catholicism in Germany in 1809 and to Anglicanism in London in 1819. Shortly thereafter he became an Anglican missionary.)

Schauffler came to America in 1826 to prepare for a career as a missionary to the Jews in the Near East. He enrolled in Andover Theological Seminary, a Congregationalist school at Andover, Mass. During his seminary years, he received financial help from the Female Jews Society. He was ordained as a missionary to the Jews at the Park Street Congregational Church, Boston, on November 14, 1831. Moses Stuart, professor of Hebrew at Andover, preached the ordination sermon. A month after Schauffler's ordination, Hannah Adams died; but her society continued to send money to Schauffler for twelve years. The twenty-seventh and last report of the Society, issued at the end of 1843, states that $147 was sent to Schauffler during 1843 and that his work was seriously handicapped by lack of funds. The Female Society of Boston and Vicinity for Promoting Christianity amongst the Jews went out of existence shortly thereafter.

In its early years, Andover Theological Seminary was a center of intense missionary activity. Practically all the missionaries of the American Board of Commissioners were trained there during these years. The American Tract Society was born on the Andover campus. It was natural, therefore, that the professors and students at this institution would have a special interest in Jewish conversion.

The Palestinian missionaries Fisk and Parsons were graduates of Andover. While Schauffler was studying there, he organized special prayer meetings, held every Friday evening, for the salvation of Israel. These gatherings were known as the "Jews Meeting."

There was also Jonas King, 1792-1869. King was graduated from Williams College in 1816 and from Andover Seminary in 1819. Pliny Fisk wanted his classmate to go with him to Palestine; but King decided to become a home missionary. He entered the employ of the South Carolina Female Domestic Missionary Society at Charleston, S.C. He worked for this society about six months, chiefly among the sailors in the port of Charleston, but he also "visited some families of Jews and reasoned with them from their scriptures respecting the Messiah."[1]

These Jewish contacts must have been very stimulating, for King determined to return to Andover and prepare for service in the Jewish field. He spent a year at Andover studying Hebrew and a year in Paris learning Arabic. He then joined Fisk in Palestine and remained with that mission for three years. Dissatisfied with the results he was achieving in the Holy Land, he went to Greece and missionized among the Catholics of that country for the rest of his life. He gained fame in Greece both as a missionary and as an American consul.

Andover Seminary seems to have taken little or no part in the activities of the ASMCJ, probably because it was felt that the Congregational descendants of the New England Puritans and the New York Presbyterians, Dutch Reformers, and Baptists represented different cultural and, also perhaps, theological backgrounds.

There was a group within the Presbyterian Church which believed that non-Presbyterians had too much voice in the management of the ASMCJ. They wanted a Jewish missionary enterprise which would be one hundred per cent Presbyterian. Following the liberal-conservative split of 1837, which divided the denomination into "New School" and "Old School" factions, the "Old School" or conservative faction decided to begin a Jewish work of its own. The retiring moderator of this group's 1839 General Assembly suggested that it send missionaries to American Jews. A motion to that effect passed unanimously. Lack of funds compelled the "Old School" Presbyterians to delay the beginning of their Jewish campaign until late in 1846.

The activities of the ASMCJ and the Boston Female Society prompted the formation of four additional "Jewish" societies in 1823 in Boston, Portland, Providence, and Northampton, Mass. None lasted more than two years or accomplished anything of importance.

The first Canadian missionary society, devoted primarily to the conversion of Jews, was not organized until 1840. Efforts prior to that date to convert the few Jews in Canada were sporadic, unorganized, and ineffective. Individual members of the Church of England in Canada sent contributions to the London Jews Society. The English society, in return, sent these contributors tracts to distribute among their Jewish neighbors. According to Louis Meyer, several Jews were baptized in Canada between 1820 and 1839, among them Henry Abraham Joseph, born in Lower Canada in 1803 and baptized in 1836, "a retired slave dealer and free thinker," and David Baruch, baptized in Halifax in 1838.[2]

The events narrated on these few pages represent the sum total of the known efforts to involve Christians in the conversion of the Jews of the United States and Canada in the third and fourth decades of the nineteenth century. The record speaks for itself. Little was done. Nothing was accomplished.

Chapter Seven

The ASMCJ "Domestic" Period (1840-1870)

The Frey fiasco of 1836-1839 caused the ASMCJ Board to abandon whatever intention it may have had of continuing to engage solely in the publication and distribution of missionary tracts to the Jews. Its determination to gain Jewish converts remained strong. The Society continued its search for some successful method of approach to the Jew.

For about a year and a half, the Society experimented with several different techniques.

> In 1840, the Society were enabled to make themselves useful in a limited degree, by administering to the necessities of several destitute Jews in this city, who had manifested a willingness to receive Christian instruction.[1]

This practice was soon abandoned and another plan adopted. A school for Jewish children was opened, not for the purpose of converting them, goodness no!—but purely "for their temporal benefit."[2] At first the school had an enrollment of fifteen pupils. When their parents discovered the nature of the school's sponsors, all but three of the children ceased to attend. The Board, "finding themselves without sufficient funds for the school's support, were compelled to discontinue it."[3]

At the annual meeting in May, 1841, the Society decided to cease thinking in terms of settlements and tracts and schools and alms-giving, and to launch a fund-raising campaign for the purpose of employing missionaries to bring the message of Christianity to American Jews in the most direct manner possible. It was resolved

> to open a new fund, for the purpose of meliorating the condition of the Jews otherwise than by a settlement, and solicit subscriptions and donations for the said fund, to be disposed of for the Jews, as such, irrespective of any profession of Christianity on their part, as may appear fit and proper.[4]

In January, 1842, Matthew A. Berk, who seems to have been a Hebrew Christian, was engaged as fund-collecting agent for the Society and "an eminent German convert from Judaism," the Reverend J. C. Moritz of Danzig, was invited to come to the United States as the Society's first missionary.

Why Berk was not appointed a missionary for the ASMCJ is not clear. In 1842 a *History of the Jews*, supposedly written by him, appeared in New York. The preface was by ASMCJ's President Brownlee. A second edition was printed in Boston in 1846. The Reverend William Jenks of that city wrote the preface to the second edition. In neither edition is there the slightest indication that the real author of the book was James A. Huie of Edinburgh, Scotland, who published it in Scotland in 1841. Nothing more is heard of Berk after 1846.

The twenty-third annual ASMCJ meeting was held on May 13, 1842. After announcing that Moritz had declined its invitation, the Board stated it was now trying to persuade the Reverend J. A. Hausmeister of Strasburgh, Alsace, to come to America as its missionary. Several large auxiliaries had been established in Eastern cities and liberal contributions made to the missionary fund. Shortly after the 1842 meeting, the Society began to publish the *Jewish Chronicle*, first as a four-page quarterly and later as a thirty-two-page monthly. It appeared regularly until the middle of 1855.

THE ASMCJ CONCENTRATES EXCLUSIVELY ON AMERICA JEWRY

In 1842 the Society took legal steps to change Article Two of its charter, the article which had caused it so much difficulty in the past. The change was effected without opposition from any source. Article Two, as revised, now declared:

The objects of this Society shall be,

1. To invite and receive from any part of the world, such Jews as do already profess the Christian religion, or are desirous to receive Christian instruction, to form them into a settlement, and to furnish them with the ordinances of the Gospel, and with such employment in the settlement as shall be assigned to them; but no one shall be received unless he comes well recommended for morals and industry, and without charge to the Society; and both his reception and continuance in the settlement shall be, at all times, at the discretion of the Directors.

2. To meliorate the condition of the Jews otherwise than by a settlement and to establish a fund for the temporal relief of distressed Jews, and for such other aid to the Jews as such, irrespective of any profession of Christianity on their part, as may appear expedient to the Board of Directors.[5]

The Society continued to include the settlement scheme among its objectives but, as a matter of fact, no further attempt was ever made to implement this idea. Two failures were enough. Also the second paragraph of Article Two was written in very generalized language in an' obvious attempt to conceal the real designs of the organization. Its official magazine, the *Jewish Chronicle*, used much more easily understood terminology:

It is proposed to devote the fund now in progress of being raised . . . to the employment of missionaries to labor among the Jews of the United States, to the temporal relief of indigent and deserving individuals of that denomination, to the circulation of tracts, bibles, and testaments among them, and to the communication of Christian instruction through any other appropriate channel.

Hausmeister of Strasburgh also refused to come to America. In October the Board, unable to secure a competent Hebrew Christian to perform the duties of a missionary, selected for that purpose a non-Jew, James Forrester. Forrester went to work in typical missionary fashion. He visited "the poorer classes of Jews . . . for the sake of giving a little charity, in one instance the sum of 25¢, and to talk a great deal about the Messiah."[6] Forrester resigned in August, 1845, convinced that he had been a failure as a missionary. In his letter of resignation, he wrote

Believing, as I do, that [Hebrew Christians] are better qualified to visit and converse with their brethren according to the flesh than I am, and knowing that your funds are low, and that you have a num-

ber of laborers in the field to support and little to do it with, I therefore tender you my resignation as City Agent for the Jews, hoping
that God, for Christ's sake, will enable me earnestly to pray, while
I have breath, for the salvation of the elect of God, whether Jews
or Gentiles.[7]

He continued to serve as a member of the Board after leaving the employ
of the Society.

One Jewish leader watched these developments with great indignation.
Isaac Leeser, 1806-1868, outstanding Philadelphia rabbi, was considerably
wrought up by the ASMCJ missionary program. In 1841 Leeser had written an one-hundred-page pamphlet, "The Claims of the Jews," in which he
had condemned Christian efforts to convert Jews. In April, 1843, he began
to publish a monthly magazine, the *Occident*. In the very first issue, he
devoted five pages to the "American Society for Meliorating the Condition of the Jews, and Its Organ, the '*Jewish Chronicle*.' "

> We would have been much pleased could our first number have ap-
> peared without a complaint against any portion of the American
> people. . . . Prejudice in its worst form, dislike for our religion, is
> still a characteristic of the vast multitude, and the effect of this pre-
> judice is seen in the revival of the association mentioned above, in
> former days known as the "A. S. M. C. J.," and the revival, too, of
> its organ, "Israel's Advocate," under the humbler title of "Jewish
> Chronicle." We had believed, and so written to our friends in Europe,
> that the Society had died for want of members, want of means, and
> want of converts; since for nearly 18 years we had heard nothing of
> its operations, or even its whereabouts, except that now and then a
> man formerly well known, though not to us, as the Rev. J. S. C. F.
> Frey, came forth from his domicile somewhere in New York or New
> Jersey, lecturing to his Jewish brethren in the Christian churches.
> Except for the labours of this curious being, equally famous for
> length of name as for the number of creeds he has professed, and a
> stray report once in a long while in papers which we did not read;
> there was like from Baal on Carmel, "neither voice, nor any to answer,
> nor one that regarded." But with the general attention lately paid to
> religious matters in America, this "bubble of the earth" has also crept
> again out of its chrysalis state, and has raised funds, employed mis-
> sionaries, and printed a paper.

In the May *Occident*, Leeser relates that he attended an April 19 meeting at which a Philadelphia ASMCJ auxiliary was organized. On this occasion, the ASMCJ organizer declared that the Reform synagogue recently established in London was founded as a result of the revelation of

the errors of Talmudic Judaism in the publications of the London Jews Society. While Leeser had no liking for the innovations of recently born Reform Judaism, he denied this allegation vigorously.

> How will our friends of the new congregation of Burton street relish the declaration that their reform is a legitimate result of a society, the object of which is the destruction of the Jewish religion? For our part, we should be sorry indeed were anyone to describe any act of ours as the result of such unfriendly advice; as we hope that they will boldly deny the assumptions of the missionary. We will merely say, that this is not the first time that the opponents of Judaism have gloried over the secession, and have feigned to discover therein a gradual approach to Christianity. We think that, much as we differ from the gentlemen who have too hastily adopted the new form of worship, they will be grieved as much as we were mortified to hear such motives ascribed to them; and, if they feel inclined, we offer them our magazine to reply to these unfounded charges.

In July, 1843, the Board undertook the financing of the education of Charles Reineman, a young Hebrew Christian, born in Bavaria and converted to Methodism there. His father later came to America and invited his son to join him. After young Reineman landed in New York, his father refused to support him unless he renounced his Christian faith. Reineman appealed to the ASMCJ for help. The Society sent him to Marshall College, Mercersburgh, Pa. One of his classmates there was another young Hebrew Christian, Joseph Stern, converted in Germany in 1842, who became a successful minister among the Germans in Ohio. In 1845 it was reported that Reineman had been transferred to Rutgers College so that the Board could keep in closer touch with him. This is the last time his name appears in the Society's annals.

Also in July, 1843, the Reverend Isaac Peter Labagh, a young non-Jewish Episcopalian, was engaged to collect money, organize auxiliaries, and preach to the Jews of New York City in a mission house rented for that purpose. From November, 1843, to May, 1844, he lectured every Saturday and succeeded in converting and baptizing one Jew. Two auxiliaries which he established drew the following banter from Leeser:

> Auxiliaries called "The Broadway (N. Y.) Tabernacle Ladies' Society for Promoting Christianity among the Jews" and another at Rochester, N.Y., called "The Rochester Auxiliary Ladies' Jews Society" have been formed. The former dates its birth from Oct. 6, 1843, and the latter has been in existence since summer. We have not heard of any Jewish congregations in the western part of New York;

we cannot therefore know against whom the ladies of Rochester mean
to direct their attacks. It is possible that the "Jewish Chronicle" may
enlighten us.[8]

In September, 1843, Brownlee was smitten by a paralytic stroke and
had to leave the active ministry. He resigned as ASMCJ president. Milledoler, who had given up the presidency of Rutgers College in 1840 and
had returned to New York, was named his successor.

The Fall of 1843 was also noteworthy for another reason. Frey patched
up his differences with the ASMCJ and agreed to go out for it again on a
money-raising jaunt. He toured the "south-western" states and returned
to New York on November 20.

> Owing to the rapidity with which he felt compelled to travel, and
> the great scarcity of money, but little was accomplished by him in
> the collection of funds for the Board. He has, however, prepared
> the way for more effectual labours by another agent, under more
> favorable circumstances.[9]

This was the last time Frey attempted to obtain financial support for or
from the ASMCJ.

The twenty-fifth ASMCJ annual meeting was held May 7, 1844. Re-
ceipts for the past year were: $1,903.28; expenditures, $1,872.71; total
assets, mainly bonds and notes, $5,521.11. During the year, seven New
York Jews had become Christians. Two had been converted by the
Baptists, two by the Methodists, two by the Lutherans, and one by the
ASMCJ. The Society now had ten auxiliaries.

Before the end of 1844 another Hebrew Christian was added to the
professional roster. Silian Bonhomme, a Frenchman, was employed as a
traveling agent. In the 1845 report he is listed as a Methodist, and in the
1846 report as a Episcopalian. In the 1847 report he is again referred to
as a Methodist. He served as agent and missionary until 1855. Then he
entered the employ of the Board of Foreign Missions of the Presbyterian
Church. He was almost constantly ill but, whenever his health permitted,
he labored for the cause. His last recorded effort on behalf of the conversion of Jews is an article published in the *Prophetic Times* magazine
in 1876.

The Board presented its twenty-second Report at the twenty-sixth annual meeting on May 8, 1845. Year's receipts were: $3,722.61; disburse-
ments $3,131.05; cash on hand, $591.56. Eight new auxiliaries had been

formed. The Reverend Nehemiah Altman, Hebrew Christian, United Brethren minister, native of Baden, Germany, had been added to the staff in March. He resigned the following November to accept a call to a church in Circleville, Ohio.

The guest of honor at the 1845 annual meeting was the well-known English Hebrew Christian missionary, the Reverend Ridley H. Herschell, 1807-1864. Herschell came to England from Russia about 1826 and was converted in April 1830 by Erasmus H. Simon. In 1842 Herschell founded and became the guiding genius of the non-conformist British Society for the Propagation of the Gospel amongst the Jews, an organization which is still functioning and is now known as the International Society for the Evangelization of the Jews.

Herschell came to the United States, at the request of the ASMCJ Board, to deliver lectures and collect money for the Society. He brought with him his younger brother Victor, who was on the verge of accepting Christianity, and had Victor placed in the home of a Philadelphia Presbyterian minister. Then he went about lecturing and collecting from May 6 to July 16. He was a very successful lecturer and collector. His tour extended from Baltimore to Montreal. To show its appreciation, the ASMCJ made him an honorary vice president.

The 1845 report mentions that Henry I. David, Hebrew Christian student at Princeton Theological Seminary, had worked for the Society three months during the past year. He also labored for the ASMCJ in New Jersey during the first six months of 1846. David's later career does not provide much encouragement for those who believe that a Jew's espousal of Christianity improves him spiritually.

Following his ordination as a Presbyterian minister, David was employed as a teacher of classics by several wealthy Philadelphia families. About 1851 he went to New York. After residing there for sometime, he returned to Philadelphia and applied for permission to plead before the Pennsylvania Supreme Court. He claimed that he had already received such permission for the New York State Supreme Court, although he presented no evidence to sustain this claim. Nevertheless the Pennsylvania Supreme Court granted his request.

David proceeded to swindle a number of Philadelphians out of large sums of money. To avoid arrest, he took ship to Australia. A windstorm forced the ship to dock in Rio de Janeiro. Following the old adage about "the ill wind," he settled in Rio and continued his swindling activities. When the Argentines began to react somewhat unpleasantly, he sailed for England. There he committed bigamy, swindled, and indulged in a number of other illegal procedures which resulted in his being disbarred from practicing in English law courts. In 1861 the Pennsylvania Supreme Court removed David's name from its lawyers' list and gave him one year in which to clear himself of all the charges made against him at home and abroad. He returned to Philadelphia a short time thereafter. Whether he was able to resume the practice of law is not known. The last public mention of the Reverend Henry I. David is on page 202 of the June 19, 1863, issue of the *Jewish Messenger*, which tells that David had been caught once more practicing some sort of confidence game on gullible Christian acquaintances.

In August, the Society rented a mission house at the corner of Second Street and First Avenue, New York City, to serve as headquarters for the Society, living quarters for its converts, and a preaching facility for its missionaries. The twenty-third Report explains that the house was obtained so that the Society might maintain a close watch on its protégés.

> The early friends of the American Society have not yet forgotten the repeated disappointments that formerly chilled their interest in the cause and led some of them even to entertain doubts, of which they can scarcely divest themselves after a lapse of fifteen or twenty years, as to whether a converted Jew can also be an honest man. . . . In our day especially, when the Jewish mind both in this country and in Europe is extensively tainted with infidel sentiments, and many acute, crafty, homeless adventurers find themselves suddenly, to their own amazement, let loose from the restraints even of rabbinic conscience and law, to push their fortune in the wide world, though it be by preying on the sympathy, often dormant, but still imperishable, of the Christian Church in the seed of Abraham—the Jewish mission, which at such a time fails to protect itself by the most likely methods from the assaults of deceivers, is sure to have a troublous career while it lives and to come to a speedy and shameful end.

At about this time, Bonhomme founded the "Brotherhood of Jewish Proselytes." Its membership included Forrester, Labagh, Joseph Stern, Berk, Reineman, P. J. Schory, a Hungarian Jew who had been baptized in Constantinople, and others. It did not last very long. Frey, who, in December, 1844, had organized the American Baptist Society for Evangelizing the Jews, behaved in a very unbrotherly manner. He established a rival "Brotherhood of Jewish Converts" and tried mightily to weaken the influence and numbers of the ASMCJ-sponsored group. His counterattack was a complete success. Within a few months both brotherhoods had ceased to exist.

Also in August, 1845, John Neander, a German convert, landed and went to work for the ASMCJ. He is not to be confused with the famous Hebrew Christian ecclesiastical historian, Johann August Wilhelm Neander, born David Mendel, 1789-1850, whose entire life was spent in Germany and who was never a professional missionary. "Our" John Neander was originally Marcus Hoch. He labored for the ASMCJ in New York, Philadelphia, and Baltimore. On June 28, 1846, the General Synod of the Dutch Reformed Church gave him a limited ordination of "missionary to the Jews." He left the ASMCJ in January, 1849, to go to work for the New York Presbytery.

For about two years, the ASMCJ had a board member who was a Hebrew Christian, but neither a missionary nor a clergyman. He was Isaac C. Mayer, a New York merchant. Mr. Mayer and the ASMCJ born Christians were not happy with each other. With what seems to have been a sigh of relief, the January, 1846, *Jewish Chronicle* announced that, at the November Board meeting, "Mr. Isaac C. Mayer, the Jewish member of the Board, tendered his resignation, which was unanimously accepted."

On November 11, the ASMCJ welcomed "ex-rabbi" John Leopold Lichtenstein and his family from Strasburgh, Alsace. He was appointed superintendent of the ASMCJ mission house. Less than a year later, he left the ASMCJ and entered the Presbyterian ministry. A letter written to the *American Israelite* in 1855 states that Lichtenstein was, for a time, with an Albany church but was dismissed for some sort of unspecified misconduct.[10] According to Louis Meyer, he was in later years "a prominent Presbyterian minister, writer, and lecturer in Cincinnati."[11]

Shortly before the 1846 annual meeting, another Hebrew Christian laborer was added, "ex-rabbi" German Lutheran minister, Reverend John H. Bernheim. He worked for a short time as ASMCJ traveling agent in New England. He died at Newburyport, Mass., in September, 1847. His family was left so destitute that a special collection had to be taken up in Newburyport to move it to Philadelphia.

The twenty-third Board Report was presented to the twenty-seventh annual meeting on May 13, 1846. Frey is again listed as a director for life "for services rendered." Erasmus H. Simon, of Long Island, is also listed as a life member. The two archenemies of the Society had returned to the fold. They had probably decided to let bygones be bygones and to renew their endorsement of the enterprise with which they had been associated, in one way or another, for a quarter of a century.

When Lichtenstein left in September 1846, the superintendency of the mission house was turned over to the Reverend John C. Guldin, non-

Jewish pastor of the German Evangelical Mission Church. Guldin was dismissed and the mission house vacated on May 1, 1847. The reasons for this are told in the twenty-fourth report.

> It must be confessed, that the difficulties in the way of successful management [of the mission house] are both numerous and formidable, arising from the character of too many of those who seek to avail themselves of the privilege of the Home, and the necessity of qualifications in the Superintendent that are very rarely found united in any one man. . . . The experience of the last twelve months has sufficiently shown that the plan does not commend itself to the judgment and sympathies of the American churches.

The churches' objection to the mission house becomes clearer as the report continues. It was suspected that ASMCJ was trying to establish a new Protestant sect, a separate Hebrew Christian Church, and that the mission house was to be the headquarters of this new sect. Many Protestant leaders refused to support the ASMCJ because they believed it was adding to Protestant diffusion and disharmony. The Board denied vigorously any intention of establishing a Hebrew Christian Church.

> The Board would have it distinctly understood, that it is not at all their desire or their wish to organize a separate church of converted Jews. . . . And as to the particular evangelical denomination with any convert shall connect himself, that is a matter in which this Society takes not the slightest interest.

On June 13, 1847, the ASMCJ baptized convert Bernhard Steinthal. Steinthal was schooled to be a chazan and melamed in Germany by two famous rabbis, Nathan Marcus Adler, 1803-1890, who became chief rabbi of England in 1842, and Samson Raphael Hirsch, 1808-1868, staunch opponent of Reform Judaism. After serving as cantor-teacher for five years, Steinthal joined the Reform group of Samuel Holdheim, 1806-1860, then landesrabbiner of Schwerin. After serving as cantor for three and a half years in Ludwigslust, Steinthal quit because he found Reform Judaism too cold. He then tried to go into business but encountered so many difficulties that, two and a half months later, he left for America. In New York City he met an ASMCJ missionary. Within a few months, he was converted, publicly baptized, and enrolled as a student at Andover Theological Seminary. He graduated from Andover in 1849 and went to work for the ASMCJ in September in Philadelphia. He left the Society in June, 1850, to become a missionary for the Presbyterian Board of Foreign Missions.

The Reverend Abraham David Cohen, for a short time Baptist minister at St. Helenaville, near Beaufort, S.C., was appointed ASMCJ missionary at Charleston, S.C., in October, 1847. Before his conversion Cohen was a housepainter.

> The reverend apostate never changed his religion from conviction, but merely out of gratitude to a Christian benefactor. This was his own private declaration in Charleston.[12]

He began his ASMCJ career on January 1, 1848 and resigned in January, 1849, to become pastor of a Baptist church. Cohen was still alive in July, 1903. He had retired from the ministry and was living in Baltimore.

During his brief stay with the ASMCJ, Cohen gained a genuinely sincere convert. He attracted into Christianity Herman Baer, born in Bavaria in 1830, the son of a chazan. Baer came to Charleston in April, 1847. Although converted by a Baptist, Baer joined the Methodists. He obtained employment with the *Southern Christian Advocate* as a compositor and proofreader. In 1852 he became a teacher in the preparatory department of Wofford College, a Methodist school in Spartanburg, S.C. He received an A.B. from this college in 1858 and an M.D. from Charleston Medical College in 1861. He served as a surgeon in the Confederate army. After the war he went into the wholesale drug business in Charleston. He frequently wrote for Methodist periodicals. In 1888 the Methodist Publishing House put out his book titled *Jewish Ceremonials*. Baer died in Charleston on January 2, 1901.

Another ASMCJ convert of this same period ended his Christian experience in a quite different manner. Bonhomme got hold of a young German immigrant, Solomon Fuld, who was living in Baltimore with his brother. After Bonhomme converted young Fuld, his extremely irate brother had Solomon arrested on some pretext and thrown into jail. Bonhomme succeeded in getting the convert out of jail and into the Episcopal theological seminary in Alexandria, Va., on March 28, 1848. Just how close Solomon came to being ordained is not recorded; but that his liking for Christianity was only temporary is clear from a statement written by him for the July 6, 1869, *Jewish Messenger*:

> Born and educated in the Jewish faith, I adhered faithfully to it, until in an unhappy moment of absence of mind, occasioned by a brain fever, I embraced Christianity. . . . Since the time that my health and mental faculties returned, I have never ceased with deepest penitence to regret that unfortunate step. . . . To give honor to my Heavenly

Father, I now declare myself, solemnly and publicly, a true Israelite who will forever acknowledge the God of Israel as the only true God of all nations, who hath never imparted His divine dignity or Deity to any living being. My Heavenly Father never died. My Redeemer lives in Heaven and He will redeem Israel at a time pleasing in His eyes. This is a true and faithful confession in which I shall live and die.

In the Spring of 1848, the Society received five pounds from a minister in Tecumsith Parsonage, Canada West. He had gotten this money from a neighboring backwoodsman. This country gentleman, expecting to meet his Maker ere long, prepared for this event by making out his will in July, 1844. One section read as follows:

And further more I Leve and bequeth to the Jewish Missionary Society forty pounds for helping to Convay Coppes of the Scripture and sending Missionaries to the Jews for if we have bee made particular of there Spiritual things I think it my duty to minister unto them in Carnal things and if I can Convay part of this said forty pounds Before my death I will mark it paid on the back of this Will.

In December, 1847, being yet in the land of the living, the poorly schooled philanthropist brought the minister the five pounds as first payment. Presumably he then made a notation on the back of his will that his estate now owed the Jews only thirty-five pounds.

The Board submitted its twenty-fifth report to the twenty-ninth annual meeting, May 10, 1848. In the past year, the Society received $5,395.34, spent $5,406, and was now $405 in debt. An appeal was issued to other missionary societies to cease working among American Jews, because their activities were hampering the fund-raising efforts of the ASMCJ. This appeal got no response.

McGREGOR SAVES THE DYING

The Society's future looked very bleak. No conversions were being made. At the annual meeting in May, 1849, the treasurer reported past year receipts, $5,585.08; disbursements, $5,572.72; balance in treasury, $12.36. Five months later the treasury was empty and most of the ASMCJ employees had been dismissed. Only four were left and they were leading a very precarious economic existence. The Board was greatly discouraged. "There was a universal want of confidence throughout the country in any scheme whose object was the colonization or the evangelization of the Jews."[13]

At this critical juncture, everything seemed to be in readiness for the funeral of the American Society for Meliorating the Condition of the Jews. But it was not to be. The Society was destined to struggle on for more than twenty additional years. The Reverend Edwin R. McGregor, Presbyterian, volunteered to give up what he later described as "a flourishing pastorate" to attempt to resuscitate the dying organization. His offer was accepted. The Board agreed to keep on trying. McGregor accomplished the seemingly impossible. During the nearly six years that he managed the affairs of the ASMCJ, the Society made a truly remarkable financial and prestigewise comeback.

The first addition to the missionary roster under McGregor's management was the Reverend G. D. Bernheim, son of the late ASMCJ employee, the Reverend J. H. Bernheim. Young Bernheim had been educated at the Lutheran Seminary in Lexington, Ky., and was working for the American Bible Society in Charleston, S.C. He became ASMCJ's Charleston missionary in April, 1850, and served in that capacity for about three years. His later activities are not known. Louis Meyer reported, in January, 1908, that Bernheim was "still alive, though very aged."[14]

Next, the Society acquired a young convert who was associated with it to the end of its days. Name: Moses Frankel. Born: Prussia, 1831. He was converted by the Reverend Mr. McGregor, baptized and renamed. Moses Frankel, Jew, became Morris Julius Franklin, Presbyterian. He studied under private tutors and at Newburgh Academy for two or three years and then entered New York University. He got an A.B. in 1855 and then entered Union Theological Seminary. He graduated from Union in 1857 and got an M.D. degree in 1858.

Whenever the ASMCJ needed money, Dr. Franklin was willing to undertake a tour in its behalf. In 1860 he was the Society's Recording Secretary. He served as a surgeon in the Union Army from the beginning to the end of the Civil War. Until 1884 he earned his living in New York City as physician and druggist. In that year he yielded to the age-long yearning of his people and went to Jerusalem, where he spent the remainder of his life. The missionary urge was still in his blood. For many years he was president of the Jerusalem Hebrew Christian Brotherhood. In 1903 he sent a message to an American group which was trying to organize a Hebrew Christian association.

> I rejoice to know that the blessed Redeemer has put it into your hearts to take up a work which, under less favorable circumstances and almost insurmountable difficulties, I alone sought to keep alive during the last thirty years of my residence in the United States.

Dr. Franklin was still alive and writing prescriptions for the Jerusalem sick in February, 1907.

Those who attended the thirty-first annual meeting in May, 1850, learned that the Society had collected $5,600 during the year and converted one Jew, i.e., Moses Frankel, alias Morris Julius Franklin.

In the next three months, seven more workers were added to the payroll. In January, 1851, the *Jewish Chronicle* boasted:

> Whatever may be said by the missionaries of other Boards, we know from our observation that the statements made by our laborers may be confidently relied on; and if other missionaries do not meet with anything like the same success, which we know they do not, it is not the fault of the field.

The same issue announced that two more Hebrew Christian workers had been added to the staff, Louis Waldenburgh and Abraham Tymim, "a converted rabbi."

Waldenburgh was employed as a colporteur in New York by the Society until the crisis of 1855. When the ASMCJ revived in 1859, he was re-employed and retained until the crisis of 1861. In 1863 he was hired again and was on the payroll until 1869.

"Rabbi" Abraham Tymim was a gentleman of many names and heaven alone knows which was the correct one. Among the other names he used were Abraham G. Wiplich, Johannes Wiplech, Abraham Diamond, Abraham Tumim, Abraham Timim, Abraham Tymin, and Abraham Tamin. Born in Galicia in 1797, he was converted by the London Jews Society Hebrew Christian missionary, Michael Alexander, 1799-1845, who later became first Anglican bishop of Jerusalem. Before coming to the ASMCJ, he had worked as a missionary in Cracow, London, Berlin, and Hamburg. His association with the Society was over before the end of 1854.

From March, 1857, to March, 1859, "Rabbi" Tymim's name appears often in the *American Israelite*. Some of Isaac M. Wise's statements about Tymim are inaccurate. Out of the welter of facts and fiction, these truths seem to emerge:

Tymim was ordained a deacon in the Episcopal Church by the Bishop of Detroit in May, 1856. He took out first papers for citizenship in New York City, June 23, 1856, under the name of Abraham G. Wiplich. Shortly thereafter he courted a recent immigrant, Rose Fuchs, and married her under false pretense, stating he was a Jewish merchant. They were married by a rabbi and kept a kosher home. In the Spring of 1857 his wife gave birth to a son. In the meantime, she had discovered, much to her chagrin, that she was married to an apostate. He traveled about lecturing in churches and collecting.

In the March 20, 1857, issue of the *Israelite*, Wise poured out his wrath upon Tymim:

> A man with a long beard, who calls himself Mr. Diamond, Tummim, or Mamsertomeh, and several other names, is between fifty and sixty years old, speaks a broken German, and a very poor English, and pretends to be the Agent of some Missionary society for the conversion of the Jews—mark this man; he is a cheat and an impostor. He is a travelling comedian, who imitates, in the churches, the old and forgotten ceremonies of the Synagogue; sings the peculiar melodies of the Russian Jews, and cuts many kinds of tricks before high heaven to amuse a parcel of curious folks, and get their money, which he spends on liquor. Diamond (what a wrong name!) pretends to convert Jews; but this is plainly and positively not true. He said to the Jews that he works for money, he never tried to convert a Jew, and he himself goes to the Synagogue during the autumnal feasts; but this preaching and harlequinade is his business! he says. On being shown an article of the "Israelite" against his clique, he always says, "Why does that man not let us alone? He works for money, and we work for money." We consider it our duty to expose the impostor to the public gaze and to caution the community against a scoundrel who makes money by lying and cheating! in the most sacred matters of humanity—in religion.

In February, 1859, Tymim took up residence in Cincinnati as missionary for the London Jews Society. His missionary career and life came to an end on March 11, 1859. He had been treating his wife very badly. A few days before his death he had threatened to shoot her. He died so suddenly that the coroner suspected that his wife had poisoned him. An autopsy showed that Tymim died from natural causes. In the March 25 issue of his weekly, Wise wrote a suitable obituary:

> When the intestines of the late Mr. Tymim were chemically dissolved, they were found to contain: Hypocrisy 25%, Dimes of credulous women 10%, Fiction and falsehood 15%, Prayer meetings and revivals 4%, Christianity 1%, Impertinence 20%, Imposition 14%. The rest consisted of pious sighs and religious fraud. Learned men were astonished at the peculiar phenomena thus exposed, and came to the conclusion that he was dead right after he died and long before it, as individuals of that kind only vegetate.

Between February and May, 1851, the ASMCJ engaged another missionary and two student colporteurs.

The missionary was Hebrew Christian Louis C. Newman. Converted in England, he worked in Constantinople for the London Jews Society until he came to America to labor for the ASMCJ. He severed this connection prior to May, 1854. In February, 1858, he became missionary for the Philadelphia Protestant Episcopal Association for the Promotion of Christianity among the Jews, with which he was associated for many years.

In October, 1853, Newman wrote an article for the Baltimore *Clipper* in which he described the ceremonies traditionally associated with Yom Kippur. This resulted in the appearance of one of the most vicious anti-missionary pamphlets ever written in the United States. Joseph Simpson of Baltimore, "a citizen of the United States of the Hebrew confession," angered by Newman's description of some of the Orthodox ceremonies, issued a thirty-six-page booklet on December 20, entitled "The Missionary Scape-goat, employed by Brutal Convert-Hunting Nimrods, Riding on a Beastly Crowing Rooster." The front cover of the pamphlet was appropriately decorated with a goat perched on the back of a rooster.

Simpson's attack on Newman was boorish and senseless. After trying, in the first half of the brochure, to prove that Newman was an ignoramus (only suceeding in demonstrating that he himself was not far removed from such), he devoted the second half to an attack on Prohibition and Bible reading in the public schools. He concluded his tirade by stating:

> The scribbling of L. C. N. did appear at a time of highest political excitement . . . and appeared in a paper which was the political organ of the cold Bible and open water company. Without impeaching the intention of the editors, still the political party who is using the paper as its organ is responsible for its political designs, and the appearance of the scribbling with the circumstances and persons connected, justifies the supposition that it was intended by the party to serve its political design, and shows that the convert hunters, confederated and combined with foreign agents, are meddling with our republican and political questions, to serve a foreign political purpose, as in truth, the convert-hunting concern altogether is not an American production, but smuggled in by foreign agents who have their factories here, and receive orders from their masters abroad, how to transact their business here.

He accused the British of using missionaries as the means whereby they hope to gain control of Palestine. He charged that the missionaries are anti-Catholic, opposed to the naturalization of the Chinese and hindrances in the establishment of friendly relations between the United States and

Japan. In the light of subsequent events, some of the charges made by Simpson in the second half of his pamphlet seem to make much more sense than does his attack on Newman in the first half.

The two student colporteurs were Sigismund Uhlfelder and Ephraim Menachem Epstein, both Hebrew Christians. Uhlfelder is not mentioned after June, 1852,

Ephraim M. Epstein, 1829-1913, was one of the finest persons converted from Judaism to Christianity in the United States. He was a sincere, good man. He came to America from Russia early in 1850 to escape military service. While working for a farmer near New York City, he was converted by an ASCMJ missionary and given part time employment as a colporteur. In 1853 he enrolled in Andover Theological Seminary. He graduated from Andover in 1856 and was licensed to preach by the New York (Old School) Presbytery. In the Fall of 1856 he enrolled in the New York University medical school and received the M.D. degree in October, 1859. From then until May, 1862, he worked as a medical missionary among the Jews of Monastir, Turkey, for the Canadian Presbyterian Church. He then gave up his missionary career and worked solely as a physician in Leavenworth, Kansas, and Cincinnati. His medical career was temporarily terminated in a tragic manner. A druggist mistakenly administered morphine instead of quinine to Epstein's sick son and the boy died. Epstein was affected so deeply that he gave up his medical practice and became a member of the faculty of Heidelberg College, Tiffin, Ohio. Here he became involved in a religious controversy which caused him to lose his academic position. He then went to Vermilian, S.D., where he established and became first president of a college which is now the University of South Dakota. Later he taught at Bethany College, Bethany, W. Va. During the 1890's he resumed his medical career. In 1896 or 1897, he joined the staff of the Chicago medical journal, *Clinical Medicine*. He was associated with this journal until his death, January 26, 1913.

In May, 1851, the Board presented its twenty-eighth Report to the thirty-second annual meeting. During the past year, $10,968 had been collected, more than the Society had gotten in one year since the glorious days of 1825; and one Jew, probably Epstein, had been converted. In addition one non-Jewish infidel had been reclaimed and five Roman Catholic children had been persuaded to attend a Protestant Sunday School. "Thus the waves of Christian influence are widening, encouraging our hearts and strengthening our hands."[15]

In February, 1852, the Reverend James Cohen entered the ASMCJ employ. He had been a missionary in London. His parents were North African Jews who converted before he was born. He was sent to America by the London Jews Society in 1847 to organize auxiliaries in the United States and Canada. He secured the cooperation of the Church of England in Canada, but he did not do as well in the United States.

Cohen suffered a setback in Albany, N.Y., in December, 1847, when he tried to organize an LJS auxiliary in that city. It was announced that a meeting would be held in the church of a Dr. Wykoff at which "Rev. Rabbi Cohen from Jerusalem, a missionary of the London Society for the improvement of the condition of the Jews" would speak "with the purpose of forming a branch organization for this holy and humane work."[16] Isaac Mayer Wise had come to Albany about a year before. The situation was made to order for the cleverest and wittiest polemist American Reform Judaism has thus far produced. Wise describes what happened:

> I donned my frock coat, let my wife put a collar and white neckerchief on me to her great surprise, and at seven o'clock promptly I stood at the entrance of the church. The sexton wished to prevent my entering the lower floor. "Are you a Protestant clergyman?" he asked. "I am a clergyman, you know that full well, who protests against you all; consequently I am a protestant clergyman," I answered, and before he knew it, I had entered the lower floor. He was compelled to leave me undisturbed, or else to have me removed by the police. He wisely chose the former alternative. I took a seat near the pulpit, and when two Unitarian and Universalist ministers entered, we came to an understanding that they would second anything that I would propose, and I, for my part, promised the same. The pious men and women came in large numbers. They eyed us askance. The church was entirely filled. Dr. Wykoff, in company with other prominent personages, entered at eight o'clock. A little, dark, well fed man, with small, black eyes and a suspiciously large nose, walked in with them. The proceedings opened with prayer and song. Thereupon someone arose and moved that the meeting organize itself, with Dr. Wykoff as chairman. This was carried. Wykoff now noticed me sitting opposite the pulpit. He had to explain the object of the meeting. He coughs and stammers, and somehow or other he can not do it successfully, for he and I are friends. At last, however, the words were out, and the unfortunate Jews was spoken of pityingly in the usual stock phrases. He finished and said, "Does anyone wish to speak on the subject?" The intention was to introduce the missionary at this point, who was to speak his piece; but I anticipated him. "I ask for the floor, Mr. Chairman." Wykoff made a wry face; but he could not refuse me the floor. Nor did I wait for his decision, but began to speak at once. It was the first time that the voice of

a Jew had been heard on this question, and I could count with assurance on the undivided attention of the public. I surrendered myself completely to my emotions. I analyzed the subject thoroughly from the moral standpoint. I chastised covetous affectation and hypocritical symptoms of piety with all the power at my command. I refused determinedly, in the name of the Jews, all monetary support, because we ourselves provide for our poor, our widows, and orphans, etc., and rear our children. There are no rowdies, streetwalkers and gamblers among us. We need no help and accept none. I had determined to treat the subject also from the theological standpoint; but the repeated applause from the gallery convinced me that this was not necessary. I contented myself with stating that I was prepared to prove that the Jew could be converted to Christianity neither by gold nor cunning, neither by persecution nor force, but I considered it unnecessary to do so at present. I then moved that the meeting adjourn sine die. The Unitarian minister arose with solemn mien and seconded my motion.

The Chairman could not do otherwise than put the motion. "All those in favor of adjournment will say aye." A rousing aye thundered from the gallery. "All those opposed will say no." Outside of a few women, no one had the courage to say no. The men recognized how the public in the gallery felt. Wykoff, happy to be released from his uncomfortable predicament, declared the meeting adjourned. The play was over, the audience went home, their faces a yard long. No similar meeting ever again took place in Albany, and whenever a missionary did come to town, Dr. Wykoff brought him to me, that I might explain matters to him. . . . Then he sent him away in peace. . . .

This Cohen remained in Albany a while, and later on came again. He was harmless, and never attempted to convert the Jews.[17]

After Cohen joined the ASMCJ in 1852, he was stationed in Albany until the calamity of 1855. He probably heaved a deep sigh of relief when Wise left Albany in April, 1854, to become rabbi of a synagogue in Cincinnati. Sometime after joining the ASMCJ, Cohen abandoned Episcopalianism and became a Presbyterian minister. From 1855 to 1862 he was Professor of Hebrew at the Presbyterian Theological Seminary in Columbia, S.C. He retired in 1862 and moved to Greenville, S.C. In December, 1865, he was drowned when a stagecoach in which he was a passenger overturned on a dark and stormy night while crossing a river near Greenville.

Between February and May, 1852, the ASMCJ hired five more Hebrew Christian employees. None played much of a role in the Society's history but one, Julius Strauss, was bitterly castigated in the August, 1852, *Jewish Chronicle:*

There is a tendency among Jewish converts to Christianity to emigrate to America, and especially of those persons who have some little knowledge of the general sciences and Christian theology. The latter, not deemed competent to do missionary work at home, procure commendatory papers of their personal friends, urging their employment as missionaries to the Jews upon Christians in the United States. Many come without money, and throw themselves upon our charity. We, in our sympathy for them, and believing their testimonials given in all good faith, are disposed in some cases to give them a trial; but very often we are imposed upon, our kindly feelings are trifled with, and our recommendations are misused. A case has recently happened.

Julius Strauss came to this country, recommended by an association which only had existence during the Great Exhibition in London [1851], by whom he seems to have been employed for six months. He came to us with one dollar in his purse. He had no friends, only one of our colporteurs was acquainted with him, who testified to his upright general deportment. He begged some employment as a laborer under our auspices. His promises were fair, and his willingness to do anything to aid the cause among the Jews repeated over and over again. We deemed it safe to give him a trial. In less than six weeks' time, the tenor of his letters began to shake our confidence in him. We watched him. In four weeks more, to our astonishment, we saw a notice of his licensure by a Presbytery. We knew then his determined course. A letter was written to draw him out. He assumed unwonted self-importance, refused to fulfill his engagement, and was immediately informed that his services to this Society would be speedily terminated.

Three instances of this kind in the course of two years are making us feel suspicious of foreign credentials of so-called converted Jews. We hope our friends abroad will use great discretion in every case of this kind; it will save us much annoyance.

What influence persons hostile to this Society had in shaping his course of ingratitude we know not; but we deem it exceedingly strange that any respectable religious body should take up a foreign Jew professedly converted, and license him to preach the gospel, without knowing him three months ,and then recommend him as a competent laborer among the Jews. Such hasty action by a grave body is very singular.

We wish to say to the friends of the cause, since Mr. Strauss has refused to give up the official papers in his possession, that his labors ceased with this Society, July 1, 1852.

After this date, newly licensed minister Strauss labored for the Presbyterian Board of Ministers in New York City.

The twenty-ninth annual report, May, 1852, shows that in the past year $12,634 was collected and seven Jews converted. There are 19 employees; 9 missionaries, 3 students, 4 colporteurs and 3 agents. 16 are Hebrew Christians.

In 1850 a learned young Jew, Emanuel Marcussohn (also spelled Marcuson and Markeson), left Europe and came to New York City. He asked Rabbis Raphall, Leeser, and others to help him find religious employment. All agreed he was a well-educated and deserving person. He obtained a position as chazan-shochet in Augusta, Ga. Later he became spiritual leader of an Orthodox synagogue in Montgomery, Ala.

Bonhomme of the ASMCJ became acquainted with Marcussohn in Montgomery and persuaded him to attend the Wednesday night prayer meeting of the Reverend J. C. Davis, a Methodist minister. Marcussohn then asked Davis to teach him English and also to enlighten him concerning the doctrines of Christianity. For about two months, Davis gave Marcussohn daily and secret instruction in language and theology. At the end of June, 1852, Marcussohn informed Davis that he wished to become a Christian. On July 10, the day his contract with his synagogue expired, Marcussohn went to live with a Methodist minister named Oliver. The Methodists gave him seventy dollars to pay off his debts. Later he was housed and fed by Judge B. S. Bibb, a prominent member of Davis' church. Still later he was sent to a farm operated by A. McGehee. To all these individuals Marcussohn stated repeatedly that he wanted to become a Christian and a missionary.

Davis wrote to ASMCJ's McGregor to ask him help prepare Marcussohn for a missionary career. McGregor instructed Davis to send Marcussohn to the Reverend G. D. Bernheim, ASMCJ missionary in Charleston, S. C. The August *Jewish Chronicle* announced the conversion of "Rabbi Markeson" of Montgomery, Ala. Davis gave Marcussohn twenty dollars to get to Charleston. There Bernheim paid his board, bought him new clothes, and prepared to baptize him, when, much to the amazement and chagrin of all the Christians involved, Marcussohn suddenly disappeared.

On September 9, Marcussohn appeared at Leeser's office in Philadelphia and denied this whole story. Not only did Leeser believe him, but he devoted eight pages of the September *Occident* to a denunciation of the *Jewish Chronicle* for its allegation of Marcussohn's conversion. He published an open letter from Marcussohn to McGregor, dated Philadelphia, September 16, which the *Jewish Chronicle* refused to print.

McGregor was naturally bewildered by all this. He wrote to Davis on October 8 to find out whether or not Marcussohn was telling the truth. Here is part of Davis' reply, sent McGregor on October 15:

I need not say that I an astonished at (your letter) respecting Mr.
Marcussohn. If he has imposed upon myself and the other ministers
of this city, the imposition was never more artfully carried on, or
more successfully practiced. If such be the case, I would suppose that
he is no new hand at the business. But so unwilling am I to admit
fully the statements against this young man, that I must demand
more information upon the subject.[18]

When Davis received, in return, a copy of the September *Occident*, both
he and Oliver sent letters of protest to that magazine, which letters Leeser
refused to publish. He helped Marcussohn get a position with a congregation in Pittsburgh. Bonhomme visited Pittsburgh several months later and
related the story to the president of Marcussohn's synagogue. That dig-
nitary refused to take any action, stating he had received letters from
several Jews in Montgomery praising Marcussohn highly. And there the
matter rested. Marcussohn later occupied pulpits in Cleveland and Nashville. Many of his sermons and letters were printed in later volumes of
the *Occident*.

On September 22, 1852, the venerable president of the ASMCJ, the
Reverend Phillip Milledoler, died. His presidential successor was the
Reverend John Forsyth, 1810-1886, then professor in the Classics Department of the College of New Jersey. Forsyth served as ASMCJ president
until its demise in 1870.

The thirtieth report of the Board, May, 1853, states that receipts for
the past year were $13,219 and 14 Jews had been converted. It says there
are 165 Hebrew Christians in the United States and more than 100 of
these had been converted through the influence of the ASMCJ.

Among the missionaries listed in this report a familiar name reappears,
that of John Christian Gottlieb Adolph Jacobi. He had come back to
the ASMCJ to be its Missionary Agent for Louisiana, Mississippi, Alabama,
and Florida. What had he been doing since the collapse of the New Paltz
project in 1831? He had moved to St. Louis and published a German
newspaper. For a while all went well. He became a quite successful small-
fry politician. In 1849 he got an appointment to the postal service. When
this term of office ended, he was unable to find other work. Finding himself without money or employment, he returned to the profession which,
more than twenty years earlier, had provided him a comfortable living.
He followed the missionary calling until he died in 1874. After the 1855
ASMCJ depression, he went to work for the Episcopalians. He still retained his interest in ASMCJ affairs. He is listed among the vice presidents
in the 1859 and 1860 reports.

Later in 1853, two more Hebrew Christians were added to the ASMCJ roster, Louis Taussig and Gideon R. Lederer. Taussig was employed in Philadelphia as a colporteur for about a year.

The main claim to fame of Gideon R. Lederer, 1804-1879, is that he was one of the very few polemists who engaged Isaac M. Wise in literary combat and successfully returned blow for blow. Lederer was born in or near Budapest. He, his wife and sister were converted by missionaries of the Church of Scotland in 1842. He worked for that denomination's Jewish missionary society in Hungary from 1845 to 1853. In August, 1853, he became ASMCJ missionary in Hartford, Conn. He resigned a few weeks later when he learned he would have to raise his own salary. In November he was engaged by the New York City Tract Society as its missionary to the Jews. He held this position for the rest of his life.

In 1853 McGregor organized the "Prayer Alliance for Jewish and Gentile Christians," composed mainly of ASMCJ workers. Bonhomme was secretary. The Alliance lasted less than a year.

That same year another anti-ASMCJ tract appeared, written by a Presbyterian minister favorably disposed toward Jewish missions, the Reverend Robert F. Burns of St. Catherine's, Canada West. His pamphlet, published in Toronto, was titled "The Jewish Society of New York Arraigned at the Bar of Public Opinion." Burns wrote:

> The society is not in very good odour. It has been discarded by all the old school Presbyterian churches and the only agents of any worth which it had are now laboring in connection with the Home Missions Board of that church. It gets little support in New York where its facts and its history are best known.[19]

In November, 1868, Burns is listed as a vice president of the Western Hebrew Christian Brotherhood of Chicago.

The thirty-first annual Board report presented May, 1854, shows $14,677.50 collected during the past year and twenty-nine converts obtained. This was the most successful year in the entire history of the Society. It was also the beginning of the ultimate end. Although the Society survived for sixteen more years, after 1854 it went steadily downhill. At this time the ASMCJ had fifteen Hebrew Christians on its staff.

A short time after the establishment of the *American Israelite* in July, 1854, its founder and editor, Rabbi Isaac Mayer Wise, began a series of weekly fulminations against the ASMCJ. He called its missionaries "lazy vagrants," "shameless humbugs," and many other uncomplimentary names.

A sample of his anti-ASMCJ writings is the set of accusations he set down in the *Israelite* for October 6, 1854:

1. They use bribery, paying well for every convert.
2. They desert them when worn out, sick or decayed in life.
3. They send agents into mad-houses to convert the insane to Christianity.
4. They teach children to disobey their parents.
5. They employ persons with "aliases," outcasts who do not dare use their own names.
6. They take advantage of famine, pestilence and sword; these are their words: "Jews are all the more accessible under the horrors of war."
7. They never name the convert until employed by them as a preacher.
8. They constantly repudiate as dishonest those whom they have once boasted of as pure and holy converts.
9. They "bear false witness against their neighbor" by stating that the Jews persecute those who enquire into the merits of other religions.
10. They "lay up treasures in this world," i.e., receive fat salaries out of money bequeathed by devout persons for other purposes.
11. They issue a paper with a false name.
12. They preach one doctrine and practice another.

All these charges were well-founded. Most of these same accusations could be leveled against many other missionary societies which have specialized in trying to convert Jews.

In October, 1854, the *Jewish Chronicle* commented upon Wise's attacks:

> Our thanks are due to the "Israelite," a Jewish paper, for the extensive notice it is giving from week to week to our humble journal. . . . Notoriety is the life of any journal and we take this occasion to speak favorably of the "Israelite." It is ably and enthusiastically conducted.

THREE YEARS OF SUSPENDED ANIMATION

Then came the fateful annual meeting of May, 1855. Exactly what transpired there is veiled in mystery. Whatever the circumstances were, the members refused to allow McGregor to continue as professional director of the ASMCJ. This precipitated a fight that racked the Society for the next three years. The *Jewish Chronicle* suspended publication and all the employees were dismissed. It seemed that the oft-delayed end had come at last.

Isaac Mayer Wise assumed full credit for the supposed demise of the ASMCJ. On August 17, he asked: "Where is the 'Jewish Chronicle' of New York? We have not received this paper for several months past. Is the 'Jewish Chronicle' no more?"[20] Two weeks later, he exultantly announced: "The 'Jewish Chronicle' of New York and the Apostate Club are dead, dead, dead!"[21] On November 14, he proclaimed:

> The "Israelite," simply by exposing them to the public gaze, broke down the New York society to ameliorate the condition of the Jews, and their organ, the "Jewish Chronicle."[22]

Although the *Israelite*, on May 20, 1859, announced the resumption of ASMCJ activities, Wise seems to have forgotten this when he wrote his *Reminiscences* in 1874. Wise's version of the episode on pages 272-273 and 310 of that volume is a picturesque combination of fact and fancy.

While Wise's articles may have stirred up considerable resentment against the ASMCJ among his Jewish readers in New York and elsewhere, they had little to do with the 1855 breakdown of the Society. It was not the astuteness of Wise but the lack of astuteness of the Reverend Edwin R. McGregor and his hired hands that probably created the 1855 storm. The Society did not come back to life until December, 1858. It maintained only a paper organization for the next three and a half years. In June, 1858, it emerged from obscurity long enough to assure the general public that a sham "converted Jewish rabbi," George Solomon Boas, who was preaching and collecting money in Boston at that time, was not connected with the ASMCJ.

THE RESURRECTION

The ASMCJ probably never would have been resurrected had not Seth Grosvenor of New York died toward the end of 1858. When his will was read the Society learned, to its great delight, that Grosvenor had bequeathed it ten thousand dollars. In December the Society decided to reorganize, although the Board did not resume meeting until March, 1859. A list of the Board members appeared in the N.Y. *Tribune* on March 25. The feeling of the general public toward the ASMCJ is indicated in the editorial which appeared in the *Tribune* on that same date:

> That the Society is, and long has been, a gross humbug, we cannot doubt; that good men, with good intentions, have lent their names to it, we have never questioned. As the Jews pay largely toward the support of Christian and Infidel paupers and foundlings, while rarely

or never allowing one of their own faith to become a public burden, we cannot regard the name of this Society as either appropriate or respectful. It is, we presume, a proselyting society, and ought to be entitled accordingly. That it does little or nothing may not be the fault of the managers; but it costs something, and should either be made to effect something, or given up. As it is and long has been, it is a naked satire on Christian philanthropy.[23]

In September, Lederer revealed that

when the Society broke down in 1855, it was considerably in debt to the publishers of its periodical and some of its missionaries; but we understand that there is a hopeful prospect of ample means to liquidate all such claims during the present year, and to employ some colporteurs.[24]

These claims were paid off when the Grosvenor bequest money was eventually received. Some additional income was obtained through tours made by Dr. Franklin and Bonhomme. Instead of reviving the *Jewish Chronicle*, the Society adopted as its official publication the *Israelite Indeed*, the magazine being published by Lederer.

In October, 1859, opposition to the ASMCJ developed in a sudden and totally unexpected manner. McGregor's supporters reorganized and announced they were the genuine ASMCJ and that the group headed by Forsyth had usurped powers and privileges to which they were not legally entitled. The rebels elected the Reverend Asahel Abbott their temporary Corresponding Secretary and demanded that the executors of the Grosvenor estate pay them the ten thousand dollars bequeathed to the ASMCJ. After considering the matter carefully, the executors decided that Forsyth's group was entitled to receive the legacy and that the money was to be turned over to them. Abbott promptly contested this decision by instituting a court suit.

So matters stood when the fortieth anniversary of the ASMCJ was celebrated, May 6-7, 1860. The Board announced that the Society was "recovering from the extreme prostration which had well-nigh amounted to actual dissolution." Since 1858, it had been promised or had received $11,783.36, of which $10,000 was to come from the Grosvenor estate, $51 in dues, and the rest from the tours of Bonhomme and Franklin. It made light of Abbott's attempt to gain control of its funds, said that his "whole claim is without a shadow of right," and declared

they would not have referred to it except to prevent any apprehension which might without this explanation, be excited in the minds of those unacquainted with the facts of the case.

During the year the Society's workers had made one convert.

The Board soon discovered that it had taken Abbott's suit much too calmly. Early in July a deputy sheriff called at the office of the Society, located in the building of the American Bible Society, and presented a court judgment against the Society in Abbott's favor for more than twelve thousand dollars! This really took the Board by surprise, as the original suit instituted by Abbott was still on the court docket and untried.

> Upon examination it was found that (Abbott) had begun the [second] suit without recognizing in any manner the present officers, and served notive on Cyrus T. Frost, of Yorkville, who had not informed us of the notice, nor, so far as we can learn, made an effort to defend the suit and protect the Society, and thus the judgment had been entered up by default.[25]

An attorney was engaged by the Society. For several weeks a legal battle raged between the Society and Abbott which resulted in a complete annulment of the judgment. But the Grosvenor money was still tied up and the Society was unable to make use of it. The denial of the use of this money plus the unanticipated expense of the court fight forced the Society to dismiss its three colporteurs.

These unpleasant facts were reported at the forty-first anniversary meeting in May, 1861. During the past year $884.07 had been collected. The treasury held a balance of $85.93. Not much hope was held out for a resumption of activity in the immediate future. "Until the present convulsions of our nation [i.e., the Civil War] are passed, we can not anticipate any enlargement of the Society's operations."

By October, 1863, the Society had gotten hold of the Grosvenor money. No annual reports have been found for 1862, 1863, and 1864.

The Society observed its forty-fifth anniversary in May, 1865. The report issued at that time states:

> The Board of Managers regret that their report cannot present evidence of any increased efficiency during the years 1863 and 1864 now in review. The universal absorption of the public heart and liberality in the efforts called forth by our national convulsions has been super-added to the obstacles previously existing and referred to in former reports. . . . The Society . . . for ten years has not been able to find a man who would undertake the duties of the Corre-

sponding Secretary's office and devote his whole strength to the
work. . . . In the absence of a Secretary, the Board of Managers have
made no effort to solicit funds, and have confined their action to
taking care of the funds providentially placed in the Treasury . . .
and using the income in the support of their long tried and faithful colporteur, Louis Waldenburg. . . . The Society now holds invested $8,500 bearing interest, adequate to support one colporteur,
and has no other reliable income. Until an income from churches and
donations can be obtained, the Society can not safely enlarge its
expenditures.

In December, 1865, the ASMCJ hired its last missionary, Hebrew Christian Siegfried Kristeller. He worked for the Society until 1868 and then
became minister of a Methodist church on Long Island.

"DEAD, DEAD, DEAD!"

The ASMCJ situation got steadily worse. No annual meetings seem to
have been held after 1865. In March, 1866, Forsyth wrote to Lederer
that the London Jews Society had sent the ASMCJ ten-pounds' worth
of tracts. In this letter President Forsyth expressed the hope that the
condition of the Society would improve. "We must try to put forth more
effort than we have made for years past. . . . I wish that we could soon
have a meeting of our Board."

In 1869 the ASMCJ placed its affairs completely in the hands of Lederer. He reported in May, 1870, that, from October 1 to December 22,
1869, he had aided ten families of converted Jews with relief money in
the amount of $112. He does not speak of this with any great amount
of pride.

> This office brings us a great deal of trouble, hatred and enmity
> instead of honor and gratitude; for many of the recipients are not
> satisfied with the amount received; they think we could do more. The
> fact, however, is, that if we would listen to their stories and yield to
> their demands, the funds would be exhausted within a short time.
> Besides, there are a great many who apply for aid who have no claims
> whatever on these funds and when refused they heap the most shock-
> ing curses upon our head. . . . It is often quite amusing to see the
> tricks they try to play to get something out of us.[26]

This is the latest dated reference to the ASMCJ from an authoritative
source. When Lederer's charity fund ran out, the Society finally ceased
to exist. The *Jewish Messenger*, July 1, 1870, p. 5, gives the impression
that the Society still is in being. It says there are many branches of the

ASMCJ throughout the country and that much money is being spent with little success. The Society, it states, is being kept alive through collections in churches and "the legacies of crazy old maids and bigoted deacons." The ASMCJ had probably ceased to exist before this was written.

Oddly enough, Wise, who had faithfully recorded the Society's collapse in 1855 and resurrection in 1859, took absolutely no notice of the final disappearance of the organization. Perhaps he was afraid that he might again find himself in the role of false prophet. He need have had no such fear. This time the American Society for Meliorating the Condition of the Jews really was "dead, dead, dead!"

Chapter Eight

The Conversionists' Progress
(1840-1878)

The account of other attempts by American Christians to convert American Jews in the years following 1840 will be subdivided into those sponsored by denominations and those of non-denominational agencies.

DENOMINATIONAL EFFORTS

During this period, the Disciples of Christ and the Southern Baptists expressed a desire to engage in Jewish work, but neither actually entered the field. Adherents of the Canadian Methodists, Northern Baptists, Evangelical Synod of North America, and Roman Catholicism carried on such an activity with the semiofficial approval of their sects. The denominations which carried on an active officially-sponsored program were the "Old School" Presbyterians, Reformed Presbyterians, United Presbyterians, and the American Protestant Episcopal Church. These efforts will be discussed in the order listed.

In 1867 the Kansas and Missouri conventions of the Disciples of Christ passed resolutions that more intensive efforts should be made to convert Jews; but no machinery for this purpose was set up. In May of that same year, the Southern Baptists, at their Memphis convention, adopted a resolution that "it is our duty to labor and pray more earnestly for the con-

106

version of the Jews."[1] Nearly four thousand dollars were pledged for the establishment of a mission to the Jews, but the mission was never established.

CANADIAN METHODISTS

The interest of the Canadian Methodists in the Jews centered around the Reverend Charles Freshman. Freshman was born at Micklosh, Hungary, in 1819. He received rabbinic ordination at a Jewish seminary in Prague. He came to Montreal in July, 1855, presented his credentials from the chief rabbi of Prague to Rabbi Abraham de Sola, who helped Freshman secure a position as rabbi, chazan, and shochet of a congregation in the city of Quebec. After serving this congregation for about three years, Freshman demanded a raise in salary. His request was refused. He then informed his congregants that, since they were unwilling to pay him suitably, he would leave them and enter the employ of those who would show greater appreciation. He had a hard time convincing his wife that her economic welfare required her to become a Christian, but she finally consented. To the horror and chagrin of the Jews of Quebec, their rabbi, his wife, and seven children were publicly baptized in the Wesleyan Methodist Church of Quebec on September 2, 1859.

Having received this Jewish brother into the kingdom, the Methodists of Quebec wondered what to do with him. He spoke Hungarian and German fluently but hardly any English. A letter was sent to the ASMCJ to inquire if Freshman might be employed by that problem-ridden organization. After receiving a negative response, the Canadians determined to send Freshman to Ontario as missionary to the Germans and Jews residing in that province. Meantime they kept the convert busy going from church to church to tell the deeply accented story of his conversion.

Freshman never did function as a full-time missionary to Ontario's Jews. He was ordained as a Methodist minister in June, 1860, and appointed to a church in Hamilton, Ontario. While mainly concerned with trying to change German Lutherans into Methodists, he reported in September, 1860, that he had converted a Jew. Freshman's eldest son, Jacob, became a Methodist minister in 1867 and served as his father's assistant. Shortly thereafter, Jacob took over the Hamilton pulpit and his father moved northwestward to a church in the small town of Preston. Rapidly tiring of the life of a rural parson, Freshman determined in 1869 to become a traveling lecturer. For over fifteen years he made a comfortable living talking throughout Canada. In 1884 he met a tragic end. His horse ran away, his buggy overturned, and Freshman broke his neck.

AMERICAN BAPTIST SOCIETY FOR
EVANGELIZING THE JEWS

When we left the Reverend Joseph Samuel Christian Frederick Frey in 1839 at the end of Chapter Five, he had just begun to serve as pastor of a Baptist church in Williamsburgh, L.I., for four dollars a week. But he was still determined to organize yet another society to convert Jews.

> During this period, I laboured incessantly to get a society formed. Three meetings took place which were attended by all the Baptist ministers in the city and vicinity and delegates from the churches. The subject was freely and fully discussed, and the object was approved of, but it was thought expedient that the sentiment of the Baptist denomination at large should first be ascertained. Accordingly, a committee was appointed to address the churches on the subject. As chairman of the committee, I was requested to perform the duty. I wrote two columns in three successive numbers in the N.Y. "Baptist Advocate," and requested communications. I am sorry to add that not a single line was received. Notwithstanding this disappointment, I was not discouraged; having ascertained during my former preaching tours, that the church felt a deep interest in the conversion of the Jews, but that much more may be effected by visiting the churches than by mere addresses in the public papers. I therefore resolved to visit the churches and did so.[2]

In 1841 Frey gave up his pulpit and spent the next two years lecturing in Baptist churches. He preached over nine hundred times in more than eight hundred churches and traveled over ten thousand miles. He returned to New York in the Fall of 1843, again attempted to organize a society and again failed. In April 1844, he went out on another lecture tour. When he came back in November, he was able to persuade his friend, the Reverend Spencer Houghton Cone, that the Baptists must do something for the Jews. Cone, president of the N.Y. Baptist Association, sent out a circular letter in which he pointed out that three Jews had become Baptists in New York within the past few months and this was prima facie evidence that New York Jewry was now ripe for Baptism.

In consequence, the American Baptist Society for Evangelizing the Jews was born on December 9, 1844. President: S. H. Cone. Corresponding secretary and missionary: J. S. C. F. Frey. Frey started a weekly Baptist prayer meeting for the conversion of the Jews and a Sunday meeting for Jews only at his residence. He tried to get financial support from the New York Baptists. Alas, the New York Baptists were only willing to try to convert Jews if the outer provinces provided the funds. So, in March, 1845, the Society asked Frey to make another provincial tour. "Rather than see this lovely child dying for want of food I complied."[3] He was gone seven months and collected $1,869.34. The tour carried him through Tennessee, Alabama, Georgia, Louisiana, and Mississippi. He showed true Christian understanding by preaching in African Baptist churches as well as those of the lighter complexioned kind. Naturally, he did not refuse to accept the money placed by black hands in the African Baptist collection plates.[4] In January, 1846, he began to issue a missionary magazine, *The Hebrew Messenger*.

The first and only annual ABSEJ meeting was held in Cone's church on May 15, 1846. Shortly thereafter the Society's funds were exhausted. Frey had to go forth on what was to be his last money-collecting trip. He left in July and came back in October. He journeyed through Wisconsin, Michigan, Missouri, and Illinois. He collected only $533.17.

> In justice to the churches, the Editor feels it his duty to state that the smallness of the collections was not owing to a want of deep interest in the salvation of the Jews; but to some unavoidable circumstances, especially general sickness, which prevented many from attending at the house of God.[5]

The ABSEJ collapsed early in 1847. In May, Frey and his family moved to Pontiac, Mich. He spent his few remaining years in the same capacity as he had begun long before, as a melamed. It is said that, for a time, he taught Hebrew at the University of Michigan, the first instructor in that subject at the school, although this could not be authenticated through the university records.[6] Frey died at the age of seventy-eight on June 5, 1850.

One who knew him well, the Reverend William Buall Sprague, wrote that, as a missionary, Frey had been a failure.

> His success, if measured by the number of converts to Christianity effected under his ministry, was not very great. . . . It must be acknowledged that Mr. Frey's labours, so far as respects his own people, never seemed to mature into very much of abiding fruit.[7]

Writing about Frey in the *Dictionary of American Biography*, George H. Gensmer concluded: "His life had been laborious and unhappy. At heart he probably remained a Jew, his frequent changes of doctrine and abode being so many attempts to escape from his inner misery."

OTHER BAPTIST ADVENTURES AMONG THE JEWS

In 1875 the N.Y. Baptist City Mission hired the Reverend Samuel Alman, Hebrew Christian, to convert the Jews of New York City. Alman quit in 1881 to become pastor of a New York Baptist church. He was still in the active ministry in 1909.

Other Jews attracted into the Baptist denomination during this period included Lewis Henry Salin, H. S. Ollendorff, and Abraham Jaeger.

Salin was born in Bavaria, 1829. Landed in New Orleans, November, 1849. Went into dry-goods business at Owenton, Ky. Baptized in Long Ridge Baptist Church, July, 1852. Ordained as Baptist minister, March, 1857. For forty years he was one of Kentucky's most popular evangelists. He died in May, 1897.

Ollendorff was born in Prussia in 1833. He came to this country in 1853 or 1854. In 1856 he was arrested in Hartford, Conn., for distributing counterfeit money and sentenced to four years in the state prison. The prison chaplain, a Baptist, converted him in October, 1857. The chaplain also obtained a pardon for the convert after he had been in jail for seventeen months. Ollendorff was preparing to become a missionary to his Jewish brethren when he died suddenly, at age twenty-five, in March, 1858.

The prize Baptist catch during these years was Abraham Jaeger. Jaeger, a learned Jew, came to America during the 1860's, went into the whiskey business in Milwaukee and failed. He was unsuccessful in several other business ventures. Then he decided to become a Reform rabbi. He went to Cincinnati, convinced Rabbi Wise he was an excellent teacher and preacher, and persuaded the leader of American Reform Judaism to help him obtain a position as rabbi of Selma, Ala. Wise gave Jaeger a testimonial letter.

> The undersigned herewith testifies, that Reverend A. Jaeger is known to him as an excellent Talmudist and Hebraist, fully competent to preach our sacred religion, and to discharge the rabbinical duties to the glory of God and the honor of his worshippers in light and in truth. [signed] Isaac M. Wise, Cincinnati, September, 1870.

Wise also sent a letter to the Selma congregation referring to Jaeger as "my friend whom I esteem highly. As far as rabbinical learning, ability and character are concerned, he is second to none."[8] In the *American Israelite* for September 16, 1870, p. 7, Wise wrote

We are happy to notice that our friend, Rev. A. Jaeger, was elected minister of the Selma, Ala., congregation, who will be well satisfied with the talent and zeal of the learned gentleman.

After serving in Selma for a year, Jaeger was elected rabbi in Mobile, Ala. This prompted Wise to write in the *Deborah* for June 23, 1871

> The election of Mr. Jaeger as Rabbi of the congregation at Mobile, of which fact we had no notice until now, is to be considered an important acquisition for the congregation, for Mr. Jaeger is an earnest and learned man, with a thinking, clear head. We congratulate the congregation.

About a year later, succumbing to a spiritual malady which has proved fatal to a number of traditional Jewish mystics after they have taken an overdose of Reform rationalism, Jaeger renounced Judaism and joined the Southern Baptists. What a shock that was to Isaac Mayer Wise! His enemies gloated over the apostasy of one whom Wise had recommended so highly. Wise was filled with rage. In his anger, he issued a statement that directly contradicted everything he had previously written about Jaeger.

> It is not true that Mr. Jaeger is or ever was a rabbi. . . . Out of compassion with his poverty, we advised him to turn his attention to teaching and occasional preaching, knowing that he had considerable knowledge of Hebrew literature, and he was appointed teacher and occasional preacher in Selma, Alabama, and afterwards in Mobile. But he never was a rabbi, holds no papers to this effect, never was called so by any Jew, and, as we are told, was not successful even as a teacher. The fact is, that Mr. Jaeger is as thoroughly a rationalist as there is one in this country, and can not possibly believe one word of all the mysticism which he professes.[9]

This sounds just like what it really was: The anguished outcry of a man whose confidence and judgment had been abused and who was ashamed to admit the truth.

In a letter to Wise, dated August 20, Jaeger tore Wise's statement to shreds and showed the obvious inconsistency in Wise's attitude toward him before and after his conversion. Many years later, a Hebrew Christian missionary cited this case as a concrete example of what he termed "the pathological attitude of Jews toward Christian Jews."[10]

In January, 1873, a Chicago firm published a 295-page book by Jaeger, titled *Mind and Heart in Religion: or, Judaism and Christianity. A Heart's Experience and a Popular Research into the True Religion of the Bible,* an account of how and why Jaeger became a Christian. At this time Kaufmann Kohler, 1843-1926, famed Jewish theologian, was rabbi of Chicago's Sinai Temple. After reading the book, Kohler wrote to Jaeger: "I knew, when you became a Christian, that you had lost your heart, but now, after reading this book, I am convinced that you also lost your mind."

In May, 1873, Jaeger addressed the Southern Baptist convention held in Mobile. Then he became professor of Hebrew at the Southern Baptist Theological Seminary at Greenville, S. C. In July, 1877, the N.Y. *Herald* reported that Jaeger had left the Baptists and become an Episcopalian. He was ordained an Episcopal priest. In June, 1898, Jaeger's bishop defrocked him "for good and sufficient reasons." Maybe after that, Jaeger realized he might have been just as well off if he had stayed in the whiskey business.

EVANGELICAL SYNOD OF NORTH AMERICA

The Evangelical Synod of North America was organized near St. Louis, Mo., in 1840. It was composed mainly of German immigrants, formerly adherents of the State Church of Prussia. In 1934 it merged with the Reformed Church of the United States. This combination was known as the Evangelical and Reformed Church. In 1957 the Evangelical and Reformed Church merged with the Congregational Christian Church to form what is now known as the United Church of Christ.

In January, 1861, the Reverend Johann C. Seybold, 1827-1902, wrote an article in the ESNA's official publication, the *Friedensbote*, urging the synod to establish a Jewish Mission Society for the purpose of converting the German Jews of the Middle West. In May, 1863, the synod's Eastern District, meeting at Bethlehem, Ind., organized such a society and appointed Seybold as its missionary. As Seybold was about to begin this new career, he received a call to a St. Louis church and accepted it. The Eastern District then engaged the Reverend A. Strauss, German Hebrew Christian of Jonesboro, Ill., as its Jewish missionary. Strauss worked in this capacity for several years. He died in February, 1868, and the interest of the Eastern District in converting Jews died with him. In 1872 the balance remaining in the Jewish Mission Society fund, amounting to $492, was sent to the Berlin headquarters of the synod's German counterpart to be used by that group in the work of its mission to the Jews of Palestine.

ROMAN CATHOLICS

The American Roman Catholic Church has never given official approval to any organized effort to convert the Jews as such to Roman Catholicism. Protestants, Jews, Muslims, and atheists are all lumped into one category, that of "unbelievers," all of whom the Church attempts to convert, without placing any special emphasis upon the conversion of any particular sect or nationality.

Individual Catholics and Catholic groups are permitted to concentrate their missionary activities upon one section of the population or a particular geographic area. In the period now being discussed, at least one Catholic church tried to bring the Catholic message to the Jews in its neighborhood. On February 7, 1874, "ex-rabbi" Professor Emanuel H. Schlamovitz began a series of German lectures at the Church of the Holy Innocents, Thirty-seventh Street and Broadway, New York City, on "Evidences of Christianity." It was announced that these lectures were being given for the benefit of the Jews. It was soon discovered that Schlamovitz had never been a rabbi. Converted through the London Jews Society, he had once been an Anglican and was now a Roman Catholic. Within a few weeks, the lectures ceased and Schlamovitz gave up the missionary business. He married a non-Jewish lady of means and, thereafter, lived the life of a gentleman of leisure.

The Schlamovitz incident marked the literary debut of Adolph Benjamin, a recent Jewish immigrant, whose antimissionary activities made him hated and feared by the Jewish missionaries in the twenty-eight years he spent combating their efforts. Benjamin is one of the unsung heroes of American Jewish history. He did more damage to the cause of Jewish missions in America than any other Jewish individual or group of individuals in his time, before or since. In the Schlamovitz case, Benjamin wrote a letter to the N.Y. *Herald*, February 15, 1874, p. 7, exposing the professor's ignorance of rabbinic lore.

This concludes the account of those American denominations which carried on semiofficial programs directed at the Jews between 1840 and 1878. We shall now consider the official campaigns carried on by two major denominations, the Presbyterians and the Episcopalians, to capture American Jewish souls.

"OLD SCHOOL" PRESBYTERIANS

Three branches of the Presbyterian Church took part in this crusade: Old School, Reformed, and United Presbyterians.

As noted in Chapter Six, the "Old School" Presbyterians in 1839 decided to send missionaries to American Jewry but, because no funds were available at that time for this purpose, the work did not actually begin until 1846. The missionary zeal of the denomination was stimulated greatly by the conversion to Presbyterianism of two bright young Jews, Victor Herschell and Isidor Loewenthal, both destined to suffer martyrdom for their adopted faith.

Victor Herschell, born in Russia in 1821, was brought to America in the Summer of 1845 by his brother Ridley, as mentioned in the history of the ASMCJ. He was baptized in Philadelphia in April, 1846, and sent to Lafayette College, a Presbyterian school at Easton, Pa. He returned to England in 1849, was ordained as an Anglican curate, and served as curate in a small English town for a number of years. In 1856 he was sent to Jamaica as missionary to the blacks on that island. On October 11, 1865, an anti-British revolt broke out at Morant Bay, where Herschell was preaching. A mob of blacks seized him, cut out his tongue, and beat him to death.

Isidore Loewenthal was born in Prussian Poland in 1826. He had to flee in 1846 because of a revolutionary pamphlet he had written. He arrived in America in the Fall of 1846 and became an itinerant peddler of household wares in Pennsylvania and Delaware. He became friendly with a Presbyterian minister in a small town near Wilmington, Del. His friend had him appointed instructor in foreign languages at Lafayette College on January 1, 1847. Victor Herschell was his roommate. Deciding to become a Christian, Loewenthal was baptized in the Fall of 1847. He received the A.B. degree from Lafayette in June 1847, taught for three years in a preparatory school at Mt. Holly, N.J., entered Princeton Theological Seminary in the Fall of 1850 and graduated therefrom with honors in June, 1854.

> He was below middle size in stature, but lithe and wiry. He had a large hooked nose, a fine black eye, and raven black hair. He was a quiet, modest man, and a man of thorough consecration.[11]

Loewenthal asked to be sent out as a foreign missionary. He was assigned to the difficult missionary post at Peshawar, India, at the entrance to the Khyber Pass, gateway to Afganistan. He arrived at Peshawar late in 1855. In this isolated spot, the young Hebrew Christian labored diligently for nine years to master the many languages and dialects of that polyglot region. He learned to preach in Pushtu, Persian, Kashmiri,

Hindustanee, and Arabic. He had completed a translation of the New Testament into Pushtu and was beginning to translate the Jewish Bible into the same language when he was killed.

Afflicted with migraine headaches, he would take long walks before dawn. One morning late in April, 1864, as he was returning from one of these strolls, he was shot down by a servant who declared that, in the dim light, he mistook Loewenthal for a thief. Whether this was true or whether the servant was bribed by his fellow tribesmen to kill the hated missionary will never be known. Loewenthal is buried in Peshawar near the road leading to the Khyber Pass. The inscription on his tombstone reads as follows:

> Sacred to the memory of Rev. Isidor Loewenthal. He translated the Scriptures into the Afghan tongue, and was shot by his own watchman. "Well done, thou good and faithful servant."

In December, 1846, the New York presbytery began to sponsor and finance a Jewish mission in New York City on behalf of the Board of Foreign Missions of the "Old School" Presbyterians. The first missionary, non-Jew Reverend Matthew R. Miller, served until 1852 and then went to a church in Washington, Ohio.

Early in 1849, John Neander left the ASMCJ and went to work for the "Old School" Presbyterians. After Miller departed, Neander was given full charge and continued until the effort was discontinued in 1876. Neander had a fair knowledge of Hebrew and was an eloquent speaker. In 1854 he became pastor of the German Presbyterian church in Williamsburgh, L.I. For twenty-two years he was both minister and missionary. He retired from his church in 1881 and died in 1885.

Between 1850 and 1858, Bernhard Steinthal, Julius Strauss, and Silian Bonhomme were employed for short periods. They labored in New York, Philadelphia, and Baltimore. After 1858 Neander was the only "Old School" Jewish missionary.

In 1853 the Board of Foreign Missions asked the "Old School" General Assembly to set up a separate organization for converting the Jews. The debate which followed is described in the *Jewish Chronicle* for August, 1853, pp. 29-32. The Reverend Mr. Henry moved that the request be tabled. The Reverend Gardiner Spring, whose levelheaded suggestions had created consternation within the ASMCJ in 1827, seconded the motion. Spring expressed serious doubts concerning the sincerity of Jewish converts. He felt that the conversion of the Jews had best be left to the Lord.

Let the Jews occupy that warm place they have had and which they must ever have in all Christian hearts. The great difficulty under which they labor is want of employment. They come among us, and are eager to get some profitable employ; it is easy to convert them, perfectly easy, nothing is easier, if you will support them. The great majority of those professing to be converts are under pay as agents of the Jews' Society [the ASMCJ]. The Jewish mind needs to be raised, to be cultivated, to be enlightened. Yet let me not be mis-understood. I am not objecting to efforts on behalf of the sons of Abraham; I would not throw a stone in the way; I wish them God speed; but I can not consent . . . to call the Church to this as a special duty of the present day.

After considerable debate, the matter was referred back to the BFM for further consideration. Never again did it come up before the "Old School" General Assembly.

REFORMED PRESBYTERIANS

The Jewish activities of the Reformed Presbyterians, a small group of Scotch Covenanters, were restricted to the employment of Silian Bon-homme in Philadelphia in the years following 1858.

UNITED PRESBYTERIANS

The United Presbyterian Church was organized in Pittsburgh, Pa., in 1858. In 1861 it decided to enter the Jewish mission field when sufficient funds would be available.

In 1863 non-Jew Reverend Abraham C. Tris came over from Holland to obtain employment with the ASMCJ. Finding that society all but dead, he volunteered to establish a Jewish mission for the United Presbyterians. His offer was accepted in 1864. He was authorized to collect funds in the churches for the establishment of a mission in New York City. He began his work in 1865 and met with such small success that, by 1867, the United Presbyterians had lost their interest in him and his Jewish mission.

He then went into business for himself by organizing an independent society, "The American Christian Society for Promoting Christianity among the Jews in the city of New York and elsewhere." In addition to being missionary to the Jews, Tris was, after 1870, pastor of a New York Presbyterian Church. For a short time he published a missionary magazine, *The Star of Bethlehem*. The ACSPCJNY collapsed in 1876. Tris moved out West. In 1903 he was serving as a minister somewhere in Kansas.

CHARLES GOLDBERG

Before turning from the Presbyterians to the Episcopalians, a story will be told that is probably unique in all of Jewish history. It is the story of a Hebrew Christian minister who, at the request of his Jewish friends, helped establish a Jewish congregation and conducted its first High Holyday services.

Goldberg was born, July 27, 1820, in Fraustadt, Poland, the youngest of seventeen children of an Orthodox rabbi. To avoid military service, he came to the United States about 1845 and worked in the Middle West as an itinerant peddler. While traveling through Missouri, he became ill and was nursed back to health in the home of a Cumberland Presbyterian, a sect established in Kentucky in 1840. His benefactors' minister persuaded him to become a Christian in 1847 and also a Cumberland Presbyterian minister. He was ordained almost immediately and began to preach in Galveston, Tex. A short time later he moved to a church in Clarksville, Tex.

When the Civil War broke out, Goldberg was a language professor at Daingerfield College, Daingerfield, Tex. He enlisted in the Confederate army as a chaplain and served throughout the war in that capacity. After the war, he went back to Clarksville. Later he served churches in Columbus and Washington, Ark.

Texarkana, Ark.-Tex., was founded in 1873. A year later Goldberg came to Texarkana to serve as Presbyterian minister and also taught in the city's first public school. By September, 1876, the number of Jews in the young community had reached a sufficient number to hold High Holyday services. The Reverend Charles Goldberg was invited to conduct the services. The Texarkana *Democrat* printed the following account of this unusual happening:

> Our Jewish fellow citizens, in celebrating their New Year, the first day of the month Tishri, on Tuesday and Wednesday last, had the opportunity of forming a synagogue for the first time in this place and of holding public prayers. They requested Rev. Charles Goldberg, a Christian minister and a convert from their faith, a resident at this place, to deliver a discourse to them on the import of the day and the duties that devolve upon them as Israelites, which the reverend gentleman did, both in Hebrew and English, to the entire satisfaction of all hearers, both Jews and Gentiles. We hear the sermon spoken of in the highest terms by all.

On October 6, 1876, Wise reprinted this news item in the *American*

Israelite with the added comment, "There appears to be a mistake somewhere."

Goldberg was greatly beloved by both the Jews and non-Jews of Texarkana. A number of Jews who remembered him well stated to the author that he never attempted to preach Christianity to any of his Jewish friends. He tutored a number of Jewish boys in Hebrew to help them prepare for their Bar Mitsva ceremony. When he died on November 30, 1890, he was not buried in the cemetery of his church, the Pine Street Presbyterian Church, but he was buried in Texarkana's non-sectarian Rose Hill Cemetery.

The author was told in 1938 by two brothers, elderly Jews whose father had been president of the Jewish congregation at the time of Goldberg's death, that Goldberg, on his deathbed, sent for the rabbi and president of the synagogue, recited Viddui, the Jewish deathbed confession of faith, and asked to be buried in the Jewish cemetery. Much as they respected Father Goldberg, as he was known in the community, the synagogue board refused to grant him this privilege.

Mrs. Mattie Goldberg Wallace of Ozan, Ark., elderly daughter of Goldberg, told the author a different story in 1938. She wrote:

> At the funeral of my father, the officiating minister declared that his last words were, "I know in Whom I have believed, that He is able to keep me against that day." As many Jews were at the funeral, and as they had told my father, when he talked of Christianity to them, that at the last he would say the words in the Jews' phylacteries, these last words were a great relief to me.

It is not possible to determine which of these conflicting statements is correct. If Mrs. Wallace's story is the true one, how would one account for her father's not being buried in the cemetery of the church he helped to establish and of which he had been pastor for sixteen years?

THE EPISCOPALIANS

At the triennial convention of the Episcopal Church, held in 1841 in New York City, Bishop Hopkins of Vermont presented a petition, signed by a number of Hebrew Christians, asking for a rector and a Jewish missionary chapel. The petition was received enthusiastically and granted. The Episcopal Board of Missions was ordered to include the Jews in its missionary program and to prepare a Hebrew translation of the Episcopal prayer book. Both instructions were carried out. The Jewish Division of the New York Public Library has a copy of this Hebrew Episcopal Book of Common Prayer, a unique relic of a short-lived venture.

At the 1844 convention, the Episcopalians approved a plan of action for the Jewish work. The Reverend Isaac P. Labagh, a young Episcopalian on the staff of the ASMCJ, was persuaded to leave that organization to take charge of the new enterprise. He resigned from the ASMCJ in May, 1844, but did not begin his Episcopal work until 1845. On Good Friday, 1846, a special collection was taken in New York's Episcopal churches for the purpose of purchasing a Jewish chapel. The response was so generous that Labagh was able to secure the Church of the Redemption on Sixth Street, between Second and Third Avenues, for his work. The activities in the new quarters had hardly gotten under way when, in 1847, Labagh resigned to become rector of a Haddonfield, N.J., church. He was succeeded by non-Jew Reverend Thomas Cook, who labored diligently but unsuccessfully. The Episcopalian interest in the project waned rapidly. In December, 1852, Cook gave up because of lack of money. For a number of years the chapel was unoccupied. Small contributions that continued to come in were forwarded to the London Jews Society.

SAMUEL ISAAC JOSEPH SCHERESCHEWSKY

Samuel I. J. Schereschewsky, 1831-1906, is the most outstanding person of Jewish birth who has been professionally associated with any American Christian denomination. A brilliant scholar, a saintly idealist, a person of unquestionable integrity and sincerity, Schereschewsky is the kind of Jewish convert Christians dream about but seldom find.

Schereschewsky was born in Tauroggen, Lithuania, on May 6, 1831. He studied in the yeshivot of Krazi and Zitomir. Intending to become a Reform rabbi, he enrolled in the University of Breslau. Drawn toward Christianity by one of his university professors, he gave up the idea of becoming a rabbi, returned to his native town and earned a living for a time as a melamed. Still wishing to become a Christian, he left for the United States in the summer of 1854. Arriving in New York, he was welcomed cordially by John Neander, Dr. Morris Franklin, Gideon Lederer, and Julius Strauss.

While preparing for public baptism, the young man lived with Lederer. Because Lederer, formerly a Presbyterian, was now a Baptist, Schereschewsky consented to join Lederer's church. He became a Baptist at Eastertime in 1855. But he did not remain a Baptist very long. Wishing to become a minister, he was persuaded by Strauss to enroll in the Western Theological Seminary, a Presbyterian school in Pittsburgh, Pa. He entered the seminary in the Fall of 1855. He graduated in 1858 and was licensed to preach by the Allegheny presbytery.

Dissatisfied with certain Presbyterian beliefs, Schereschewsky decided to become an Episcopalian. In the Fall of 1858 he enrolled in the General Theological Seminary, New York City, and finished the course in the Spring of 1859. During this academic year, the Episcopalians tried to persuade him to devote himself to working among New York's Jews; but Schereschewsky had made up his mind that he wanted to work among the Chinese.

In July, 1859, he sailed for Shanghai with Bishop Boone, first Episcopal bishop in China. He received priestly ordination from Boone in Shanghai in October, 1860. In 1875 he published a translation of both the Old and New Testaments in the Mandarin dialect. In October, 1877, he was consecrated as Missionary Bishop of China. On April 14, 1879, he laid the cornerstone of St. John's University in Shanghai, which became one of the outstanding institutions of learning in the Far East. In August, 1881, he suffered a stroke. This forced him to give up his bishopric in 1883 and to return to the United States in 1886.

Determined to translate the Bible into Wen-li, the classical Chinese language, he returned to the Orient in August, 1895. After remaining in Shanghai about eighteen months, he moved to Tokyo, where he spent the rest of his life. He finished his Wen-li translation in 1903, which was published by the American Bible Society and is still the standard Chinese Bible translation. He was absorbed in the task of preparing a Chinese reference Bible when death halted his labors on October 14, 1906.

Schereschewsky was a thorough student of Hebrew, Greek, and Chinese. He was one of the outstanding modern Oriental scholars. During the last twenty years of his life, fever ridden, completely paralyzed below the waist, unable to write in long hand, he sat at his desk toiling away at the work he loved so much, patiently typing out the translation of the Bible in Roman letters with one finger, a finger which trembled and ached as he used it. He was a devout Christian and a high-minded servant of God and man.

Although Bishop Schereschewsky never engaged actively in missionary work among the Jews, he took a keen interest in such endeavors. His name is listed among the patrons of a number of Hebrew Christian Brotherhoods and Episcopal conversionist organizations. In 1903 he wrote to the First Hebrew Christian Conference of the United States:

I need hardly say how deeply I am interested in the matters you propose considering. . . . Although it is not in my power to be present, I can still sympathize with your meeting together, and trust that it may bring the solution of many questions and the maturing of the best methods of carrying on the cause of Jewish Missions. I hope that your minds and hearts may be clearly illuminated, so that you may see clearly what it is best to do for the gathering in of Israel.[12]

CHURCH MISSION TO THE JEWS

Unable to persuade Schereschewsky to work for them among the Jews of New York, the Episcopalians engaged an old hand in this business, Hebrew Christian John Christian Gottlieb Adolph Jacobi. After the 1855 ASMCJ decline, Jacobi worked for the Episcopalians in Hartford and New Haven. In December, 1856, he became an Episcopalian deacon. By July, 1858, he was laboring for the New York City Episcopalians. In 1859 the triennial convention granted Jacob's request that the denomination's official sponsorship of Jewish missionary work be revived. The new effort was named the Church Mission to the Jews. Jacobi was put in charge and was authorized to collect funds in any and all Episcopal churches.

Its third annual report, August, 1861, states that Jacobi had converted eleven male and six female Jews and had persuaded a large number of Jewish children to attend Christian Sunday schools. Jacobi resigned in 1862 to become an army chaplain. For two years he was stationed in the smallpox hospital in Washington, D.C. He then returned to New York; but there is no evidence that he went back into Jewish missions work. He is listed in July, 1868, as a vice president of the Hebrew Christian Brotherhood. He died in New York City in February, 1874.

The work of the Church Mission limped along in rather halfhearted fashion for about a year after Jacobi left. In 1863 a representative of the London Jews Society, the Reverend Buchan Wright, addressed a large gathering in the Church Mission's chapel and berated his audience for having allowed the chapel to fall into disuse. Next day a meeting of Episcopal clergy was convened to discuss ways of reviving interest in Jewish conversion. As a result of Wright's speech, it was decided to open a mission school for Jewish children.

The school was opened on Second Street about May 1, 1863, with an initial enrollment of thirty Jewish children. The principal was Hebrew Christian John Goldberg. German-born, thirty-seven-year-old Goldberg was converted in London in 1857 by the LJS. He came to the United States a few months later and worked for the New York State Colonization Society, whose purpose was to Christianize Africa by sending American blacks to Liberia. Goldberg continued to work for this organization during the years he also attempted to Christianize the Jewish children of New York.

As long as the missionaries confined their efforts to converting adults, the Jewish community of New York paid little attention to them; but, when they began to proselyte little children, the Jews became righteously and violently angry. Marcus Bondy, a wool merchant, began a campaign against the mission school. Rabbi Samuel M. Isaacs, 1804-1878, rabbi of Congregation Shaaray Tefila and editor of the *Jewish Messenger*, joined in. Week after week, he editorialized that free Hebrew schools must be established to ward off the missionary menace.

The more the rabbi thundered, the more the school seemed to prosper. In November it had 102 pupils. In March, 1864, it had nearly 200 pupils. Mr. Cohen, editor of the *Jewish Herald*, also began to denounce the school week after week. Finally the papers' tirades had the desired effect. On April 1, 1864, the board members of eleven congregations met at Rodeph Shalom synagogue on Clinton Street to take appropriate action.

A number of ways of dealing with the problem were advanced, attacked, and defended: The parents of the children should be visited. The parents should not be visited. Warning circulars should be printed and distributed. The circulars should not be distributed (too much publicity for the school), but proper announcements should be made in the various synagogues. Synagogue announcements would do no good, because those who had to be reached did not attend the synagogue.

The final decisions of the meeting were: The parents will be visited. Circulars will be distributed. A committee, made up of the presidents of the congregations, will raise a fund for the organization of a system of free Hebrew education in New York City. This system will include primary and elementary schools and an institution of higher learning to be known as Montefiore College.

The Hebrew Free School Association of the City of New York was formally organized on Sunday, May 8, 1864. On that same day, the mission school suffered a disastrous blow. As a result of the circulars, the school attendance had decreased considerably. About fifty children, many of them Christian, continued to attend.

On this Sunday morning, while the teachers were expounding the doctrines of Christianity to their young listeners,

a robust Jew, armed with a stick, rudely entered the room, and with terrible cursing and swearing, drove out the children, insulted Mr. Goldberg, the Hebrew teacher, threatening to kill him, and made otherwise such noise, that hundreds of people gathered before the house, and after five minutes the crowd became so dense that First Avenue became impassable and the cars stopped. . . . Finally a policeman made his appearance, helped the teacher into the house, and after a while the crowd dispersed.

Neither did they stop here. On the next morning, a half dozen or more sturdy butchers, whose slaughter house is in the immediate vicinity of the school, guarded the entrance of the latter, and drove off the children as they came in parties of three or more to enter the school. Several bold ones, however, could not be frightened away, and forced their way through the vigilant guard, while some slipped in unobserved. The zealots outside then began to fling stones into the room, whereupon the pupils and teachers fled for safety into the yard, but the persecutors entered the neighboring yard and pelted their victims from that place. This method of reasoning proved so effectual that the next following days, scarcely half a dozen children were in attendance. . . . At present, about twenty pupils attend the mission school, and there are hopes and even promises from many fathers, that after a few months the institution will be as well frequented as before the riot.[13]

The strain on Goldberg's nerves was too great. He left the school. It ceased operating soon thereafter.

In 1871 Goldberg left the Colonization Society. He worked here and there as a missionary to the Jews. He died in Providence, R.I., in April, 1903. The first Hebrew Free School in New York City opened on Friday, June 16, 1865. It was a pioneer effort in the field of Hebrew education for American Jewry. It had a staff of five teachers and an enrollment of three hundred students. Much of the credit for its establishment belongs to a despised "meshumad" named John Goldberg.

The mission school idea was down but not out. In 1866 the Episcopalians opened another one under the direction of a non-Jew, Miss Martha J. Ellis. Miss Ellis' school lasted about forty years and attracted thousands of Jewish children. In its early years it reported an enrollment of 150 Jewish and 50 non-Jewish children. In 1868 the Hebrew Christian Brotherhood had a school. In 1876 the Baptists supported a school for a short time.

For the last hundred years a children's school of some kind has been part of the standard program of practically every American Jewish mission. While most missionaries have claimed that the children have come with the consent of their parents, there have been many instances in which it has been proven that this claim is untrue. Many of the parents have been unaware of the missionary purpose of the schools. Some Jewish fathers and mothers, being either irreligious or anti-religious, have not been greatly concerned about the religious welfare of their children and have allowed them to go to the mission schools because of the Christmas parties and toys and presents and the like. The rest have been drawn from poor immigrant families of traditional backgrounds. It has been a rarity to find an American-born Reform Jewish child in a mission school. In 1875 the *Jewish Messenger* complained that some East Side children attended a missionary school on East Eighth Street in the morning and the Hebrew Free School on Avenue C in the afternoon.[14]

PROTESTANT EPISCOPAL ASSOCIATION FOR THE PROMOTION OF CHRISTIANITY AMONG THE JEWS

About the same time that Jacobi revived the New York Episcopal work in 1858, another Episcopal effort was started in Philadelphia by the diocese of Pennsylvania. It bore the imposing name with which this section begins.

The Association engaged as missionary the Reverend Louis C. Newman who had left the ASMCJ in 1854. Newman worked for the Pennsylvania Episcopalians for almost twenty years. An unfriendly contemporary described him as

> a stolid, heavy looking personage, with a skull as spherical as a billiard ball, and a face possessing all the fineness of expression that centers in the surface of a dumpling. The effect of his phiz is heightened by the gold spectacles that bestride his nasal bulb.[15]

In 1862 the bishops of Pennsylvania and New Jersey allocated their diocesan Good Friday contributions to the society. Rabbi Leeser condemned this action vigorously.[16] From then on until he died in 1868, Leeser wrote many articles in the *Occident* and in the secular press ridiculing Newman and his society. In 1867 the New Jersey bishop again issued a pastoral letter instructing his clergymen to contribute all future Good Friday collections to the cause of Jewish evangelization. Leeser addressed a letter to the bishop, printed in the Philadelphia *Inquirer*, April 25, 1867. In very sarcastic language Leeser accuses the bishop of feeding the fires of anti-Semitism by stressing the conversion of the Jews on a day commemorating their alleged connection with the crucifixion of Jesus.

The eleventh report of the Association, issued in 1870, states that Newman has converted twenty-nine Jews since 1858. In the past year he converted one female and collected $3,027.44. The bishop of Pennsylvania is president and the bishop of New Jersey and the famous liberal preacher, Phillips Brooks, 1835-1893, are listed among the vice presidents.

Newman is last mentioned in 1877. The Philadelphia Association was merged with the national Church Society for Promoting Christianity among the Jews when the latter Society was founded in 1878.

"WE DON'T LIKE AN APOSTATE"

American Jewry should be grateful to the secular press of this country for the important part it has played in nullifying the efforts of Christian missionaries. From the birth of the ASMCJ in 1820 to the present time, the overwhelming majority of American newspapers have followed an editorial policy of opposing efforts to proselytize Jews. There has been no more effective antidote to the propaganda of the missionaries than that which has been provided by the vigorous pens of their fellow Christians, the newspaper editorial writers.

The Philadelphia *Sunday Mercury* stated in August, 1870: "We don't like an apostate. What is more, we never expect to." It was referring to Newman. In April, 1873, the Philadelphia *Sunday Dispatch* editorialized:

> The conversion of the Jews is still a matter of absorbing interest to sundry Christians who do not know what to do with their money. A meeting of the Society to Promote Christianity among the Jews was held recently at an Episcopalian church, and a report was made of what had been done, or rather what had not been done, during the previous year. Formerly the officers of the Society were able to report occasionally that by immense effort a stray Jew had been converted. But, during the last year, business was exceedingly dull, and not an apostate has been gained. The Society, in fact, despairing of finding a sufficient number of Jews in Philadelphia to affect unto conversion, has extended its jurisdiction over New York and Boston, in which places its colporteur went up and down looking for somebody to become an example of conversion.
>
> But although in those cities, particularly in Boston, diligent effort was made, nothing resulted except the distribution of books, the delivery of addresses, and advice given to the Hebrews, who did not adopt it. All this cost $4,294.33, and, pecuniarily speaking, the investment does not offer many dividends. All this was apparent; but, so long as the zealous will contribute, the managers of this Society will find an opportunity to spend the money, although they know that it is thrown away and the whole thing is a sham.[17]

On January 21, 1877, the *Dispatch* again derided the Episcopal efforts to convert the Jews. It singled out for especial ridicule Bishop Stevens of Pennsylvania, who, on January 14, 1877, had repeated a conversionist sermon he had first delivered in 1860. The *Dispatch* ended its attack with this bit of appropriate free verse:

> Are there no Christian beggars at your gates?
> Nor any Christian poor about your lands?
>   Oh! teach the orphan boy to read;
>   Oh! teach the orphan girl to sew;
> Pray Heaven for an honest heart,
>   And let the honest Israelite go!

NON-DENOMINATIONAL EFFORTS

We now turn our attention to the conversionist efforts of non-denominational agencies in the years 1840-1878. In addition to the already fully described ASMCJ, these included the Maryland Ladies' Society for Promoting Christianity among the Jews, the Pennsylvania Society for Evangelizing the Jews, the New York City Tract Society, the Montreal Tract and Bible Society, and the various Hebrew Christian Brotherhoods.

THE "NEW YEAR'S GIFT"

The Maryland and Pennsylvania societies were probably adjuncts of the ASMCJ. All that is known concerning the Maryland organization is found in a fourteen-page pamphlet published in Baltimore, January 1, 1843, and titled "A New Year's Gift to the Maryland Ladies' Society for Promoting Christianity among the Jews." The writer uses the pseudonym, "The Right Reverend Rabbi, Hebrew Republican Citizen-Soldier."

The Baltimore *Sun* announced the Society's formation on November 12, 1842. Aroused by this news item, the "right reverend rabbi" wrote a satirical sermon which he published as a New Year's present to the Maryland female proselyters.

He based his sermon on the obscene story told about the pagan prophet Balaam in the Babylonian Talmud.[18] It says that Balaam organized "female associations for public prostitution" to wean the Israelites away from their religion. The "rabbi" clearly infers that the ethical and moral motives underlying the formation of female missionary societies are not on a much higher level.

The telling of this story and the moral lesson which it conveys takes up the first nine and a half pages of the pamphlet. The author then asserts that attempts to convert Jews are violations of the principle of religious freedom. He continues:

> Believe me, dear ladies, that I am not prompted by any wrong motives in presuming to address you. You will greatly do me wrong if you suppose I am capable to draw an inference between you and those females mentioned in that part of Scripture I have called your attention to. Be assured that I am well convinced of the purity of your intentions; in the meantime truth and candour dictates to represent to you the effect produced in the Hebrew mind in suffering yourselves to be the tools of the insidious missionaries, and I most uprightly and most candidly confess, that I have never in my life met with anything so ridiculous and contemptible as the "Mission" you are engaged in. One thing I can assure you, that I am fully convinced that should a Reverend Rabbi, even with the longest beard imaginable, dare to propose to Hebrew females to organize themselves in a society for the purpose to meddle with church affairs of other denominations, the male part of the Hebrew community will shave his head and pour cold water on his smooth skull in order to cool his inflamed brain, and lodge him in the "Mad house" until his sound reason is restored, and the female part will take him to the washing tub and lodge him amongst the foul linen and dress his extraordinary superior Rabbi-ship in the very style he truly merits. I sincerely confess that I am inclined to suppose that prudent and decent females have quite enough to do to employ their precious time to prudently attending to their domestic affairs. It seems that you have too much leisure time and do not know how to employ your time usefully; permit me then to propose something, which I am sure will produce a quite effective remedy for this serious contagious evil, and if you accomplish what it is intended for, you will actually be the greatest benefactors of the human family under the present circumstances.[19]

He then alleges that there are more prostitutes in Christian than in non-Christian countries; and he suggests to the Christian ladies that they should try to improve the moral standards of their own fallen sisters before they try to win the Jews to their faith. Finally, he pays his compliments to the missionaries:

> I would consider it a sin in not opening your eyes to the enormity of the imposition practiced upon your chaste and delicate feelings by these designing and filthy sets of Missionaries. Tell them, if you please, that "Charity begins at home"; let them first look into their own bosoms and examine themselves well and ask whether they themselves are real Christians? Whether they are not instigators for sinister purposes? and whether it was not better for them to go forth amongst countless thousands of pretenders to Christianity, among their

own clique and who are a disgrace to Christianity and a reproach to the human family, and instil and plant christianity in its noble sense, and not using it as they do for disgusting, contemptible, sectarian, designing tricks; let them do this, and they will have enough to do without trying to patch and mend the Messiah's breeches. Tell them again, if you please, to try and promote good morals, and to remove all kind of prejudice, and as good citizens, encourage peace and harmony among the different members of the community. Let them do this, and the Jew, although a Jew, surely will go the whole hog with them.

The effect produced by this tongue-in-cheek New Year message is not recorded. No further mention has been found of the Maryland Ladies' Society for Promoting Christianity among the Jews.

THE PENNSYLVANIA SOCIETY

The short-lived Pennsylvania Society for Evangelizing the Jews was founded in Philadelphia in August, 1843. Its first and last president was the Reverend Stephen H. Tyng, 1800-1885, conservative Episcopalian and, in his prime, the most eloquent preacher in America. Many prominent ministers and laymen were members of the Society. In October, Leeser described it as a "powerful association of intellect and wealth."[20] Shortly thereafter he announced gladly that the Society had been dissolved on the ground "that the number of Jews in this country is hardly sufficient for a separate organization."[21]

NEW YORK CITY TRACT SOCIETY

The American Tract Society was organized in May, 1825, mainly to publish missionary tracts. Among its early officers were many who were also active in the ASMCJ. In 1844-1845 the Society employed Hebrew Christian colporteurs in New York City and then abandoned this activity.

The New York City Tract Society, an offshoot of the American Tract Society, dates from February, 1827. Its very active female branch was started in 1829. It hired its first missionary in March, 1833. In 1864 it adopted a new name, the New York City Mission and Tract Society. In recent years it has shortened its title to the New York City Mission Society. It entered the Jewish field in 1853 and left that field, with a deep sigh of relief, in 1925.

Its first Jewish missionary was Gideon Lederer, who went to work in November, 1853, and remained with the Society until he died in 1879.

He had a lackluster sort of personality and spent most of his time distributing tracts and conversing with prospective converts.

In 1870 he claimed that, in sixteen years, he had converted sixty-nine Jews. Of these four had died, two were Christian ministers, three were preparing for the ministry, three had returned to Europe, and one (Schereschewsky) was a district missionary in China. Lederer was very kind to Schereschewsky and arranged for his baptism, but he very definitely was in no way responsible for Schereschewsky's decision to become a Christian. It is likely that the actual number of Jews Lederer induced to become Christians was much less than sixty-nine.

Lederer organized public discussions between Jews and Christians, weekly prayer meetings, a number of Hebrew Christian Brotherhoods, and, from 1857 to 1871, he published a monthly magazine, *Israelite Indeed*.

Isaac Mayer Wise thought he had killed the ASMCJ and its *Jewish Chronicle* in 1855 and, with them, all past, present, and future attempts to convert American Jews. He was so sure of this that, in January, 1857, he declared, "In America, missions to the Jews are bankrupt."[22] In July of that same year, much to Wise's amazements and disgust, missionary Lederer started putting out his magazine. For a few months, Wise ignored the new publication. Then, on October 16, he took careful written aim at Lederer and fired, hoping that his tirades in the *Israelite* would cause the *Israelite Indeed* to collapse. Week after week he fired volley after volley; but none of his penned shots accomplished their purpose. Lederer and those who assisted him responded by taking aim and firing at Wise and his *Israelite*. Wise called upon the Jews of New York to get rid of Lederer. He said that, if Lederer were in Cincinnati or he in New York, he would make short work of the apostate.

The Jews of New York City paid little attention to Lederer or to Wise's plea; and so the literary battle continued. The longer it raged, the more vituperative it became. At the beginning, Wise hurled at his opponents such epithets as ignoramus, renegade, outlaw, hypocrite, and the like, while Lederer and his helpers tried to be mild and reasonable. Finally, Lederer lost his temper and, after vainly exhorting Wise to watch his language, he bestowed upon his adversary such encomiums as "Hungarian coach driver," imbecile, liar, and infidel. Wise and Lederer finally ceased their wrangling in 1866. In all likelihood both were thoroughly tired of the useless conflict and were willing to call it a draw.

Lederer's chief backer in the publication of *Israelite Indeed* was Theodore Dwight, who had been interested in the ASMCJ. After Dwight died in 1866, the magazine became a financial burden. In 1871 it went bankrupt.

Lederer was poorly paid by the Tract Society and often complained bitterly about his meager salary. Nine of his ten children died during his lifetime. He seems to have been very sincere, he worked hard, suffered much, and accomplished little.

MONTREAL TRACT AND BIBLE SOCIETY

For a short time in 1859, the Montreal Tract and Bible Society employed a Jewish colporteur, David Silverstein. He was caught embezzling Society funds and was discharged. Early in October, he went to Essex, a village in northeastern New York and, claiming to represent the Montreal group and the London Jews Society, he preached in the churches of the little town and collected money. In a very short time he courted and was about to marry a local non-Jewish girl when it was learned that there was a woman in Plattsburgh, N.Y., whom he had introduced as his wife. Then a letter was received from Montreal stating that Silverstein's wife and two children had left that city in July and gone to England. A warrant was sworn out for his arrest but, before it could be served, he fled. He was captured in Rutland, Vt., and brought back. Charged with "attempted bigamy," he was found not guilty for lack of sufficient evidence. Nothing is known about the later doings of David Silverstein.

THE HEBREW CHRISTIAN BROTHERHOODS

Practically all Hebrew Christian Brotherhoods have been organized either as an advertisement for some Jewish missionary society or as a means of affording a livelihood for one or more Hebrew Christian missionaries. Far from promoting friendlier relations in missionary circles, these organizations have often intensified existing rivalries and hatreds. Genuine brotherhood has been conspicuously absent.

Hebrew Christian associations established by the ASMCJ and by Frey during his Baptist years have already been mentioned. Six more such groups were born and died in the United States between 1855 and 1878. They lasted for periods ranging from three months to two years.

BROTHERHOOD No. 1

The future of the Jewish missionary cause in America seemed very bleak when the ASMCJ went into sudden eclipse in May, 1855. Gideon R. Lederer gallantly came to the rescue of his stranded Hebrew Christian brethren. A meeting was convened at a Methodist Church on Norfolk Street in New York City that same month. It was attended, Lederer states, probably very imaginatively, by 50 unconverted Jews, 60 converted Jews, and about 150 non-Jews. The gathering brought into being the American Hebrew Christian Association. President, John Neander; vice president, Charles T. Weissel; secretary, Morris Franklin; and treasurer, Lederer. That night Lederer dreamed a beautiful dream:

> We dreamed of a happy future; we saw our "Brotherhood" growing as fast as mushrooms; saw a gathering of thousands, bending their steps towards a plain but large building over the door of which we read: THIS IS MY HOUSE, A HOUSE OF PRAYER FOR ALL NATIONS, written in many languages.[23]

But, alas, "Three months after that night of golden visions, the 'Brotherhood' was 'sought and not found.' It died of the dangerous disease of denominational differences."[24] In an earlier account, Lederer wrote:

> Owing partly to the withdrawal of some brethren whose engagements carried them far away from the centre of population—the city of New York—and partly to some other circumstances, which, for reasons known to ourselves, we would not like to become public, the monthly meetings were sparingly attended, and gradually died away.[25]

In this and subsequent New York brotherhood attempts, the Reverend Charles E. Harris was very active. Harris was born in London in 1830 and baptized in Montreal in 1851. He was ordained a Methodist minister in 1858 and served in churches in New York and Brooklyn for many years. He was president of Hebrew Christian Brotherhoods No. 2, No. 3, and No. 4. He is listed as a vice president of No. 5, the Chicago effort. He was active in a number of Brotherhoods after 1878. He seems to have been a natural born Hebrew Christian Brotherhood joiner. He was still alive but retired in 1903.

BROTHERHOOD No. 2

Lederer's dream still haunted him. He wanted an American Hebrew Christian Church which would take over the task of converting the Jews. In the Fall of 1859 he persuaded Jacobi to help him promote the formation of a Hebrew Christian social club, with the hope that out of it would come a Hebrew Christian church. Instead the result was another

American Hebrew Christian Brotherhood. President, Harris; vice president, L. C. Newman; secretary, Franklin; treasurer, Lederer. The Brotherhood soon perished. Lederer lamented: "Alas! We failed again; we failed signally, and we came to the conclusion that, so long as we shall remain a scattered nation, we shall also remain divided."[26]

BROTHERHOOD No. 3

In 1865 John M. Goldberg and Siegfried Kristeller, the last missionary employed by the ASMCJ, persuaded Lederer to try again. Kristeller wrote:

> It was no easy task to persuade Brother Lederer to make another effort on a subject in which he had failed twice. . . . Still he yielded to my demonstrations and we commenced the meetings at his house.[27]

The meetings, more or less of a social character, sometimes drew as many as twenty-five Hebrew Christians and lasted about a year.

BROTHERHOOD No. 4

This one came into being in May, 1868. President, Harris; secretary, Goldberg; treasurer, Lederer. Both Jewish and non-Jewish Christians could belong. A charter was obtained from the New York state legislature. Weekly meetings were held at the Cooper Institute. One of Lederer's converts, Brother Ginsburg, was engaged as missionary.

There were at this time a few Hebrew Christians training for the ministry in the Chicago area. The New York Brotherhood planned to use them as a nucleus with which to build a Chicago branch. A Chicago organizing meeting was called for the third Monday in May, 1869. Lederer and Kristeller were invited to attend. Through a misunderstanding, the New Yorkers arrived on the second Monday. A meeting was hastily convened on Wednesday, May 13. Some forty or fifty persons were present, both Jews and Christians. After the New York visitors had spoken, a heated discussion ensued between them and a number of Jews who wanted no Hebrew Christian Brotherhood in Chicago. The project was also strongly condemned a few weeks later in a Chicago *Tribune* editorial. On Friday, May 15, Lederer attended the service at Sinai Temple and created such a disturbance that he was ejected. The Chicago branch did not get under way until October.

The first anniversary of the Hebrew Christian Brotherhood was celebrated at the Presbyterian Church of the Reverend Howard Crosby on May 31, 1868. Received during past year, $2,184.78; expended, $1,651.53, for the missionary's salary, hall rent, and "aid for poor brethren." The June 5 *Jewish Messenger* expressed astonishment that the "Reverend Dr. Howard Crosby, a man of sterling piety, unaffected worth and sincerity," should associate himself with such an enterprise. In the June 12 issue, the *Jewish Messenger* stated that "the society had been formed almost on the ruins of the ASMCJ."

During the Summer of 1868, the "brothers" quarreled so violently that most of them dropped out. By the end of 1869, Hebrew Christian Brotherhood No. 4 was no more.

BROTHERHOOD No. 5

As mentioned, Chicago's Western Hebrew Christian Brotherhood got under way in October, 1868. It, too, had both Jewish and non-Jewish Christians as members, including the world-famous evangelist, Dwight Lyman Moody, 1837-1899. During its brief existence, the Western Brotherhood employed four missionaries. One of these was Charles E. Reider.

"Ex-rabbi" Charles E. Reider was converted during a Chicago revival conducted by Moody and Edward P. Hammond between 1862 and 1866. He claimed that he had been a rabbi in Chicago. This, said I. M. Wise in 1876, was a lie. "No RABBI in this country has turned apostate, and those Christianity peddlers who call themselves rabbis are liars, willful liars."[28] Reider was small, black whiskered, wore spectacles and had "a tongue slicker than grease."[29] After the Western Brotherhood collapsed, Reider was pastor of churches in Pittsfield and Knoxville, Ill. He left the latter community rather abruptly as the result of some illegal real estate transactions. Then he made a comfortable living soliciting funds for non-existent Jewish missions, Christian Bible societies, and Baptist churches. The cause to which Reider dedicated his services depended largely on which one of them happened to come to his mind first as he began his spiel. Needless to say, not one cent that was collected ever went to the cause for which it was given. Then, as a sort of change of pace, in 1876 he began to deliver lectures in churches around the country in the guise of "a converted rabbi from Jerusalem."

> Reider is a fraud; he is no rabbi; never was one, never was in Jerusalem, was not converted by Mr. Moody. His name is not Reider; he is a common tramp who defrauds Christians by confessing a conglomeration of lies.[30]

Credit for the rapid dissolution of the Western Hebrew Christian Brotherhood belongs to Rabbi Bernard Felsenthal, 1822-1908, of Chicago's Zion Temple and his good friend, Robert L. Collier, a Unitarian minister. Felsenthal delivered speeches to Jewish groups and wrote many letters to the press explaining the contempt that Jews feel toward Hebrew Christians who try to save Jewish souls. So devastating were Felsenthal's statements that Lederer accused him of having himself been a missionary! In the *Israelite Indeed* for May, 1869, Lederer wrote:

> We greatly suspect that Rabbi Felsenthal was once an inmate of Palestine Place, Bethnal Green, London, enjoyed the hospitality of the London Society for promoting Christianity among the Jews, was, out of gratitude, baptized, and, after an amelioration of his circumstances, turned rational rabbi in Chicago. We do not say that we know these things to be so, but that we suspect it, and our suspicion is based, first, upon the fact that Rabbi Felsenthal seems to know so much of the affairs of missions among Jews, while one who was not closely connected with the institutions would hardly obtain so much information; and, secondly, because he comes out with such a degree of enmity of which a two-fold renegade only is capable.

In February, 1869, Collier preached a forceful sermon on "The Folly of Converting the Jews." He said,

> I wish to affirm here tonight, in the full knowledge of what I say, that rationalistic Judaism is nearer in its tenets to primitive Christianity than the Christianity of the orthodox churches.[31]

For this bold statement he was bitterly condemned by the Chicago *Advance*, a religious weekly, which addressed him as "Rabbi" Collier and suggested he turn his church into a synagogue.

The oratorical and literary efforts of Felsenthal and Collier had the desired effect. Before the end of 1869, the Western Hebrew Christian Brotherhood dismissed its missionaries and went out of business.

BROTHERHOOD No. 6

This attempt was initiated by as dashing a pirate as ever roamed the missionary world, Mordechai Rosenthal, alias Max Louis Rosevalley.

Here is a precis of Rosevalley's life as he told it in a sixty-six-page booklet he published in June, 1876, under the title "A Short Sketch of the Life and Conversion of a Jew": Born, Wuertemberg, Germany, August 17, 1828. Received M.D. degree from University of Heidelberg. Came to

U.S. during the 1850's. Served in Union army as surgeon during entire Civil War. After war was in charge of yellow fever hospital in Galveston, Tex. Baptized in February, 1876, by head of gospel mission in Albany, N. Y. Few days later began to preach on streets of Washington, D.C. Left in April for New York City where he continued to preach and organized Hebrew Christian Association.

This is Rosevalley's story as he told it in 1876. In later years he polished it up considerably. He had been not only a successful surgeon but a famous actor. He published hundreds of thousands of copies of the pathetic story of "Charlie Coulson," a mythical "dying drummer boy," through whose influence he had been converted during the Civil War.

Here are the actual facts, gathered from many sources: Rosevalley was born in Laupheim bei Ulm, Wuertemberg, Germany. In the years before the Civil War, Rosevalley was jailed in Germany for robbery, escaped and fled to the United States. Arrested for thievery in New Orleans and other southern cities prior to the outbreak of the conflict. When war began, enlisted in Louisiana militia as surgeon; but was discharged because he was caught stealing merchandise from store of Hyde and Goodrich in New Orleans.

Then began an espionage career which, for bold double-crossing, has seldom been exceeded in annals of warfare. Went to Washington, offered himself to Union army as spy, was accepted, returned south, repeated same offer to Confederates, was accepted and, for a time, made comfortable living serving as spy for both sides. His knavery was finally suspected. Had he not exited speedily from Mobile, Ala., he would have been hanged.

Next stop: Richmond, Va., Here he obtained position in office of Confederate provost marshal. Enhanced his income by stealing discharges of disabled soldiers from provost marshal's office and selling them for handsome price to able-bodied males. Was arrested for this, found guilty, and sent to Castle Thunder prison. After release from Castle Thunder, returned to Mobile under assumed name. To avoid possibility of re-arrest, had article published in Mobile paper stating that, some months before, he had been hanged as a spy.

Next known episode: February 5, 1869, Rosevalley was sentenced to twelve years in Albany, N.Y. penitentiary for possessing and passing counterfeit money. Through efforts of evangelist Edward P. Hammond, Rosevalley was pardoned by President Grant on February 8, 1876, became a "Christian," and joined Hammond's religious carnival as one of its most prized side-show performers. Although his name is on the prison records as Moritz Rosevalley, he was referred to in the evangelistic billings as Moritz Rosenwald.

In March, Hammond and his troupe arrived in Washington, D.C. Here "Rosenwald" attempted to convert some Jews, who made such a fool of him that an exasperated and chagrined Hammond fired him. Then he went to New York and, toward the end of April, organized a Hebrew Christian Association.

In July, Rosevalley summoned his Hebrew Christian brethren to a meeting to set up in New York City an "Operative Jewish Converts' Institution" similar to that of the London Jews Society. The meeting was attended by Morris Franklin, Isaac S. Nathans, another genuine rascal, and a number of other Hebrew Christians and Jews. The meeting developed into a verbal free-for-all. Franklin accused Rosevalley of being a money-grabbing impostor who was bringing discredit on sincere Hebrew Christians. The two almost came to blows. Then a young Jew got up and bitterly condemned all efforts to convert Jews. The meeting broke up in utter confusion without accomplishing its objective. This was the end of Brotherhood No. 6 but marked only the beginning of Rosevalley's "Christian" career.

Before continuing the account of the adventures of this missionary rogue, one paragraph will be devoted to Isaac S. Nathans.

Nathans has been described as

> a man of medium height, with an extremely foreign cast of features, a shock of unkempt brown hair, and a bushy, ragged brown beard. He has a cast in both eyes, which gives him a very peculiar look, walks with a shuffling gait, and has a most unprepossessing appearance. He can not speak or write English correctly.[32]

He was for a brief time rabbi of Congregation Adas Jeshurun of Philadelphia. He was discharged when the congregation discovered his rabbinical diploma, signed by a Pressburg rabbi, was forged. Another Philadelphia rabbi declared at that time, "This pseudo-rabbi is a self-overrated fool, with little learning, but an abundance of impudence." After posing, in various communities as a convert to Catholicism, Unitarianism, and infidelity, as suited his mood and purpose, he came to San Francisco where, pretending to be a pious Orthodox Jewish scholar, he began to publish a magazine, *The Voice of Israel*, a mixture of "bad Hebrew and worse English."[33] The magazine was a failure and Nathans left San Francisco to avoid being arrested by his creditors. He appeared in New York about the middle of 1875 and greatly pleased Bishop Horatio Potter by converting to Episcopalianism. Potter licensed him as a lay reader, gave him an office at Bible House, and prepared to use him as a missionary. By the end of July, 1876, Potter discovered Nathans' true character and abandoned him. Nathans then became a shoemaker.

And now back to Rosevalley: In January, 1877, he was arrested in New York City for making and passing counterfeit ten-dollar bills. Somehow he avoided going to jail. In April he conducted a revival in Cleveland, Ohio, and in August in Bay City, Mich., collecting money to build a synagogue in New York for converted Jews. The Bay City ministers announced to their congregants that all contributions would be acknowledged in the New York *Jewish Messenger*! In September, the pastor of a church in Lansing, Mich., where Rosevalley was conducting a "meeting," caught him dipping his hand into the collection plates. In January, 1878, Rosevalley came to East Toledo, Ohio, with his "daughter." After collecting forty dollars at a meeting which he addressed, he and his "daughter" sneaked out of town without paying their hotel bill. A short time thereafter they were expelled from a Columbus, Ohio, hotel when they were discovered occupying the same bed, with a half-filled bottle of whiskey within easy reach. Many of the facts thus far narrated were published, on May 21, 1879, in the Fall River, Mass. *Daily News* while Rosevalley was in the midst of a revival campaign in that city.

In May, 1878, Rosevalley began to publish a little magazine, the *Hebrew Evangelist*, in New York City. He had the audacity to send I. M. Wise a story for publication in the *Israelite*, which Wise indignantly rejected. For almost six years, Rosevalley went about lecturing "in costume" to American Christian audiences on the rites connected with Yom Kippur and similar highly enlightening subjects.

At some time prior to April, 1884, Rosevalley's American missionary career terminated in an unpleasant manner. This is how Adolph Benjamin described the decline and gall of Rosevalley:

> When, at the height of success, he was bragging . . . about converting a few million Jews to Christianity, a couple of ungodly detectives took a marked interest in that dispenser of salvation, no doubt for the purpose of becoming converted themselves. They accordingly paid him frequent visits. Finally they commenced to study the New Testament. Imagine their surprise and horror when opening it to find it interleaved with counterfeit five-dollar greenbacks. They immediately changed their minds. Instead of becoming converted themselves, they were instrumental in converting the great St. Rosevalley

into a convict in a striped suit who is still "doing time" in an Ohio penitentiary.[34]

After being released from prison, Rosevalley left the United States and became a missionary in England. It was in these latter days that he invented the heart-rending tale about "Charlie Coulson." Writing in the *Jewish Missionary Herald* in 1932, the Reverend David G. Thirtle, missionary to the Jews in Leeds, England, states:

> The story of Dr. Rosevalley's conversion is a remarkable one. He had been called upon to amputate an arm and a leg for a drummer boy, and was met by the latter's refusal to receive an administration of chloroform. The boy said to him: "Christ is my strength! He will support me while you amputate." Thereupon the doctor wanted to give him some brandy; but this also was refused in the same direct way.
> During the subsequent operation, the lad did not utter a groan, but simply prayed, "O Jesus, blessed Jesus, stand by me now!" That night the Jewish surgeon could get no sleep, for whichever way he turned he seemed to see the soft, blue eyes of the Christian lad; and, when at last he did seek to close his eyes, the boy's words kept ringing in his ears.
> Such is but the beginning of the remarkable story of God's dealings in mercy with this man of the Hebrew race. The incident thus recorded made an impression which could not be effaced; and in quick succession other occurrences came along to bring the first conviction of sin, and finally conversion to God through faith in Christ. The whole story is told in "Charlie Coulson, the Drummer Boy," published by the Drummond Tract Depot, Stirling, Scotland.
> As soon as Dr. Rosevalley became converted and realized what had happened, he resigned his commission in the U.S. Army and began to devote his powers to the preaching of the Gospel among the Jews first in the United States and then in Europe. For the purpose of his work in Europe, he took up his residence at Leeds, and some of the earliest missionary work among the Jews of that city was done by him and with his help.

When Rosevalley died in 1892, he left the sum of two hundred pounds for the erection of a memorial to "Charlie Coulson"! This money, together with additional funds, was used by English Methodists to build the Roseville Road Memorial Hall in the Jewish section of Leeds. A memorial tablet to "Charlie" was placed in the building. To this day, "Charlie Coulson the Drummer Boy" is one of the tracts distributed by societies that try to convert Jews. Max Rosevalley's soul goes marching on. Glory, glory, Hallelujah!

THE EVANGELISTS

The beginning of modern fundamentalist professional evangelism dates from about the time of the Civil War. This is, therefore, an appropriate place to comment upon the efforts of such evangelists to convert Jews. The conducting of church and community revivals by these professionals has been and continues to be a major religious business, a favorite means of raising money for and increasing community interest in fundamentalist Christian beliefs and activities. One of the best examples of this is suave, smooth-talking Billy Graham and his entourage, who have parlayed his good looks and outworn theology into a multimillion-dollar business that has exerted a strong influence upon the religious thinking of many Americans from the most lowly to a former occupant of the highest political office of the land.

Whenever such evangelistic Bible-thumping rabble rousers as Edward P. Hammond and William (Billy) Sunday conducted a revival in a community with a large Jewish population, they usually set aside one service as "Jewish Day," and on that occasion made a special appeal to the Jews. Local Jewish missionaries were invited to participate in the service. These "Jewish Days" did not produce many Jewish conversions, although occasionally a Jew would come forward to say that he had seen the light.

The great Dwight L. Moody was a different type of evangelist. His exhortations were not of the spellbinding kind. They were quiet and sincere appeals to the human heart and mind. Moody did not ordinarily employ spectacular gimmicks or attempt to direct his message toward any particular group.

The only time that Moody departed from this norm was during the 1893 Chicago World Fair. During the Fair he conducted a revival designed to reach not only English-speaking people but also the foreigners who visited the exposition. For this reason, he organized special meetings on the Fair grounds for Germans, Poles, Bohemians, Frenchmen, and Jews. These meetings were conducted in the languages of the nationalities they were designed to reach. They supplemented many other types of gospel gatherings held at the same time. There were separate meetings for men, women, and children, temperance meetings, soldiers' meetings, jail meetings, open-air meetings, cottage meetings, prayer meetings, all-day meetings, and all-night meetings. The foreigners' meetings were simply part of an all-encompassing evangelistic enterprise. A number of prominent foreign evangelists assisted Moody. Pindor from Silesia preached to the Poles; Monod from Paris to the French; Stoecker, the notorious anti-

Semite from Berlin, to the Germans; and Joseph Rabbinowitz from
Kishinef, Russia, to the Jews.

In 1876 Moody was asked if he had made any Jewish converts. He
replied, "Well, several have stood up and professed Christ, but I can not
say that I put much faith in converted Jews."[35] This distrust was em-
phasized further when Moody imported Rabbinowitz for the World Fair,
when he might have used any one of a hundred American Hebrew Christians for the same purpose. Rabbinowitz held his American confreres in
utter contempt. The *American Hebrew* commented on this on August
4, 1893:

> There is no doubt whatever that Rabbinowitz is one of the very few
> men, converted to Christianity, who are sincere in their conver-
> sion. . . . Mr. Rabbinowitz . . . is an unobtrusive person out of whom
> certain missionaries in this country sought to make capital. He ex-
> pressed to Mr. Adolph Benjamin his utter contempt for renegades
> who pose as missionaries; and was surprised that persons of such
> meagre knowledge of the sacred tongue should be allowed to occupy
> the field. "It is no wonder," said he, "that American missionaries fail
> to have the desired effect, since they themselves are entirely ignorant
> of what they preach. Besides, they are men who stand very low in
> the esteem of their own admirers." It will be remembered that Rab-
> binowitz has been reported as having made 50,000 or more converts.
> To the question as to how many he had won over to Christianity, he
> answered modestly, "About 200 in all." Asked how it was that the
> numbers had been so exaggerated, he replied vehemently, "I told
> you that Jewish missionaries are not to be believed under oath."

Dwight L. Moody, quite unintentionally, contributed a greater service
to the cause of modern Jewish missions than any other American before
him or since. He did this by founding, in 1889, the Chicago Bible Institute, renamed, after his death in 1899, the Moody Bible Institute. A high
proportion of the most active American missionaries to the Jews during
the last seventy-five years have been trained in this school. Since 1923
it has conducted a special training course in Jewish missions. During these
many years, the Moody Bible Institute has exerted a powerful and, in the
main, a wholesome influence upon those who formulate the policies of
American missions to the Jews. The MBI leadership is keenly aware of
the seamy histories and questionable practices of many Hebrew Christian missionaries of the past and present. It is trying very earnestly to
raise the levels of missionary integrity and performance in this specialized
area.

Chapter Nine

Denominational Efforts
(1878 to the Present)

From 1880 to 1910 the number of Jews in the United States jumped from about a quarter of a million to over two million and in Canada from about two thousand to seventy-five thousand. The number of Christian agencies seeking to convert the Jews increased in like proportion during this period. Twenty-nine American denominations established Jewish missionary enterprises in these three decades. In addition, hundreds of independent societies and thousands of individuals sought to turn the Jew from his ancestral faith.

Since 1910, the interest of the American Christian world in the overt evangelization of the Jews has decreased considerably. The reasons for the rapid increase and just as rapid decrease are clear. The increase was a direct result of the great influx of Jews into the United States and Canada from Europe, primarily eastern Europe. The decrease is the direct result of the meager number and poor quality of those Jews who have been induced to see the light. Although there are now more than five and a half million Jews in the United States and three hundred thousand in Canada, there is only one major Christian denomination and a few very minor ones in the United States and Canada that are actively engaged in spreading the gospel among American Jews. Many would like to do so, but their desire is more sentimental than practical. There is a steadily diminishing number of independent missionary ventures designed primarily to obtain American Jewish converts.

In 1937 the International Missionary Council established a Jewish section known as the Christian Approach to the Jews, which tried to persuade the various evangelical denominations to abandon their traditional methods in favor of having the witnessing to the Jews done through the neighborhood churches. This method also proved to be very ineffectual. When the International Missionary Council was absorbed by the World Council of Churches in 1961, the Christian Approach to the Jews was a casualty of the merger. The World Council has no section devoted to the proselytizing of Jews. Instead it has a section with the task of promoting helpful dialogues between Jewish and Christian thinkers and of improving the relationships between the Christian and Jewish communities.

This chapter will be devoted to a consideration of the various denominational attempts since 1878 to convert American Jews. The next chapter will concern itself with a few of the major independent ventures having the same objective.

THE BAPTISTS

Northern Baptists

In 1845 the main American Baptist group split into two denominations, the Northern Baptists and the Southern Baptists. Although the Northern Baptists are now known as the American Baptist Conference, the former designation will be retained here in order that there may be a clear differentiation between the activities of these two denominations in the Jewish mission field.

The Northern Baptist Convention and its Women's Home Missionary Society made occasional efforts between 1875 and 1933 to support missionaries to the Jews; but this work never had the wholehearted support of the individual members nor did any particular effort last for very many years.

One notorious missionary who worked for Northern Baptists was the Reverend Aris Lichtenstein, who was employed by New York City's Mariners Temple from 1891 to 1896. Lichtenstein's real name was Hirschman. He was born in Russia about 1848 and converted while living in the village of Pudavitch-Podolia. He married a Christian girl, became a government informer, and was driven out of his native village by its irate Jews. He went to Austria, married again, returned to Russia, was again forced to leave, and migrated to America. Here he was baptized again and married and deserted his third wife.

Ex-informer Hirschman now transformed himself into "ex-rabbi" Lichtenstein. As "ex-rabbi" Lichtenstein, he began his missionary career at the Mariners Temple in September, 1891. Adolph Benjamin, the Jewish missionary nemesis, attended the first gathering and reported that Lichtenstein

> gave expression to utterances which were of such a disgraceful character as to bring a blush to the cheeks of a large number of Russian Jewish girls who were present, attracted, no doubt, by curiosity. . . . The language used in connection with the Christian Saviour and his birth was of such a vile, obscene character . . . as has more than once awakened the murderous passions of Russian toward Russian in their country when addressed toward one another.[1]

Lichtenstein obtained converts by paying them ten dollars to be converted and fifty cents for every meeting they attended. He taught them the "Christian" way of life by engaging them in drinking bouts and taking them to houses of prostitution. He boasted that he spent his missionary pay on liquor and women. On one occasion, a "convert" appealed to Benjamin to expose Lichtenstein and was told that Lichtenstein was "too far below his dignity to handle."[2]

After being discharged by the Mariners Temple in 1896, Lichtenstein made his living working as a missionary in and around St. Louis until he died in July, 1923. In later years, his New York misconduct seems to have been forgiven or forgotten, because, from 1915 until his death, he was a leading light of the Hebrew Christian Alliance of America and for a number of years its General Secretary. This is surprising because, on the whole, the HCAA made a serious effort to keep the ethical and moral character of its membership on as high a level as circumstances permitted.

The modernist influence is so strong among Northern Baptists that, for the past forty years, the denomination has made no effort to convert the Jews as such. In 1938 the executive secretary of the American Baptist Home Missionary Society stated:

> The philosophy of our faith demands that we shall be active evangelists among all people. . . . So far as Jews are concerned, we have no policy of evangelism among them as a group. . . . Our testimony to them will come only in the normal and natural contacts through which individuals come into touch with individuals or groups of our people. In other words, we have no formal program for evangelizing the Jews as a people.[3]

Seventh-Day Baptists

The Seventh-Day Baptists are a small, intelligent, aggressive group of Christians who observe the Jewish Sabbath. Having less than one hundred churches and ten thousand members in the United States, they support two colleges and a publishing house. From April, 1889, to December, 1899, their publishing house issued a peculiar magazine called *The Peculiar People*. This magazine was unique in that it was the only missionary publication printed in North America in the nineteenth century that consistently advocated the so-called "Judaizing" doctrine, a doctrine that permits a convert to Christianity to remain within the ranks of Judaism. It was edited by men who believed themselves to be Gentile by birth and Jewish Christians by religion.

Corliss Fitz Randolph, an eminent Seventh-Day Baptist leader, has written:

> Our attempts to work among the Jews have not met with any marked success. So far as I know, our relations with them have always been cordial; but, with but two or three exceptions, we found that those who seemed interested were so from unworthy motives—adventurers.[4]

Southern Baptists

The Southern Baptist Convention, largest, most powerful, most influential Baptist denomination in the United States, did not go into the Jewish field until 1921. In that year its Home Missions Board in Atlanta, Ga., set up a Jewish Department and put Hebrew Christian Jacob Gartenhaus in charge of this special work.

Gartenhaus came to this country from Austria in 1915 and was baptized in Leopold Cohn's Brooklyn mission in 1916. After graduating from the Moody Bible Institute in 1919, he entered the Southern Baptist seminary in Louisville, Ky. When he finished there, he went to work for the Home Missions Board.

In 1949 the Southern Baptists, deciding that the amount of time, effort, and money it was putting into the Jewish Department was not justified by its meager accomplishments, abolished the department and discharged Gartenhaus. Since then, Gartenhaus has continued to live in Atlanta. He set up his own independent effort, the International Board of Jewish Missions, Inc., and has made his living by lecturing to Christian audiences about how to convert Jews. His lack of tact and his arrogance combined in 1931 to cause the Hebrew Christian Alliance to drop him from its membership. In later years he was re-admitted to the HCA and served as its president from 1948 to 1950. His most important accomplishment during the years he labored for the Southern Baptist Convention was probably his persuading Hebrew Christian Hyman Appleman to become a Baptist.

The Moody Bible Institute considers Hyman Appleman the most successful Hebrew Christian evangelist of our time. Appleman never made a really serious effort to convert Jews. He spent almost his entire life conducting revival meetings among fundamentalist Christians. In this he was extremely successful and because of this he was greatly envied by his fellow Hebrew Christians.

Appleman was born in Moghiliev, Russia, in 1902. He was brought to Chicago by his parents in December, 1914. He got a B.A. from the University of Chicago and a law degree from De Paul University in 1921. This intellectual effort was too arduous. Shortly after becoming a lawyer, he suffered a nervous breakdown. While recovering from this affliction, he was converted in 1925 in Denver, Colo., by a Disciples of Christ minister. In November of that year he enlisted in the army. In 1927, while stationed at Walter Reed Hospital, Washington, D.C., he met Gartenhaus, who persuaded him to become a Baptist. He left the army in 1930 and received Baptist ordination at Lawton, Okla.

He attended Southwestern Baptist Seminary, Fort Worth, Tex., from 1930 to 1933. From 1934 to 1942 he served as State Evangelist for the Texas Baptist Convention. He then went into business for himself and did very well, conducting evangelistic campaigns throughout the United States, Great Britain, and many parts of Europe.

With the help of Harry A. Ironside, pastor of the Moody Memorial Church of Chicago, he established in 1945 the American Association for Jewish Evangelism, with headquarters at Winona Lake, Ind. The new venture was staffed by a number of former employees of J. Hoffman Cohn's American Board of Missions to the Jews. For several years there was a great bitterness between the AAJE and the ABMJ. Charges and countercharges of corruption and mismanagement were hurled by leaders of each against the other. In 1950, shortly before he died, Ironside directed Appleman to stop using Ironside's name in his attacks on J. H. Cohn and he also resigned from the AAJE board.

From 1952 to 1954, Appleman was president of the Hebrew Christian Alliance. During his presidency he tried to change the nature of the organization. Since its establishment in 1915, the HCA had been primarily a society of Hebrew Christian missionaries and their wives which met once a year in various cities for three or four days at the expense of the fundamentalist Christians of the community where each meeting was held. The HCA members paid for this brief annual vacation by preaching in the churches of their benefactors and, by means of the collection plates, helped their hosts defray the costs of the HCA gatherings. Appleman attempted to make the HCA an out-and-out missionary effort, which would raise money from Gentiles and use it to convert Jews. His effort did not succeed. Appleman became seriously ill in 1954, was named Honorary President of the HCA, and thereafter ceased to be intimately involved in its activities. Once Appleman was out of the way, the HCA went back to being what it had been pre-Appleman, a non-aggressive fraternal organization of mostly professional Hebrew Christians.

Recovering from his illness, Appleman continued his career as traveling evangelist and also continued in high favor at the Moody Bible Institute. He became less and less active in the American Association of Jewish Evangelism. By 1959 a non-Jewish Baptist minister, J. Palmer Muntz, had succeeded Appleman as head of the AAJE.

Since dissolving its Jewish Department in 1949, the Home Missions Department of the Southern Baptist Convention has made no further organized attempt to convert American Jews. It is, however, one of a sizable number of American fundamentalist denominations that support missions to the Jews in the State of Israel.

THE EPISCOPALIANS

Church of England in Canada

There were branches of the London Jews Society in Canada from 1847 on. These branches maintained separate existences until 1882, when they were united as the Canadian Auxiliary of the LJS, with headquarters in Montreal and a Canadian secretary. The LJS Canadian headquarters and secretary were maintained until about 1930 and were then discontinued.

In 1902 the LJS took over a Presbyterian mission to the Jews of Montreal, together with its missionary, Ignatz Trebitsch.

Ignatz Trebitsch was born in Hungary in 1870. After traveling about the world, he began to edit a Spiritualist magazine in Budapest in 1897. This venture speedily failed and he began to travel again. In London he was attracted into the missionary business. He allowed missionary Arnold Frank, Anglican missionary in Hamburg, Germany, to convert him on Christmas Day, 1898. In 1900 Frank sent him to Canada where he went to work for the Presbyterians and, subsequently, the Anglicans. The archbishop of Montreal gave him Anglican ordination on Christmas Day, 1902. On this occasion he changed his name from Ignatz Trebitsch to the more euphonious Ignatius Timothy Trebitsch-Lincoln. In March, 1903, he resigned as missionary and returned to England.

He then became, in rapid succession, a country curate, politician, member of Parliament, oil-well driller, forger, war spy, thief, and, prior to the advent of Harry Gurgason, alias Prince Michael Romanoff, the most amazing and persistent illegal immigrant with whom the U.S. Immigration Service has ever had to deal. He ended his days as Abbot Chao Kung, head of a Buddhist monastery in China. He died in a Shanghai hospital on October 7, 1943.

Trebitsch was succeeded in Montreal by another Hebrew Christian, the Reverend D. J. Neugewirtz. He, too, had been converted in Hamburg by Frank. Unlike his predecessor, he spent the rest of his life as a missionary. The most dramatic moment of his career came on Yom Kippur in 1916, when the Jews of Montreal turned out in such great numbers to bring him the season's greetings that a regiment of soldiers had to be summoned to disperse the infuriated mob.

In 1912 the London Jews Society turned the task of evangelizing Canadian Jewry over to the Missionary Society of the Church of England in Canada. This denomination operated missions to the Jews for many years in Montreal, Ottawa, Toronto, and Hamilton. The one in Toronto lasted the longest. It did not disappear until about 1960. Since then this denomination has ceased to maintain a separate evangelistic effort to the Jews of Canada.

Protestant Episcopal Church of the United States

This denomination was the only one in the United States whose governing body made an organized effort to convert American Jews between 1878 and 1882. Spurred on by the great influx of East European Jewn in the 1880's, fifteen more denominations began to engage in some sort of Jewish work between 1882 and 1895.

On January, 1878, the Board of Missions of the Protestant Episcopal Church founded the Church Society for Promoting Christianity amongst the Jews. It began by taking over existing missions in New York and Philadelphia. The one activity of the Society that remained constant from beginning to end was the mission school operated in New York City by Miss Martha J. Ellis. She had established this school with local support in 1866. In 1900 she boasted that she had had more than two thousand

Jewish pupils and that seventy of them had been baptized. Most of these children were from the homes of poor immigrants. Although Miss Ellis insisted that the children came with full parental knowledge and consent, this claim was denied vigorously by Adoph Benjamin. He declared in 1889 that, whenever a child would inform its parents that the school was designed to get converts for Christianity, the teachers would attempt to placate the angry parents and the child with liberal gifts of money, clothing, and candy.

At the height of its growth, the Church Society had missions in sixteen cities. The work of the Society among Jewish adults was conducted in such an honorable fashion that it accomplished practically nothing. A *Jewish Messenger* reporter, who went to a Sunday evening service at the New York mission in July, 1884, reported that he found present only three children and three adults. Adolph Benjamin never attacked the Episcopal efforts to reach Jewish adults, which is a clear indication that their efforts were both ethical and fruitless.

Many Episcopal clergy were strongly opposed to the Church Society. This opposition came to a head in 1897. In that year, New York's Bishop Henry Codman Potter, a liberal, fearless humanitarian, recommended to his diocese that its Good Friday offering, which had been for years turned over to the Church Society, be devoted instead to educational work among southern blacks. Although the Church Society struggled on for seven more years, the action of Bishop Potter marked the beginning of the end. In 1904 the Church Society's treasury became exhausted and the Society had to quit. Miss Ellis' school continued for a few more years through the support of a small group of faithful contributors.

In 1919 the Board of Missions created a "foreign born Americans division" "to convert the discontented foreigner in the United States to a sound principle of Americanism through Christian helpfulness." The division's head was instructed to seek to proselytize Italians, Scandinavians, Czechs, Slovaks, Welsh, Syrians, Hungarians, Mexicans, Russians, Orientals, and Jews. In response to Jewish protests, the reply was that the main purpose of the effort was not to convert but to Americanize the foreign born and that the Episcopalians would attempt to win over only those Jews unaffiliated with the synagogue. Shortly thereafter the denomination's General Convention adopted unanimously a resolution that the Americanization program was not intended to be a conversionist effort so far as Jews were concerned. In March, 1920, the Federal Council of Churches issued a statement condemning the use of "Christianization" and "Americanization" as synonymous terms. This ended the controversy. The

Episcopal "foreign born division" made no direct effort to convert American Jews.

Although, during the last seventy years, individual dioceses and churches have made sporadic efforts to reach the Jews, the Protestant Episcopal denomination as a whole has made no such effort since the demise of the Church Society.

For hundreds of years, there has been a fixed prayer in the ritual of the Anglican Church, a prayer recited every Good Friday, asking God to help the Anglicans convert all "Jews, Turks, heretics, and infidels." When the American branch broke away from the Church of England during the Revolutionary War, this prayer was retained in the American Episcopal prayer book. About 1913 liberal-minded Episcopalians began to suggest that this phraseology be changed. In 1922 the Joint Commission on the Revision of the Prayer Book recommended a substitute phrase, "all who know Thee not as Thou art revealed in the Gospel of Thy Son." The recommendation was adopted and the revised prayer book, published in 1928, contained the prayer in its new form.

THE LUTHERANS

Norwegian Lutherans

The Zion Society for Israel, conversionist effort of clergymen affiliated with the Norwegian Lutheran Synod, was organized in June, 1878. For the next eighty-five years, it tried to convert Jews in eastern Europe, Palestine, and the United States.

From 1878 to 1881 the Society employed no missionaries. It supported missions already in existence in Russia and Palestine. In 1881 it sent a missionary to Europe. Work was begun in the United States in 1882. A mission was opened in Baltimore. A second mission was opened in Chicago in 1902. In this same year the Zion Society discontinued its European operations and concentrated its attention upon the Jews of the United States.

In 1918 Hebrew Christian John Resnick, 1874-1924, was appointed General Superintendent of the Society. In the six years of his administration, the Society's income and influence expanded considerably. It opened missions in Minneapolis, St. Paul, Omaha, and Brooklyn. Resnick was able to secure financial backing and active support from five other Lutheran bodies, the Lutheran Free Church, the Augustana (Swedish) Synod, the Iowa Synod, the Joint Synod of Ohio, and the United Danish Lutheran Church.

In March, 1933, Elias Newman, 1888-1967, was appointed director of the work in Minneapolis and St. Paul. He held that position until 1950. Newman was one of the ablest and most intelligent American Hebrew Christian missionaries. Before coming to the Zion Society, he was successively a Baptist minister in Latrobe, Pa., and a Presbyterian missionary to the Jews in Montreal, Chicago, Damascus, Syria, and St. Louis. He received Lutheran ordination in order to work for the Zion Society. A sincere fundamentalist Christian, he fought valiantly during the 1930's against the anti-Semitic activities of a number of prominent fundamentalists, including Arno C. Gaebelein, Gerald B. Winrod, William B. Riley and others.

In 1945 sentiment began to grow in Lutheran circles that the Zion Society should be taken over by the National Lutheran Council, the overall coordinating body of American Lutheranism. One of the advocates of this move declared:

> The Society has labored in the face of much indifference and opposition. . . . To its earnest persistent plea for a Church related program, there has been no official, authentic response. . . . Hardships have been imposed upon the Society by the lack of official recognition and authorization of American Lutheran church bodies. One handicap is adequate training facilities for our missionaries. . . . Another serious handicap is the frequent blockade of entrance to congregations. Since the Society does not bear the official seal of the Lutheran Church, her representatives often have to reach congregations by way of a detour.[5]

At the annual convention of the Society in October, 1946, a motion to merge with the NLC was defeated by a vote of 41 to 12.

After the Zion Society delegates refused to fuse with the National Lutheran Council, the latter body established its own Commission of Jewish Missions in 1947. This affected seriously the fund-raising efforts of the Zion Society. It could no longer continue as an independent entity. At its 1949 convention it voted to merge with what had now been given the fancy designation of the Christian Approach to the Jewish People, working under the Division of American Missions of the National Lutheran Council. This department took over the management of the United Lutheran missions in Pittsburgh and Philadelphia, the independent Lutheran mission in Baltimore, and Zion Society's missions in Chicago, Minneapolis and St. Paul.

American Lutherans continued to show little interest in their denomination's attempt to convert American Jews. In 1961 the National Lutheran

Council abolished its department of the Christian Approach to the Jewish People.

For a short time the Zion Society was revived and attempted to continue as an independent entity. The attempt was not successful. On February 1, 1964, the Zion Society was merged into the Commission on Evangelism of the American Lutheran Church and went out of existence permanently.

Evangelical Lutheran Synod of Missouri, Ohio, and other States

From 1883 until about 1931, this denomination employed a missionary to the Jews in New York City. Nothing much was accomplished; but the effort did create a mighty furor in the New York Jewish community at one unpleasant point in its existence.

About the middle of May, 1899, a very foolish East Side blacksmith, wishing to play a practical joke on a young Jewish boy, branded a cross on his back. A day or so later, a sailor, whose hobby was tattooing, was requested by a group of Jewish and Christian lads to tattoo stars, anchors, crosses, and other decorative symbols on their arms. He willingly obliged. By chance he pricked the emblem of the cross on the arms of a few Jewish youths. After the frantic mothers of these children had rubbed and scrubbed in vain in a futile effort to remove the objectionable symbol from the skin of their children, they took the boys to a neighborhood doctor. This doctor, after informing the mothers that their children were branded for life, took it upon himself to notify the newspapers that the tattooing had been performed by the neighborhood's Lutheran missionary. He declared further that the children had been bribed into giving permission by gifts of candy and toys.

The result was tragic. The Jews of the East Side, many of whom bore upon their bodies scars inflicted by East European pogromists, started a pogrom of their own. Missions were stoned, street preachers beaten, and Nathaniel Friedman, the missionary in question, had to be rescued by the police from an infuriated mob.

On June 16, the anti-missionary crusader Adolph Benjamin published a letter in the *Jewish Messenger*, stating that the whole incident was a grievous blunder, an imaginary happening "created by a clever Jewish physician and his Jewish druggist to obtain cheap advertisement through our sensational yellow journalism." But the Jews of the East Side and New Yorkers in general kept right on believing that the story was true. In February, 1900, Benjamin again announced that the generally believed tale was false. Despite this, twenty-three years later, Walter Hurt, on page 289 of his book *The Truth about the Jews* wrote:

> In 1899, a Christian mission in New York City conducted a particularly aggravating crusade among Jewish children. At that time, I wrote an article on the subject, entitled "The Sign of the Cross." . . . Its viewpoint may not be without value to Christian readers, so I herewith present it in part, having deleted its more undesirable passages:
> . . . Christian missionaries in the East Side districts of New York, having nothing more bigoted or less brutal to do, are busily engaged in branding the arms of Jewish children with the sign of the cross. Babies are bribed with gifts of candy and toys, and, too young to realize the cruel consequences, they readily submit to the operation of tattooing. Wherefore are the parents panic stricken and the children thus disfigured are ostracized by their playmates."

This denomination is now known as the Lutheran Church, Missouri Synod. The Missouri Synod Lutherans also began to support the Emanuel Hebrew Mission in Chicago in 1942. After this Chicago mission ceased functioning in 1956, the denomination made no further organized effort to convert American Jews until July, 1977, when, in convention assembled, it decided to resume its efforts to convert Jews. It is, currently, the only major Protestant denomination in the United States that has reached such a decision.

United Lutheran Church

The United Lutheran Church was formed in 1918 through the merger of a number of Lutheran synods. It took over the support and supervision of two Jewish missions already established, one in Pittsburgh backed by the Pittsburgh Synod since 1906 and the other operated in Philadelphia since 1917.

The ULC opened a mission in Baltimore in 1920 with Hebrew Christian Henry Einspruch as director. Einspruch was a very high-minded and intelligent person. For many years he edited a small monthly magazine, *The Mediator*, which was the most attractive and best written periodical thus far published by an American mission to the Jews. In 1939, syndicated columnist Alfred Segal of Cincinnati made the following comment about *The Mediator* in his column "As I See It":

> It is altogether unlike the general conversionist press, what with its intelligence, what with an absence of fanaticism. It is, indeed, almost like any Jewish paper you might pick up in its worrying about the

current pain of the Jews, in its protest against the persecutions. These converted Jews haven't been able to escape the agony of Israel and don't seem to want to. They appear to be better Christians by remaining conscious Jews.

In later years Einspruch conducted his Baltimore operation as an independent mission. It went out of business when Einspruch retired in 1963. Einspruch died, at the age of eighty-four, on January 4, 1977.

In 1947, the United Lutherans placed their Jewish missions in Pittsburgh and Philadelphia under the jurisdiction and management of the newly organized Commission of Jewish Missions of the National Lutheran Council.

In June, 1962, the United Lutheran Church dissolved and its churches became part of The Lutheran Church in America, now the largest of all American Lutheran denominations.

THE METHODISTS

Northern Methodists

In 1894 the Methodists of New York City, through their Church Extension and Missionary Society, began to support the mission to the Jews established in New York in 1892 by the Reverend Arno Clemens Gaebelein, 1861-1945, non-Jew.

In 1891, while pastor of a Methodist church in Hoboken, N.J., Gaebelein began to preach once a week in Jacob Freshman's independent New York mission. A year later he became Freshman's assistant. A few months thereafter, alarmed by the dishonesty of Freshman and the insincerity of his converts, he left Freshman and opened his own mission, the Hope of Israel. His first helpers, three of Freshman's converts, drank and gambled so much that he had to dismiss them.

After becoming an official Methodist mission in 1894, the Hope of Israel Mission began to publish *Our Hope* magazine in English and *Tikvas Yisrael* in Hebrew and Yiddish. By this time Gaebelein could speak Yiddish so fluently that he was often supposed to be a converted Jew. Gaebelein was one of the principal leaders of the anti-Warszawiak campaign, to be discussed in the next chapter. In 1897 the Methodists stopped supporting Gaebelein's mission. They hired Dr. Harry Zeckhausen, a Hebrew Christian osteopathic medical missionary, as their official Jewish missionary. Zeckhausen remained with them until 1920. After that the New York Methodists stopped employing anyone for the specific purpose of converting Jews.

Gaebelein continued to try to convert Jews until 1904. From then on he made his living as a highly successful lecturer at Christian Bible conferences. For the rest of his life he continued to publish *Our Hope* magazine, which contained articles on many themes, including that of Jewish evangelism. Gaebelein eventually became persona non grata among Hebrew Christians, because in 1934 he wrote a book, *The Conflict of the Ages,* which sought to prove, on the basis of the fraudulent Protocols of the Elders of Zion, that Russian Communism is a Jewish invention.

In his autobiography *Fifty Years—Autobiography of a Servant,* published in 1930, Gaebelein discusses his ten years as a missionary to the Jews. He says he had very few serious inquirers and that most of those who attended his mission were prompted by material motives.

> The accusation from the side of intelligent Hebrews, that Jewish Missions have encouraged such a miserable spirit and mercenary motives in order to make converts, is not wholly unfounded. Many of the converts of certain missions conducted by Jewish converts are nothing but hirelings and a disgrace to both Judaism and Christianity. Yet there have been and there are genuine cases of real conversion.[6]

From about 1907 to about 1940, the Women's Home Missionary Society of the Methodist Church supported a settlement house, known as Marcy Center, in Chicago for the principal purpose of converting Jews. Until 1930 the Center was located on Maxwell Street. In November, 1930, it erected a new building on South Springfield Avenue in the most thickly populated Jewish section of Chicago's West Side.

The new Marcy Center was the most attractive mission to the Jews in America. It had excellently equipped and conducted medical dispensaries, gymnasium, Americanization classes, playground, game rooms, and many other social and educational features. Gradually it paid less and less attention to Jewish proselytization and became more and more a high type neighborhood settlement house. After 1942 it was turned over by the Methodists to the city of Chicago for administration and support. Of course, after that its program had nothing whatsoever to do with trying to convert Jews to Christianity.

The Northern Methodists now make no organized attempt to convert American Jews.

Southern Methodists

Beginning in 1884, this denomination employed Hebrew Christians to the Jews for brief periods of time. Such persons were at work in Atlanta,

Ga., from 1884 to 1887 and from 1904 to 1914 and in Memphis and Nashville from about 1927 to 1932. The Southern Methodists no longer sponsor this kind of missionary activity.

THE PRESBYTERIANS

Presbyterians, U.S.A.

This was the name long used by the Northern Presbyterians to distinguish them from their Southern brethren, who were known as the Presbyterians, U.S.

The national Board of Home Missions of Presbyterians, U.S.A., did not sponsor any Jewish work until 1908, but the New York presbytery entered the field in 1893 and, during the next seven years, had a very unpleasant series of experiences. The sad tale revolves around the names of Hermann Warszawiak and Herman Paul Faust. Although Warszawiak brought great agony to the richest and most influential Presbyterian church in America, he was never directly employed as a missionary by the Presbyterians; and so his story will be told in the next chapter.

Faust came to America in 1888 and served for a very short time as rabbi in Poughkeepsie, N.Y. After losing this position, he came to New York City and supported himself by obtaining alms from various rabbis and congregations. In 1892, two days before Passover, he got his final gift from New York Jewry, fifty pounds of matzot. Then, convinced that the Jews would no longer help him, he went to Jacob Freshman's mission and got "converted."

After being a star attraction at the Freshman mission for a number of months, he went into business for himself in December at the Allen Street Presbyterian Church. At the end of 1893, the New York Presbytery assumed official sponsorship of Faust's mission and began to pay him a salary of $150 a month. In December, 1895, the Presbytery showed it was not entirely happy with Faust by refusing him Presbyterian ordination and reducing his salary 10 percent. Later it had a change of heart and, in January, 1898, consented to grant him ordination.

In December, 1898, Faust sued the N.Y. *Sun* for libel because, in an editorial, that paper had compared him to Warszawiak. Adolph Benjamin gave the defense attorney so much damaging information about Faust that the jury not only acquitted the newspaper but placed the costs of the trial upon the plaintiff. In March, 1900, the Presbytery stopped sponsoring Faust and his mission. Shortly thereafter the Allen Street church, which had been Faust's headquarters, was sold and became an Orthodox synagogue. Faust spent the remaining eighteen months of his life lecturing in Christian churches about the Jews.

The Board of Home Missions of the Presbyterian Church, U.S.A., set up a special Jewish missions department in New York City in December, 1908. The Reverend Louis Meyer, 1862-1913, a scholarly Hebrew Christian, was named director. He was a good speaker but a poor organizer, and he held on to his job for only two years. During the last fifteen years of his life, Meyer made an intensive study of Jewish missions and was regarded as an authority in this field. Many facts contained in this book were taken from articles written by Meyer. He was, for the most part, a careful student and not given to falsehood or exaggeration, as so many so-called authorities in this field have been. He was respected by both Jews and Christians. He enjoyed the friendship of a number of Jewish scholars, notably Gotthard Deutsch and George A. Kohut.

From 1911 to 1914 the Northern Presbyterian's Jewish department was inactive. From 1914 to 1938 it was the most vigorous denominational organization seeking to proselytize American Jews. The Presbyterians called their missions "settlement houses." They operated such houses in ten major American cities. In 1920 the Jewish work was re-named the Department of Jewish Evangelization.

By 1923 the denomination had decided to employ a two-faceted approach, to win the Jews through the settlement houses and also through the local churches. The director of the department, John Stuart Conning, 1862-1946, explained the reasoning for this decision:

> Community work is more fruitful in results than the conventional Jewish missions, as the Jews resent being singled out as an object of Christian effort. The varied ministries carried on in the community center furnish manifold opportunities for a personal approach through which the Christian spirit is revealed, prejudices are broken down, and the way is opened for the Gospel. These ministries make more effective the distinctively evangelistic services which are an essential part of the program. As evidence of the fruitfulness of such methods, a speaker at a recent conference of Conservative Jews was quoted as saying that, while the old fashioned missions succeeded in demoralizing a few individuals, the new method of community approach demoralized whole neighborhoods. While community work in neighborhoods predominantly Jewish meets an essential need, and should be greatly extended, yet the majority of the Jews of the United States do not live in ghettos, but in American residential neighborhoods and within the parishes of Christian churches. For such Jewish people, the way of approach must be through the local church. There are thousands of churches that have Jews in their community and the

work of Jewish evangelization will never be overtaken until such churches are enlisted in a ministry to these Jewish neighbors.[7]

In 1931 the Department of Jewish Evangelization became a unit of the Presbyterian Board of National Missions. In 1936 Conning became secretary of this Board and the Jewish section was headed by Dr. Conrad Hoffman, Jr. Under Hoffman's guidance, the Board of National Missions turned over the financing and administration of the Jewish settlement houses to local presbyteries. On October 1, 1946, Hoffman left the Board of National Missions to become director of the interdenominational committee of the Christian Approach to the Jews of the International Missionary Council. By this time all financial support for Jewish missions at the national denominational level had ceased. "Settlement houses" remained in operation in Baltimore, Chicago, Los Angeles, and Philadelphia, all sponsored by the local presbyteries. As the years passed, the local presbyteries also stopped supporting these local missions to the Jews.

The denomination is now known as the United Presbyterians, U.S.A. and has no missionaries to American Jews at either the national or local presbytery levels.

United Presbyterians

Under the auspices of its Women's Association, this denomination operated a Jewish mission in Chicago from 1894 to 1901. In 1958 the United Presbyterians were absorbed by the Northern Presbyterians. Together they form the United Presbyterians, U.S.A.

Reformed Presbyterians

This denomination opened Jewish missions in 1894 in Cincinnati and Philadelphia. The Cincinnati mission was abandoned in 1900. The Philadelphia mission lasted for many years but no longer exists.

Presbyterian Church in Canada

This denomination, founded in 1875, operated a Jewish mission for a few years in Montreal, beginning in 1892. In 1908 a mission was started in Toronto, in 1911 in Winnipeg, and once more in Montreal in 1914.

In 1925 the United Church of Canada was formed through a merger of the Presbyterian, Methodist, and Congregational denominations. The United Church has dropped the Jewish work of the Presbyterians and has no missions specifically designed to convert Canadian Jews.

THE ROMAN CATHOLICS

The Roman Catholic Church makes no distinction between Jews and other non-Catholics. Therefore, as a denomination, it has operated no missions either in the United States or Canada specifically meant to convert Jews. It has been especially cautious in this regard because of a concern that is might be classed with those fundamentalist Protestant sects which, in the past, have aroused Jewish antagonism by inducing Jewish children to attend denominational schools intended to convert them to Christianity. However, individual priests and laymen have been permitted to carry on conversionist activities for the purpose of persuading both Jewish children and adults to become Roman Catholics.

In 1850 two Hebrew Catholic brothers, Father Marie Theodore Ratisbonne, 1802-1884, and Father Marie Alphonse Ratisbonne, 1814-1884, founded in France the order of Notre Dame de Sion, whose purposes were to convert Jews and to give Jewish children a Catholic education. This order established convents all over the world, including two in the United States at Kansas City and Marshall, Missouri, and one in western Canada. These three convents carried on no active proselyting work among Jews but confined their efforts in this direction to praying for the conversion of the Jews. During the 1960's this order of nuns formally abandoned its conversionist goal and now concerns itself with trying to improve Christian-Jewish relationships. One member of the order has stated, "Our job is to convert Christians to a new openness about Judaism and to help Jews be better Jews."[8]

In 1903 the Association of Prayer for the Conversion of Israel was founded in Paris. In August, 1907, Pope Pius X raised the Association to the rank of an Archconfraternity. About 1920 a number of Catholics, including some converted Jews, established a branch in New York City. The members meet once a month in a Manhattan Catholic church for Bible study and prayer. Since 1941 this group has been known as the Guild of Our Lady of Sion.

In the twentieth century a number of Jews converted to Catholicism have made zealous efforts to evangelize for their new faith. Among the most widely advertised of these have been:

David Goldstein, 1870-1958, converted in Boston in 1908. In 1910 he formed the Catholic Campaigners for Christ and conducted conversionist campaigns in Catholic churches throughout the United States. He made no special effort to convert Jews. In 1938 he stated that, although he had made no such special effort, his campaigns had resulted in three Jewish conversions to Catholicism.

Rosalie Marie Levy, born in Alexandria, La. Converted in 1912 in Washington, D.C., while working for the government as a typist. In 1919 she became American secretary for the Archconfraternity of Prayer for the Conversion of Israel and occupied this position for ten years. In 1929 the direction of this work was given to the Kansas City nunnery of Notre Dame de Sion. Miss Levy then moved to New York and devoted herself to lecturing to Catholic groups on why Jews should become Catholics and to attempting to preach to Jews at street meetings in Union Square.

In 1926 she was accused by the Jewish press of having persuaded a young Jewish girl, Rose Goldstein, of Newark, N.J., to become both a Catholic and a nun and to change her name to Sister Mary Agnes. The accusation was only partially true. Rose Goldstein of Newark became a Catholic in December, 1920, several months before she ever met Miss Levy. Miss Levy was one of those who persuaded her to enter the Dominican order in 1925 and become a nun. When Rosalie Marie Levy wrote her autobiography *Thirty Years with Christ* in 1942, she was working in New York as a court stenographer.

John M. Oesterreicher, born in Austria, February, 1904. Converted while a medical student. Ordained as priest in Vienna Cathedral, July, 1927. At first taught in parochial schools. From 1934 to 1938 directed Opus Sancti Pauli, a society devoted to the conversion of Austrian Jews. When the Nazis annexed Austria, he went first to Rome, then Paris, and in 1940 to the United States, where he continued to labor in New York City for the conversion of Jews. In December, 1948, he wrote a pamphlet "The Apostolate to the Jews," in which he told of efforts being made to turn Jews into Catholics by the Kansas City sisters of Notre Dame de Sion, Rosalie Marie Levy, Monsignor A. Raphael Cioffi of Brooklyn, and himself. He stated that the purpose of his pamphlet was to encourage the establishment of an institute which would have as its main purpose the conversion of Jews to Roman Catholicism.

About 1954 Oesterreicher succeeded in establishing such an institute, the Institute of Judeo-Christian Relations, at Catholic Seton Hall University in South Orange, N.J. Under his editorship, this Institute has issued a series of volumes under the general title of *The Bridge*, i.e., a means of bridging the gap of misunderstanding between Catholicism and Judaism. When one reads these volumes carefully, he discovers that Monsignor Oesterreicher's bridge is a one-way structure, subtly designed to make Catholicism attractive to Jews. Since 1965, when the Catholic Church slightly revised its position on Jews at the Vatican II conclave, Monsignor Oesterreicher has insisted that his publications are no longer intended to try to get Jews to become Catholics.

THE OTHERS

Christian and Missionary Alliance

In 1881 a New York City Presbyterian minister resigned his pastorate and organized the Christian Alliance for home mission work and the Missionary Alliance for foreign work. He did not intend to create a new denomination; but in 1916 the two Alliances merged into one organization, the Christian and Missionary Alliance, and a new denomination was born. It now has a membership of about seventy-five thousand.

In 1920 the Alliance opened a Jewish mission in New York City which still exists and presently occupies very modest quarters in a small building in the Times Square area. In 1931 the vice president of the Alliance wrote concerning this mission:

> The results have been meagre. Not more than fifty Jews have confessed faith in Jesus of Nazareth as Savior and Messiah. Of that number there are at present not more than twenty affiliated with the mission."

In the years since 1931, the mission has been even less effective.

In 1923 the Alliance opened a mission in Toronto which it ceased to support in 1927.

Reformed Church in America

This was originally known as the Dutch Reformed Church and played a prominent role in the history of colonial New York. It has about 250,000 adherents. It has never supported an official Jewish mission of its own; but it has given considerable financial support to various independent missions.

Christian Reformed Church

This denomination is also of Dutch origin. It has about three hundred thousand members. It opened a mission to the Jews in Paterson, N.J., in 1913 and in Chicago in 1918. Both missions were closed about 1960 when the denomination decided to get out of the Jewish mission business.

Reformed Church in the U.S.

This is a very small denomination, known formerly as the German Reformed Church. It operated missions to the Jews in Brooklyn from 1916 to 1926 and in Philadelphia for some years after 1921.

Catholic Church of Zion

This is a minute sect founded by John Alexander Dowie, 1847-1907. It maintains headquarters in Zion City, Ill., believes the earth is flat, and teaches that females must cover every portion of their bodies except the face to ward off immorality. Hermann Warszawiak was missionary to the Jews of New York City for this group from January to October, 1904.

Seventh-Day Adventists

This denomination, which came into being in 1845 as a result of William Miller's mistaken belief that the "second coming" would occur in 1844, is very desirous of converting Jews. However, it has made only one determined effort in that direction. From 1906 to 1916, Hebrew Adventist Fred C. Gilbert conducted a mission to the Jews of Boston. In later years he became a well-known leader of the Adventists and served as one of its international field secretaries.

Mennonites

Of German origin, this sect of the so-called "plain people" employed a missionary to the Jews of Chicago in 1917 and for a short time thereafter. Since then they have not had their own missions to Jews but they support strongly a number of independent missions, particularly one with a rather dubious reputation operated in Los Angeles by Hebrew Christian Arthur A. Michelson. For many years Michelson lectured about his work and collected many dollars in many Mennonite churches.

Church of the Brethren

This is another group of the "plain people." It, too, has been supporting a mission to the Jews of Los Angeles, a mission established in 1939 by the American Board of Mission to the Jews.

What of the hundreds of other Christian denominations which have not been mentioned because they have not attempted to convert American Jews? What is their position on the question of evangelizing the Jew?

There are fundamentalist groups which say, "We would very much like to establish missions to the Jews, but we lack the funds with which to do so."

There are denominations like the Christian Scientists and the Mormons which say, "We are anxious to convert everyone, including Jews, but we make no effort to reach out to the Jews as a special group."

And then, of course, there are liberal denominations like the Quakers who state, "We want to convert all human beings to the point of view which intelligent Christians and intelligent Jews hold in common," and the Unitarian-Universalist who wrote, "What we would like is a conversion of Unitarians into better Unitarians, Protestants into better Protestants, Catholics into better Catholics, and Jews into better Jews."

Chapter Ten

The Independents

In addition to the conversionist efforts of the Christian denominations, there have been hundreds of other organized attempts since 1880 to convert the Jews of the United States and Canada. These ventures have been sponsored either by non-denominational societies or by interested individuals. In missionary parlance, such attempts are known as "independent" missions. Rather than present a dry statistical survey of all of them, a few of the best known (and, with the exception of the Chicago Hebrew Mission, one could also say the most controversial) of these independent endeavors will be discussed.

JACOB FRESHMAN

Jacob Freshman was the oldest son of Canadian Hebrew Christian missionary Charles Freshman. He was ordained as a Methodist minister in 1867. In 1885 he established a mission on New York's East Side at 17 St. Mark's Place. He was at this time forty-one years old. One New York paper described him as "a little, wiry, enthusiastic Hungarian." He was supported by some of the most prominent New York ministers and laymen of that day. The mission was dedicated on October 11, 1885, as the "First Hebrew Christian Church in America." Among the many gifts were an organ from Colonel Jacob Estey, pious founder of the Estey Organ Company, and a hand-painted plate from Mrs. Michael J. Cramer, sister of Ulysses S. Grant, eighteenth president of the United States.

All seemed to be going well when, toward the end of 1887, a barrage of diatribes from the tongue and pen of Adolph Benjamin began to take effect. Benjamin exposed the linguistic ignorance of Freshman and the illiteracy of his converts by issuing the following public challenge to Freshman and the Jewish converts he had acquired:

> I am willing to put up against any sum, not exceeding a thousand dollars, to be equally distributed between the Young Men's Hebrew Association and the Young Men's Christian Association, if Rev. Freshman, the missionary to the Jews, will explain in grammatical Hebrew the Lord's Prayer which adorns his Hebrew Christian church in gold letters. I also challenge this year's crop of seven converts to answer one or two questions from the New Testament in either language: English, German or Hebrew. The judges are to be Dr. Howard Crosby and Dr. William Henry Ward, the former being Chairman of the Mission's Advisory Board, and the latter being a most profound Hebrew scholar. The challenge is open two weeks from date of publication.[1]

Benjamin's scheme worked well. Freshman and his parasites refused to accept the challenge and became the laughing stock of all who were not infected with the conversionist virus. From that time on, the anti-Freshman sniping became constant and most annoying to the missionary. He would not make public his financial statements and was accused, in both Christians and Jewish periodicals, of misusing the funds given him.

Then some of his converts began to talk about their "conversions." Here, briefly, are a few of their tales:

A young man named Rubin was converted in London and then came to New York. Freshman gave him ten dollars and a suit of clothes as pay for being converted all over again.

John Hoffman was born in England in 1865. He came to New York in 1884. Freshman got him a job, converted him and paid him fifty cents per testimony to tell of his "remarkable conversion." Hoffman repented and confessed in 1890.

In 1891 John Paley, 1871-1907, a leading Yiddish journalist, deliberately allowed Freshman to convert him in order to expose Freshman in the Yiddish press. He wrote that the mission staff spent most of their earnings in saloons and houses of prostitution.

The Reverend Nathaniel Nicolai became pastor of the First German Presbyterian Church, Elizabeth, N.J. He was expelled therefrom because he forged checks on the elders thereof.

Louis Schlesinger was born in Germany, 1869. He arrived in New York, 1888. Freshman gave him two dollars and a suit and baptized him in February, 1891. He became a worker in Freshman's mission. "More than once," he wrote later, "we delivered stirring testimonials with strong-smelling breaths, more than once did we hold up the holy Bible with hands yet unwashed from the touch of contaminating playing cards." He left Freshman in 1892 and returned to Judaism.

Many more such examples could be given. These stories were contained in personal affidavits, obtained by Benjamin and sworn to before a notary public. The affidavits gradually weakened Freshman's prestige and the confidence of his backers.

In October, 1892, Freshman's board informed him that it would no longer support him and that he was to be given an indefinite leave of absence. Six months later Freshman managed to get rid of the board and to go back into business at the same address on St. Mark's Place. But money stopped coming in and, in December, 1893, Freshman turned the building over to the New York City Mission and Tract Society and went out of the missionary business.

He became a Presbyterian minister and spent the few remaining years of his life as pastor of a number of Presbyterian churches. In June, 1895, he was given a D.D. degree by Ursinus College of Collegeville, Pa.

CHICAGO HEBREW MISSION

The Chicago Hebrew Mission was organized in 1889 and functioned as an independent mission until 1953. It then changed its name to American Messianic Fellowship and abandoned the independent mission approach. The AMF now works largely through local churches and concentrates, through programs in such churches and through itinerant missionaries, on trying to convert Jewish college students and Jewish drug addicts. It is the oldest existing organization in North America whose main objective is the conversion of Jews to Christianity. Throughout its entire history, it has maintained close ties with the Moody Bible Institute. Almost throughout its entire history, it has been administered by non-Jews. While there is little to indicate that its efforts have had much success, its affairs have been managed in an honorable and honest manner, untainted by scandal.

The CHM owed its birth to one who was not free of taint, Hebrew Christian Jacob Freshman. He came to Chicago in the Fall of 1887 to organize a branch of his New York mission. An organization was set up to achieve this objective. In April, 1889, this organization decided to cut its ties with Freshman and to continue on its own. At the second annual meeting, December 9, 1889, the name Chicago Hebrew Mission was adopted. From 1889 to 1891, Jane Addams, famed social worker, was a member of the CHM board. Among the five locations which the CHM occupied for short periods prior to May, 1891, was Hull House, which Miss Addams had recently purchased but was not yet ready to use.

The first superintendent of the Chicago Hebrew Mission was William E. Blackstone, who served from 1889 to 1891. Blackstone, 1841-1935, was at General Grant's headquarters during the Civil War as a Christian Commission worker. The YMCA is a direct outgrowth of this Christian Commission work, initiated and headed by Dwight L. Moody. After the war, Blackstone became an evangelist. In 1866 he moved to Oak Park, Ill., and resided there for forty years. He moved to California in 1906, was missionary in China from 1909 to 1914, and spent the last twenty years of his life in Los Angeles, venerated as an apostle of the coming of the day when there shall be neither strife, want, nor sin.

Blackstone exemplified, in life and in his works, Fundamental Christianity at its very best. He was chiefly responsible, in 1890, for the convening of the first American "good will" conference in Chicago. The daughter of Rabbi Bernard Felsenthal wrote about Mr. Blackstone and this conference:

> Mr. Blackstone came sometimes to visit my father—not, I am sure, expecting to convert him, but to discuss questions of creed. My father met him in a friendly spirit, recognized his sincerity and respecting the frank and courteous manner of his approach. As to conferences between men of opposite faiths, my father believed them quite useless; they were likely to create misunderstanding and ill feeling. However, once this conference was organized, he could not refuse to take part in it and spoke with entire frankness on the subject, "Why the Jews do not accept Jesus as the Messiah."[2]

Rabbis Emil G. Hirsch and Joseph Stolz also addressed the conference.

In 1892 Blackstone secured the signatures of the rulers of thirty-six nations, including Benjamin Harrison, twenty-third president of the United States, on a document declaring that war should be outlawed as an instrument of international policy. This documents was one of the important steps in the process that led to the establishment of the Permanent Court of Arbitration at the Hague in 1899. After the first Basle Conference, Blackstone became an ardent exponent of the Zionist dream of Theodore

Herzl. In 1916 Richard Gottheil declared that Blackstone's efforts on behalf of the Zionist cause had been of great value to the movement. While Blackstone also ardently desired the conversion of the Jews, his efforts in this direction were completely free of guile. Two Hebrew Christians served as CHM superintendents between 1891 and 1897. After 1897, the superintendents were all non-Jews. The Chicago Hebrew Mission served as a training ground for many Hebrew Christians who prepared at the Moody Bible Institute for a missionary career among their Jewish contemporaries. The MBI continues to maintain a separate department for the training of missionaries to the Jews. Such a department is also to be found at Biola, i.e., the Bible Institute of Los Angeles.

HERMANN WARSZAWIAK

The Warszawiak case is one of the psychologico-religious puzzles of modern times. We do not pretend to understand it. We can only wait and pray for the shadow cast on him, and through him on all Jewish missionaries, to pass away.[3]

So wrote Louis Meyer, authority on American missions to the Jews, in June, 1903.

Some said Warszawiak was the "American Dreyfus." Some said he was the most conscienceless rascal who ever cavorted in the American missionary field. Some said that, in the early days of his Christian career, he was honest and sincere; and that the flattery heaped upon him by Christian admirers and supporters turned his head. This much is certain: Warszawiak was the logical climax of the conversionist hysteria that swept through American Fundamentalism as a result of the European Jewish mass migration to the United States that began in the 1880's. The Warszawiak case convinced most evangelical Christians that the conversion of the Jew in America is a thankless, fruitless, and hopeless enterprise. It convinced many evangelical Christians, rightly or wrongly, that a large proportion of Hebrew Christians are a disgrace both to their people and their adopted religion.

Hermann Warszawiak was born in Warsaw in March, 1865. In 1887 or 1888 he fled from Poland to escape military service, leaving behind a wife and two small daughters. In Hamburg, Germany, in June, 1889, he stole money and other valuables from his landlady and from the family of a boyhood friend which was en route to America, and he had to skip town to escape arrest. He was baptized at a Scotch Presbyterian mission

in Breslau in October, 1889, and sent to Edinburgh for missionary training. He had to leave Edinburgh hurriedly in March, 1890, because those
whom he had robbed in Hamburg tracked him down.

He landed in New York on March 28, 1890. After preaching a few
times in Freshman's mission, he decided to go into business for himself.
As a preliminary step, on April 10 he joined the Fifth Avenue Presbyterian Church, the richest and most influential Presbyterian church in
North America, whose pastor was the greatly respected John Hall, 1829-
1898. Hall was well liked by New York's Jewish community, but he was
also firmly of the opinion that the time had come to convert the Jews.

Hall suggested to the superintendent of the N.Y.C. Mission and Tract
Society that Warszawiak be hired as its missionary to the Jews. Warszawiak was engaged and went to work on April 28, 1890. Soon he was
packing them in. As an orator he was a spellbinder. The Jews of the East
Side came in great numbers to hear him. He was short, broad shouldered,
with thick, jet-black hair, a large mouth, and thin lips. His arms were
unusually long and his shoulders so rounded that, at first glance, he looked
humpbacked. His nose was long and sharp, his eyes small and deep set,
surmounted by heavy eyebrows. He had a very broad and high forehead
and gave the impression of being a person of great intellect. He was ar-
rogant, shrewd, clever, knew how to capitalize on the weaknesses of both
Jew and non-Jew. His lectures were given in Yiddish and English. His
severest critics admitted that he was an unusual person who would have
been a great success in a more useful field of endeavor.

In the Fall of 1892 Warszawiak went to Europe and brought back his
wife. His wife's parents refused to let him have his two daughters because of his abandonment of Judaism. The Warszawiaks regained custody
of their oldest daughter in November, 1900, and of the second daughter
in the summer of 1903.

Adolph Benjamin was Warszawiak's constant accuser almost from the
very start of his missionary career. Until Benjamin died in 1902, the
destruction of Warszawiak's prestige was the chief goal of Benjamin's
antimissionary crusade. Before Benjamin died, he had the satisfaction of
knowing that his efforts had destroyed Warszawiak's effectiveness as a
missionary.

Here is a sample of the kind of affidavit that Benjamin produced repeatedly to discredit "the little Messianic prophet," as Warszawiak was
called by his doting Christian friends:

Marcus Breitstein was baptized by Warszawiak on February 28, 1893.
Then, because Warszawiak desired to become more closely acquainted

with Breitstein's wife, he sent the new Christian to Edinburgh. When Mrs. Breitstein informed her husband of Warszawiak's duplicity, he returned to New York immediately. As a result of Breitstein's conversion, his wife left him. He appealed to the head of the N.Y.C. Mission to help him get her back. Warszawiak then sent Leopold Cohn to him with the threat that, unless he kept quiet, he would be arrested and forced to return the money which Warszawiak had given him. On November 18, 1893, Mrs. Breitstein swore to the truth of this story. She declared, "If I had the means, I would sue Reverend Warszawiak for alienating the affections of my husband."

For a time such revelations as these had a boomerang effect. They convinced Warszawiak's Christian supporters that the Jews were persecuting their Jewish prophet and telling all manner of falsehoods about him. After Jacob Freshman turned his mission building over to the N.Y.C. Mission Society, this Society re-named the mission the "American Hebrew Christian Home" and put Warszawiak in charge of it on January 1, 1894. About the middle of 1894, Benjamin's unceasing stream of accusations began to take effect. In December, the N.Y.C. Mission and Tract Society announced that, as of January 1, 1895, it would sever its connection with Warszawiak. In the announcement, the Society concealed the real reason for this decision by stating that it had concluded that Warszawiak would have greater success as an independent missionary.

By this time Warszawiak had broken down his wife's objections to Christianity. She and her infant son, Herman Paul, were baptized by John Hall on Easter Sunday, April 14, 1895.

In his new role as independent missionary, Warszawiak lectured on Saturday afternoons at the Presbyterian Church of the Sea and Land at Henry and Market Streets. He began to hold his meetings there in May, 1895. To attract Jews to his gatherings, he had cards printed and distributed. On one side the cards contained a Yiddish announcement of the church meeting and, on the other side, these words in large Yiddish type:

> Whoever comes this Sabbath afternoon to our meeting at 19 Market Street will receive a free ticket to a wonderful electric picture exhibition. Come and secure free tickets. The collection of pictures is highly interesting. *The tickets to be purchased will cost 50¢.*

Large numbers of Jews came to listen and get the tickets. This spiritual deception aroused the ire of Warkszawiak's competitors. A number of other missionaries to the Jews urged Warszawiak's backers to disown him but to no avail. The board of the "American Mission to the Jews," as Warszawiak called his effort, issued a statement expressing complete confidence in the integrity of its missionary.

Thus began an amazing battle of words and deeds that raged around Warszawiak for more than five years, that divided the evangelical Christians of New York City into two camps, pro-Warszawiak and anti-Warszawiak, and that almost ruined the Fifth Avenue Presbyterian Church.

On January 1, 1896, Warszawiak opened his own mission at 424 Grand Street. On February 26, 1896, seven prominent Christian clergymen put a paid ad in the N.Y. *Tribune* to announce that they were no longer members of the board of Warszawiak's mission. The superintendent of the N.Y.C. Mission and Tract Society issued a statement giving the real reasons for Warszawiak's dismissal:

> He is a constitutional and persistent liar. . . . I have a letter from the man who baptized him [in Germany] saying that he is a liar and would lie at any time about anything. He left the City Mission a year ago last January. He resigned, but his resignation was something that had to come and it was accepted in the hope that he would improve, but he has not done so, and we will have nothing more to do with him under any circumstances. I sent him a letter last year endorsing his work in some measure, because I thought he would do better, but yesterday I sent another letter withdrawing the former one, because he has continued to lie.

The real fireworks began in November, 1896, when Hall requested the New York Presbytery to grant Warszawiak ministerial ordination. On December 14 the Presbytery denied this request by an almost unanimous vote. This caused it to be accused of anti-Semitism but it stuck to its decision. It tried to dispose of the matter by referring the problem to the session of the Fifth Avenue Church. After a thorough investigation of Warszawiak's background, the session decided to place Warszawiak on trial—not on the question of ordination but with regard to his moral eligibility to continue as a member of the church!

The trial began on April 27 and ended on June 10, 1897. Eighteen meetings were held and over fifteen hundred pages of testimony taken. The meetings were held in executive session. The specific charge: That on February 9, 10, 22, and 23, 1897, Warszawiak had visited the Hoffman House, a gambling hall and poolroom in Weehawken, N.J., and had played roulette there. The verdict: Guilty. The vote 7 to 4. Hall, who believed Warszawiak innocent, abstained. The penalty: Public dismissal from the church, effective Sunday, June 20. The principle witness against the missionary was Anthony Comstock, 1844-1915, notorious anti-vice crusader. The dismissal was carried out under very dramatic circumstances, with police surrounding the church to prevent Warszawiak's supporters from breaking up the service, which Hall refused to attend.

Warszawiak declared, "I will fight to the bitter end," and he did. He carried his battle for vindication from the lowest to the highest Presbyterian ecclesiastical courts. He succeeded, on November 9, 1899, in having the trial proceedings declared null and void by the Fifth Avenue session. His membership in the church was restored. On May 24, 1900, the General Assembly of the Presbyterian Church, U.S.A. announced that it, "without expressing any opinion on the merits of the case, does hereby terminate this unhappy case, and all the proceedings growing out of it, without any further trial."

Because John Hall had defended Warszawiak so strongly, the Fifth Avenue session demanded his resignation on January 6, 1898. Accordingly, Hall offered his resignation. But the congregation refused to allow this to happen. At a meeting on January 19, attended by more than a thousand church members, a resolution requesting Hall to continue his pastorate was adopted unanimously. On February 8, Hall officially withdrew his offer of resignation. As a result, eight elders of the session resigned as well as a number of the church's most wealthy members. Hall's health broke under the strain. He had to give up the active ministry a few months later. He died on September 17, 1898.

By December, 1898, Warszawiak's finances were in such bad shape that he filed a petition of voluntary bankruptcy: Liabilities, $29,802. Assets, none. By the end of 1903, Warszawiak's mission was closed. On January 1, 1904, he went to work for John Alexander Dowie's Catholic Church of Zion. A little while later the U.S. District Court dismissed Warszawiak's request for bankruptcy on the ground that it contained indications of fraud. About the middle of November, a board of inquiry reported to First Apostle Dowie that it had found Warszawiak to be guilty of "lying and financial crookedness." Hebrew Catholic Zionist Warszawiak was speedily excommunicated and had to seek other employment. By October, 1905, Warszawiak was out of the missionary business permanently.

One report has it that Warszawiak became a grocer. But J. Hoffman Cohn, son of Leopold Cohn, has a different story to tell about Warszawiak's later days: Warszawiak contracted tuberculosis. Through the generosity of the Guggenheim family, he was sent to a sanatorium in Colorado. There he changed his last name and became manager of one of the Guggenheim silver mines. When J. H. Cohn was about twenty years old, i.e., about 1906, the former missionary came to the Cohn home in a chauffeur driven limousine and spent an afternoon with the Cohn family. Sometime thereafter he died of tuberculosis.[4]

LEOPOLD COHN

Leopold Cohn founded what has been, financially speaking, the most successful mission to the Jews in North America.

Leopold Cohn came to the United States in 1892. Prior to 1892, his life story is part of one of the most amazing coincidences in all the annals of time. Cohn was born in Beresin, Hungary, in 1862. So was Itsak Leib Joszovics. In 1880, Cohn married Rose Hoffman and moved to Apsica. So did Itsak Leib Joszovics. Several years later, Cohn was asked to become rabbi of three congregations near Apsica. But it was not so with Itsak Leib Joszovics. He became a saloonkeeper. In 1891 Joszovics and his brother-in-law, Jacob Hoffman, were arrested for having forged the deed to a dead peasant's farm and they were found guilty. Hoffman was sentenced to two and a half years in jail and Joszovics to three years.

To avoid serving this sentence, Joszovics fled from Hungary, leaving behind his wife and children. The police published a description of the criminal which stated that he was

> 5 ft. 6½ inches tall, of wiry build, long face, brown complexion, hair, mustache, eyebrows, high forehead, eyes black, mouth regular, teeth defective, chin, round; special mark of recognition: red spot under his left eye.

Now comes the most amazing coincidence of all: This description fitted Leopold Cohn so perfectly that Joszovics might have been his twin! And what is even more remarkable is that Cohn also had a brother-in-law by the name of Jacob Hoffman who lived in Apsica and was imprisoned for forgery.

But Rabbi Cohn left Apsica for a much different reason. He became convinced that the Messiah has already come. When he informed his congregations of this belief, he lost his rabbinical position and was forced to leave Hungary.

In a 1913 New York court action, four relatives and friends of Itsak Leib Joszovics swore that Joszovics and Cohn were one and the same man. Cohn steadfastly denied this—and he got away with it. His Christian supporters and his professional Hebrew Christian colleagues said many times and in many places that this "tsaddik" was really and truly ex-rabbi Leopold Cohn.

Cohn got in touch with Hermann Warszawiak, who sent the "rabbi" to Edinburgh to be baptized and educated for missionary work. Cohn returned to New York with his wife and children on September 20, 1893. As early as October 13, 1893, Adolph Benjamin wrote in the *Hebrew Standard* that Cohn's real name was Itsak Leib Joszovics.

After working for Warszawiak for a few months, Cohn went into business for himself. He opened a small mission in the Brownsville section of Brooklyn.

In 1896 his mission began to be supported by the American Baptist Home Missionary Society. With its help he started a second mission in the Williamsburgh section. In 1898 Cohn began to publish for Christians a monthly, *The Chosen People*, which is still being issued by the missionary organization he founded. The American Baptists withdrew their support from Cohn early in 1908. The corresponding secretary of the Home Missionary Society issued a statement:

> I regret to say that I have quite lost confidence in Mr. Cohn, and the Board of the Home Missionary Society has discontinued its appropriation to his work in Brooklyn. He has alienated some of his best supporters by his refusal to have any supervision of his work in any way whatsoever. He insists upon receiving all funds, and paying them out as he pleases, appointing and dismissing appointees at his pleasure, and determining what kind of service they shall render, as if he were the only anointed one of the Lord. His insulting language, and his bad temper and general management of the work have alienated many of his best friends. I regret to be obliged to say these things, but I cannot advise anybody to put money into the enterprise as it is now conducted.

In 1909 Cohn acquired a mission house at Throop and Broadway Avenues, Brooklyn, which he named Beth Sar Shalom. Before that, in 1906, the Cohns bought a "mission" farm at Easton, Conn., which they said would be used as a summer camp for children. Instead Cohn turned it into a dairy farm from which he made profit and a summer home for himself and his family. In June, 1908, two New York Hebrew Christians went to the farm to find out if it really was being used as a children's camp. They came back to New York and reported that it was not. They returned to the farm on July 1 to continue their research. They were met by one of Cohn's sons, pistol in hand, and accused of trespassing. This son, described in a newspaper account as "Joshua, age 17," was arrested and tried on a charge of assault with intent to kill.

Cohn's son Joseph graduated from Moody Bible Institute in 1906 and then became a traveling salesman for his father's mission. Joseph, or J. Hoffman, as he preferred to be known, took over the management of the operation about 1933. Despite all kinds of trials, tribulation, and harassments from antimissionary forces, mobs, boycotts, pickets, scandals, lawsuits, adverse publicity, and what not, the Cohn mission was a great financial success and went from strength to strength.

In 1920 the mission began to publish the *Shepherd of Israel*, a four-page monthly for Jews only. Two pages were in Yiddish and two in English.

In 1924 the Cohns changed the name of their operation from "Williamsburgh Mission to the Jews" to the "American Board of Missions to the Jews, Inc." It still bears this high-sounding title.

During his early years as a missionary, Leopold Cohn mingled freely with his fellow Hebrew Christian professionals. But, during about the last thirty years of his life, he was distinctly persona non grata in Hebrew Christian circles, as was his son after him. Why? Not only because of his unsavory past and questionable present, but also because he and his son never seemed to want to give credit to any Jewish missionary effort except their own. In their publications they rarely indicated that other American missionary efforts to the Jews existed. The absence of the names of Leopold and J. Hoffman Cohn from all lists of officers and committees of the Hebrew Christian Alliance of America, founded in 1915, is suspiciously conspicuous. Yet the Alliance and its members tried to maintain a semblance of outward cordiality toward the Cohns, because the other Hebrew Christian missionaries not only disliked the Cohns but also feared them. In addition to financial strength, they had the admiration and support of some of the most powerful American fundamentalist leaders. The Moody Bible Institute, which has tried consistently to maintain a high standard of ethical performance in American home missions, never ventured to criticize the actions or ethics of the Cohns because it did not want to get involved in the kind of nasty infighting that would have been sure to follow such criticism. As Leopold Cohn grew more powerful, the Baptists decided to accept him as one of their own. He was for many years a member of the Long Island Baptist Ministers Association. In 1930 Wheaton College, Wheaton, Ill., conferred upon him the honorary degree of Doctor of Divinity.

Leopold Cohn died on December 19, 1937. Condolence messages were received from the International Hebrew Christian Alliance, the Hebrew Christian Alliance of America, and the Department of Jewish Missions of Moody Bible Institute, as well as from many Hebrew Christian missionaries who, in his lifetime, had considered him an obnoxious individual. The HCAA *Quarterly* spoke of him as follows:

> One who has been rightly called the Dean of Hebrew Christianity in America. . . . A man of rare endowments, both intellectual and spiritual. . . . Dr. Cohn was rabbi of an Orthodox synagogue in Austria-Hungary.

In 1945 the ABMJ purchased a new mission building in Manhattan at 236 West Seventy-second Street, which it used as its national headquarters until 1973, when the ABMJ headquarters was moved to Englewood Cliffs, N.J.

J. Hoffman Cohen died, age sixty-seven, on October 5, 1953. He, too, had an honorary D.D., received in 1937 from the Los Angeles Baptist Seminary. This time *The Chosen People* published no letters of condolence from missionary organizations or Hebrew Christian missionaries. This seems to indicate that, in professional missionary circles, and particularly among Hebrew Christians, J. Hoffman Cohn was disliked more than his father had been. The death of J. H. Cohn was ignored completely by the Hebrew Christian Alliance and its magazine. A non-Jew, Harold B. Pretlove, succeeded Cohn as general secretary of the ABMJ. With this the sixty-year dictatorial rule of the Cohns, father and son, over their missionary enterprise came to an end.

In October 1955, Daniel Fuchs, 1911- , a second generation Hebrew Christian, was named Director of Missionary Activities of the ABMJ. In 1968 he succeeded Pretlove as professional head of the operation. Under Fuchs' astute direction, the ABMJ has continued to prosper. It has a more respectable standing in fundamentalist Christian circles than it did under the Cohns. In a time when independent Jewish missions are very much on the wane, the money-collecting ability of the ABMJ has been little less than phenomenal. Its receipts in recent years have exceeded one and a half million dollars per annum.

In 1971 and 1972 the ABMJ received much publicity and aroused much antagonism and controversy by sponsoring a Passover TV program with strong evangelistic emphasis on six stations in the United States, forty in Canada, five in Australia, and one in Ecuador. In addition, it published a full-page ad, showing thirty-three smiling Hebrew Christians and titled, "So many Jews are wearing 'that smile' nowadays," in the N.Y. *Times* plus nine other metropolitan dailies and three Jewish weeklies. This, too, stirred up quite a storm. Many Jews canceled their subscriptions to the weekly papers. The Jewish publishers responded that principles of freedom of speech and of the press impelled them to accept the ad. The storm passed by. The papers survived. The incident is already a faint memory. There is little doubt that the ABMJ will continue its struggle for survival by using other gimmicks that are designed to get the attention of the American Jewish community, so that its reaction may be used to continue to draw a rich harvest of dollars from the pockets of naïve fundamentalist Christians.

The independent mission to the American Jew is a phenomenon which is gradually disappearing. The almost complete cessation of Jewish immigration and the breaking up of the urban Jewish ghettos are partly responsible. The major reason is that the American Christian world has come to the conclusion that the poor results of all efforts to convert American Jews are not worth the great amount of money and zeal that have been devoted to them. The overwhelming majority of evangelical-minded Christians will spend little time mourning the demise of independent missions to the Jews. While there have been some earnest and dedicated individuals laboring in this largely fruitless endeavor, the Jewish missions of this type have much too often a breeding ground for the kind of chicanery, hypocrisy, and dishonesty which is associated in the popular mind, Jewish as well as Christian, with the term "missionary to the Jews."

Chapter Eleven

The "Antis"

Emma Lazarus, gifted American Jewish poet, gave accurate expression to the prevailing sentiment in the American Jewish community with regard to so-called "converted" Jews when she wrote, in the *American Hebrew* for May 9, 1883, that such Jews are "not only the most expensive of all marketable commodities but also the most worthless."

Despite their low opinion of those who went over to Christianity, the Jews of New York and other cities were greatly alarmed by the intense efforts made in the 1880's and 1890's to win the souls of the large number of Jews who came to our shores in those decades. In order to offset the missionary efforts, many schools and social centers were established to minister to the needs of immigrant children and young people. Very few countermeasures were devised to keep the immigrant adults in the fold, because it was deeply felt that, when an older person converted, it was, in almost every instance, "good riddance of bad rubbish." And, besides, very few of the adults remained "converted" very long. In most cases they accepted a Christian sprinkling in order to obtain temporary benefit from Christian charity. There were some who underwent the ordeal of baptism dozens of times to secure such benefits.

Many antimissionary societies were formed during this period and many individual Jews did much to make the lives of the hated missionaries and the "meshumadim," the apostates, as miserable as possible. These societies drew their membership mainly from the kind of young, brash idealists who now gravitate toward such an organization as the Jewish Defense League. And as is usually the case when brawn is substituted for brain, their efforts served mainly to give the missions additional publicity. As pest killers, they did not accomplish very much. Most of the successful antimissionary efforts were the work of a number of individuals who used the power of the tongue, the pen and the law rather than the uncontrollable methods of the mob. The efforts of a few of these individuals will be described. The bravest and most successful of them was Adolph Benjamin, little-known American Jewish hero.

ADOLPH BENJAMIN

Some of the results of Adolph Benjamin's one-man antimissionary crusade, carried on for more than twenty-five years, have already been discussed. Now let us examine the life and character of the man himself.

Adolph Benjamin was born in Russia about 1847. After an elementary school education, he was apprenticed to a bookbinder. He came to the United States about 1873 and continued to earn his living by mending and binding books.

He began his antimissionary career on February 18, 1874, by writing a letter to the N.Y. *Herald* condemning the proselyting activities of a Hebrew Catholic, "Professor" Emanuel H. Schlamovitz. From then on, Benjamin's chief aim in life was to uncover all facts that would help discredit missionaries to the Jews. This was a unique undertaking and one which had neither the approval or support of many who benefited greatly from his efforts. In 1888 Benjamin complained that most Jews and Christians regarded his disclosures with either indifference or hostility. "The Jewish clergy," he declared, "look upon this matter as too profane a project to handle, while the Christian clergy consider it too sacred."

Despite all obstacles and rebuffs, Benjamin persevered. Over the years his constant stream of affidavits, letters, mission visits, and appeals to the Christian clergy achieved very positive results. No other person or group of persons ever gave Christian missions to the Jews such an indelible black eye as did Adolph Benjamin.

In addition to combating missionaries, Benjamin was an ardent worker for organizations concerned with the Americanization of the Jewish immigrants. He helped to establish schools and settlement houses for the education and enlightenment of the foreign born.

He was one of the East Side's best known and most beloved figures.

To the oppressed and poverty-stricken Jews of the New York ghetto, Benjamin brought not only a thorough understanding of their problems; but he also exhibited a thoroughly unselfish spirit and dedication that made him the uncanonized saint of the Jewish masses. In a time when most uptown New York Jews regarded their poorly educated, strange tongued, segregated downtown brethren with ill-disguised contempt, as creatures to be tolerated but not embraced, as unworthy recipients of grudgingly given charity, Adolph Benjamin made these poor cousins feel important and gave them the hope that they would eventually find themselves completely at home in the United States.

In June, 1895, feeling that he had the missionary situation in New York City well under control, Benjamin went to Great Britain and spent three years feuding with the Jewish missionaries there. He returned to America in December, 1898, and immediately resumed his role as chief nemesis of New York's Hebrew Christians.

He died suddenly on December 2, 1902. His passing was mourned by tens of thousands of East Side Jews whom he had helped. His funeral was attended by some of the most prominent Jewish leaders of the New York community.

Benjamin's enemies often accused him of being the front man for a group of wealthy New York Jews, who were determined to undermine all efforts of Christians to convert Jews. There was a small amount of truth in this charge. The "group" consisted of one man, Jacob H. Schiff, great-minded and great-hearted Jewish philanthropist. Schiff realized that the work Benjamin was doing was necessary and important and, from time to time, he gave Benjamin financial aid.

Benjamin lived and died a poor man. He accepted financial help from Schiff only because his unappreciated but successful battles against a Freshman or a Warszawiak took so much of his time and effort and money that, without such outside help, he would have been unable to buy needed food and clothing.

He was a simple man, hated by unthinking Christians and ridiculed by unthinking Jews. Many looked upon him as an obnoxious fool. His letters to the newspapers were ungrammatical and garrulous. He lacked polish and tact. The traps he set to catch his slippery prey were, perhaps, not exactly "cricket" according to the rules of the game as played by the Park Avenue set. He was fighting those who employed unholy weapons in what they claimed was a holy cause; and he had no scruples about fighting fire with fire. He, too, was a zealot. He, too, was interested in saving souls. He, too, had a mission in life; and he fulfilled that mission with a selflessness and a determination that were truly remarkable.

Three days after he died, New York's leading Jewish weekly stated editorially:

> Mr. Benjamin pursued what he made the object of his life with a devotion that cost him his worldly possessions; but his only regret was that he lacked more means of his own to sacrifice to the cause. . . . His heart was set conscientiously on the accomplishment of what was undoubtedly a holy purpose. His was, indeed, a troubled soul that now has found rest.[1]

SAMUEL FREUDER

During the last quarter of the nineteenth century, three graduates of the Hebrew Union College converted to Christianity: Samuel Freuder, ordained 1886, converted in 1891 and returned to Judaism in 1908; Max Wertheimer, ordained in 1889, converted to Christian Science in 1900 and then, in 1904, became a Baptist and worked as a missionary and evangelist until his death in 1941; and Joseph Moses, born Moses Jerusalemski, ordained in 1894, became an Episcopalian, worked as a missionary from 1901 to 1904. According to J. Hoffman Cohn, he came to Leopold Cohn for financial help at some time before 1910 because "he had found no way of making a living . . . to provide for himself and his children, and my father, himself in the midst of a desperate struggle . . . could be of no help to him."[2] J. Hoffman Cohn states further that, when this appeal to Cohn, Sr., failed, Moses committed suicide and was buried in New York's potter's field. Since this unhappy man changed faiths in 1901, no graduate of the Hebrew Union College has defected to Christianity.

Freuder was baptized at the Chicago Hebrew Mission on Yom Kippur in 1891. In 1894 he received the degree of B.D. from the Chicago Theological Seminary and was ordained as a Congregationalist minister. In 1895 he worked as a missionary to the Jews of Boston for five months. Then he supported himself by selling religious books and giving lectures about Jews and Judaism in Christian churches. In 1902 he transferred his allegiance from Congregationalism to Episcopalianism. In 1905 he became a student at a seminary in Philadelphia, preparatory to entering the Episcopal priesthood. He sustained himself by working at the Episcopal Jewish mission in Philadelphia. In 1906 he was ordained as a deacon and served his deaconate in churches in Philadelphia and New York and continued to lecture to Christians about Jews.

Several times Freuder attempted to abandon Christianity and return to Judaism, but each time his unsympathetic Jewish brethren rejected him. His spiritual burden finally became unbearable. On June 3, 1908, he created a nationally publicized sensation by publicly abandoning the Christian religion. His announcement was made at a Hebrew Christian conference held in Boston.

Freuder then obtained a position as book salesman with the Jewish Publication Society. His book *A Missionary's Return to Judaism* was published in 1915. It is the most authentic book of its kind and should be read by everyone who wants to know the truth about most missionary efforts to convert Jews.

Freuder states:

The whole Jewish missionary business, as conducted by professional converts, is steeped in dishonesty and trickery. . . . It is rotten from the core to the rind, from the top to the bottom. It is only fair to state that most, if not all, of Christian supporters of Jewish missions are unaware of the fraudulent nature of the work done, and have no inkling of its evil effects upon those who happen to fall into the missionary's net. Their missionary zeal makes them blind and deaf to anything that might disturb their sweet illusion of being instrumental in bringing the glad tidings to the "lost sheep of the house of Israel." They come to look upon any criticism of the work or the workers as inspired by Satan himself. . . . This easygoing and self-complacent attitude of his patrons is taken advantage of by the Jewish missionary. Whenever his character or the methods of his work are attacked, he promptly assumes the martyr role, casts his eyes heavenward, bows his head, and moves his lips as if in prayer for his persecutors.[3]

Careful observation, extending over a period of many years, has shown me that only one out of a thousand children that attend the mission schools is influenced to such a degree that he becomes a Christian. . . . But attendance at mission schools is fraught with great danger to the moral character of the children. The fact that the children, in most cases, come without the knowledge of their parents, and thereby are encouraged to do things by stealth and deception, is bad enough, but this is as nothing compared with the injury inflicted upon the child by lowering the religion of his parents in his estimation. . . . Children are alienated from their parents, and seeds of discord and discontent are planted in the minds of tender children.[4]

WILLIAM JAY GAYNOR

William Jay Gaynor, 1849-1913, was Mayor of New York City from 1910 until his life was terminated by an assassin's bullet in 1913.

Shortly after Gaynor assumed office, a New York missionary to the
Jews asked for a permit to hold street meetings on the East Side. On April
22, 1910, Gaynor refused the request and publicized his decision, much
to the delight of the New York Jewish community, by writing the missionary an open letter, which read in part:

> Do you not think the Jews have a good religion? . . . Why should
> anyone work so hard to proselytize the Jew? . . . I do not think I
> should give you a license to preach for the conversion of the Jews
> in the streets in the thickly settled Jewish neighborhoods which you
> designate. Would you not annoy them and do more harm than good?[5]

THE YACHNIN CASE

The traditional attitude of the Jewish community toward Christian missionaries has been one of carefully studied indifference. Once in a while
some especially heinous missionary act causes the Jewish group to forego
temporarily this complacency.

Such an act occurred in Brooklyn early in 1911. Esther Yachnin, age
fifteen, was baptized without her parents' consent at the Eighteenth Street
Methodist Church. This act received such widespread publicity that a
protest meeting, sponsored by the Brooklyn Federation of Jewish Organizations, was held at Liederkranz Hall on May 7, 1911. A resolution
was passed demanding that legal steps be taken to compel missionaries
to cease proselyting children. A few days later bills were introduced in
both the New York State Assembly and Senate which would have made
it a misdemeanor "for any person to entice or admit to religious missions
any minor under sixteen years of age without the consent of parent or
guardian." Both bills died in committee.

In 1929, Max J. Kohler made a thorough study of the legal aspects of
this matter and wrote up his findings in a mimeographed brochure titled
"Christian Conversionism among Jewish Children versus the Law of the
Land." Mr. Kohler determined that the pertinent American statutes lead
to the following conclusions:

1. The law recognizes the right of parents to determine the religion of
their minor children and to have exclusive control over their religious
education.

2. Attempts at conversionist propaganda among minor Jewish children
in this country without the consent of their parents is a violation of the
law and those who engage in such activity can be sued.

3. No missionary may give religious instruction to any minor of an-

other religion without the written and authenticated consent of the parents.

4. It is very doubtful whether even parents may legally consent to a change in the religious faith of their children as long as their children are minors.

OTHER ANTI-CONVERSIONIST EFFORTS

During the last half-century, there have been many well-intentioned verbal attacks on missionary efforts to convert Jews by Jewish leaders whose approach to the problem has often been more emotional than practical or who used this subject matter as a means of promoting some project of importance in which they were interested. A number of instances of this kind will be noted.

In January, 1929, Rabbi Israel Goldstein of New York City appeared before the national convention of the Protestant Home Missions Council and, speaking on behalf of the Synagogue Council of America and the National Conference of Christians and Jews, demanded that Protestants stop trying to convert Jews. A special committee was appointed to consider his request. A few days later the committee issued its reply:

> We desire to assure Dr. Goldstein of our hearty cooperation in the cultivating and propagating of good will, civic righteousness, social service and national loyalty between Jews and Christians everywhere. We wish also to say to him that when little children from Jewish families come to our churches, Sunday Schools, and our neighborhood houses, we believe it is desirable that they should come with the consent and approval of their parents. And furthermore, we do not believe in the conversion of men and women to Christianity by bribes or by bait. . . . We affirm that the gospel of Jesus Christ is the gospel for the whole world. . . . Not to go, therefore, to all people would be a direct violation of this central (principle) of our religion. Not to go to any group of people would be a discrimination against that group from the Christian point of view.

In March, 1946, Dr. Louis Finkelstein, eminent president of the Jewish Theological Seminary, made the headlines by declaring, at the outset of a fund-raising campaign for his seminary, that

> the conversion of American Jews to other faiths is proceeding at such an alarming rate that, within the next generation or two, Judaism may cease to have any significance in American life. . . . The stream of conversion of Jews to other faiths has become a river, particularly in the case of boys who have been overseas, all very sensitive.[6]

Dr. Finkelstein's fears, fortunately, were unfounded. Then and now, the number of American Jews who convert to Christianity is not nearly as large as the number of American non-Jews who convert to Judaism.

At its annual convention in Boston on January 30, 1947, the Rabbinical Council of America, a national Orthodox body, initiated a countrywide drive to halt the efforts of Christian missionaries to convert Jews. Its president asserted, at a press conference, that the Pope's 1946 Christmas message inviting non-Christians to enter the Catholic Church is illustrative "of a new tendency on the part of various Christian denominations to aim their missionary programs at the Jewish people." He stated further that "Jews leaving the Orthodox fold and entering Reform temples are taking the first step toward assimilation."[7] As far as positive results are concerned, this countrywide drive began and ended at the Rabbinic Council of America's 1947 convention.

In 1972 a very large number of liberal and conservative Protestant groups plus some Roman Catholic dioceses announced that, during the entire year of 1973, they would operate a project, to be known as "Key 73," to try to attract as many unchurched people as possible into membership in American Christian churches. This caused some staff members of some of the American Jewish defense agencies to charge that one of the objectives of Key 73 would be to convert Jews to Christianity. Those in charge of Key 73 vigorously denied this charge. Key 73 came and went. It made no organized effort of any kind to convert Jews. It made practically no impact on the general community. It really does not seem to have been worth the time and the money and the attention that were expended on it. The overreaction of the Jewish defense agencies gave the Key 73 fiasco an importance in the sight of the American Jewish community that was without substance and undeserved.

Chapter Twelve

Hebrew Christianity and Messianic Judaism

In July, 1975, the Hebrew Christian Alliance of America changed its name to the Messianic Jewish Alliance of America. In and of itself this was not exactly a world-shaking event. Few American Jews were aware of the existence of the Hebrew Christian Alliance, even though it had been on the American scene since 1915, and even fewer would be affected by the efforts of this organization under its new name or any other name. Nevertheless, in the fundamentalist world in which this aggregation of Jewish soul-seekers operates, the change in name had a very important significance. It was concrete evidence of a new trend in the Jewish mission field, a new approach that has become more and more popular in recent years among that fringe group of persons who consider themselves Jews ethnically and followers of Jesus Christ, excuse me, of Yeshua ha-Mashiach, religiously.

The term "Hebrew Christian" for a British or American Jew who converts to Christianity came into use early in the nineteenth century when missionary societies to convert Jews began to blossom in Great Britain and the United States. At that time it was taken for granted by Gentile Christians that a Hebrew Christian would affiliate with one of the existing Christian denominations. That such a person would want to be a Christian and yet segregate himself religiously from the Gentile Christian was considered a grave heresy. Had not St. Paul said, "In Christ there is neither Jew nor Greek"?

Such a situation arose in the early history of American Christian efforts to convert Jews. In June, 1825, Hebrew Christians Erasmus H. Simon and David Christian Bernhard Jadownicky were separated from the employ and care of the American Society for Meliorating the Condition of the Jews because, in their lectures and fund-raising appeals in various communities, they had indicated that the colony of foreign Christian Jews which the ASMCJ intended to establish in the United States would constitute the nucleus of an independent Hebrew Christian Church.

These bold spirits were far ahead of their time. Little more is heard of this particular heresy until it reappeared at the end of the nineteenth century in the person of Mark John Levy, 1855-1936, born in England as Mark Lev. He journeyed first to Australia and then to the United States, where he converted to Episcopalianism in 1887. He traveled all over the United States and Great Britain as a missionary lecturer, preaching and writing that Jews who become Christians should not be "Gentilized," i.e., they must be allowed in all ways to follow the precepts and practices of traditional Judaism, except that they shall acknowledge Jesus as the Messiah whom the Jews have long awaited. They must not be forced to accept membership in any Christian denomination.

Primarily for business reasons, the overwhelming majority of Hebrew Christian missionaries strongly opposed Levy's point of view. They feared that, if they supported it, they would be cast adrift by the church groups from whom they made their living. However, from about the time of the 1917 Balfour Declaration, a number of highly placed Hebrew Christians began to incline toward this so-called "Judaizing" philosophy. As the Hebrew Christian interest in Zionism grew, so, too, did the interest in this "Judaizing" position. Among the most prominent of the new proponents was Quaker Hebrew Christian Max I. Reich, 1867-1945, for many years head of the Jewish department at the Moody Bible Institute. The notorious "ex-rabbi" Leopold Cohn, 1862-1937, founder of the American Board of Missions to the Jews, espoused this belief in the early years of his missionary career. But he soon discovered that it was causing him to lose the financial support of some of his wealthy Christian backers, and he very quickly abandoned the concept.

In 1915 Levy helped organize and was first secretary of the Hebrew Christian Alliance of America. In 1916 he persuaded the General Convention of the Protestant Episcopal Church to adopt a resolution endorsing his position, an achievement which had been denied him by the same body in 1910. In 1917 he presented the same resolution to his Hebrew Christian colleagues in the HCAA and this group of professional converts voted it down almost unanimously. In September, 1925, he went to England and was instrumental in the establishment of the International Hebrew Christian Alliance, a federation of converts from all parts of Europe, Palestine, and America. Although Levy's fellow missionaries, as a group, did not approve of his "Judaizing" doctrine, they liked him very much as a person and often expressed complete confidence in his integrity and ability.

Beginning in 1885 with Jacob Freshman's First Hebrew Christian Church in America in New York City, there were many so-called Hebrew Christian churches established in the United States and Canada; but, until 1934, they were, without exception, nothing more than run-of-the-mill Jewish missions. The first genuine Hebrew Christian Church in the United States, one which is still functioning (although it is now non-denominational), was the First Hebrew Christian Presbyterian Church of Chicago, organized in 1934 with Hebrew Christian Reverend David Bronstein as pastor. . . . Since 1962 Bronstein's son, Reverend David Bronstein, Jr., has been the North American secretary of the International Hebrew Christian Alliance. He lives in Dunedin, Fla., and is one of the best-known, most influential, and most respected Hebrew Christians of our day. Although born and reared as a Christian, David Bronstein, Jr., like many other present-day Hebrew Christians, considers himself ethnically Jewish and is an ardent supporter of the State of Israel.

The first American Hebrew Christian Church, operated from its inception as an independent entity, was that established by Hebrew Christian Martin Chernoff in Cincinnati about 1960. Since then more such churches have come into being in Philadelphia, Washington, D.C., Miami, and a number of other communities. Their membership is not made up entirely of born Jews. A reporter who attended Chernoff's service in Cincinnati,[1] wrote that there were about fifty persons present at the service, of whom only about half were born Jews. The rest were either spouses of the converted Jews or born Christians, white and black, who had been attracted by Chernoff's teaching that, through joining his congregation, they would become spiritually Jewish.

Now these churches have begun to call themselves "synagogues" and some of their members are using the word "rabbi" when they address the pastor or lay leader of the "synagogue." Beth Messiah Congregation of Cincinnati, Beth Messiah Congregation of Washington, and Beth Yeshua

Congregation of Philadelphia have been listed in the Yellow Pages under "Synagogues." The words "Jesus Christ" are no longer used. Their saviour has now become "Yeshua ha-Mashiach." Baptism is now referred to as the Mikveh-Bris ceremony, "a rite of spiritual circumcision." Some Hebrew is used in the service. The High Holydays, Chanuka and the Passover Seder are observed with heavy Christian coloration. Well-known Christian hymns are sung and also Christianized English texts set to the tunes of familiar synagogal and Israeli melodies. This hodgepodge is known as Messianic Judaism. The cultists style themselves, naturally, Messianic Jews.

What has led to this development? First and foremost, of course, the almost complete lack of interest of American Christian denominations in sponsoring missionary activities directed solely at Jews and the disappearance of most of the independent missions to the Jews. This has made necessary a face-lifting operation, a decided change in appearance and methodology on the part of those converted Jews who want to attract other Jews into Christianity.

In addition to the Messianic Synagogues, some dynamic individuals have been hard at work concocting this strange brew. The most dynamic is a shrewd, glib, knowledgeable, completely dedicated charmer who calls himself Moishe Rosen. He was born as Martin Meyer Rosen in Denver, Colo., about forty-nine years ago in a traditional Jewish family. He was converted in 1953 while working as a camera salesman. He graduated in the Spring of 1957 from the Northeastern Bible Institute, Essex Falls, N.Y., was ordained a Baptist minister in Denver on August 28 of the same year, and went to work for the American Board of Missions to the Jews at its mission in Los Angeles. In 1966 he was brought to New York to direct the ABMJ missionary training program. His school graduated its biggest class in 1969—seven, all non-Jews. Desiring to engage in a more satisfying endeavor, Rosen went to San Francisco in 1970, still under the auspices of the ABMJ, and began to try to convert the Jewish "street people" in that city, the Jewish down-and-outers, those who, according to Rosen, were completely alienated from their parents and had been rejected by the synagogue and the Jewish community—the drug addicts, hippy rebels, loose livers, antisocial freaks. He gave his missionary effort the dramatic title "Jews for Jesus." He soon acquired a small but very vocal band of followers; and "Jews for Jesus" received widespread publicity in the religious and general press.

For about the first three years of his San Francisco work, Rosen continued to follow the long-accepted missionary line that Jewish converts, while they may consider themselves Jews ethnically and culturally, should join one of the established Christian denominations. He gradually became convinced that Jews do not need to become denominational Christians when they accept Jesus as their messiah and saviour. They can remain Jews, Messianic Jews. This change in conviction resulted in Rosen and the ABMJ parting company. The executive director of the ABMJ, Daniel Fuchs, had given Rosen's efforts in San Francisco his warm support, despite some criticism from Christian sources, but, when Rosen came out for Messianic Judaism, that was too much. It was no good for ABMJ's business. Since then Rosen has been on his own, raising funds independently, preaching, lecturing, writing, sending his singing group, the Liberated Wailing Wall, up and down the land, and making quite a name for himself in Fundamental ranks.

Another key figure in Messianic Judaism is Mike Evans, executive director of Bnai Yeshua, an outfit which draws much of its spiritual as well as financial strength from the charismatic fever that is currently surging through American Fundamentalism. The headquarters of Bnai Yeshua is in Stony Brook, L.I., N.Y. Other star performers on the Messianic Jewish circuit are spellbinder Arthur Katz, leader of Washington, D.C.'s "synagogue" Manny Brotman, and, last but far from least, popular singer Pat Boone. In an article in a widely read movie magazine, Pat has described how he and his family have been converted to Messianic Judaism. Pat, in all seriousness, believes that, through joining this movement, he has become a Jew.

Up to 1973 neither Moishe Rosen nor the Bnai Yeshua had taken a very active interest in the Hebrew Christian Alliance; but, in just two years, they, together with the leaders of the various Messianic Synagogues, moved in on the HCAA and took over completely, so completely that they were able, in July 1975, to change the name of the organization to the Messianic Jewish Alliance of America. This change was made over the bitter opposition of the old-line Hebrew Christian members of the Alliance and the keen displeasure of the heads of those independent missions to the Jews that still exist.

In October, 1975, the Fellowship of Christian Testimonies to the Jews, composed of representatives of the independent Jewish missions, passed a resolution of condemnation which deserves to be quoted in full because it describes vividly the outward structure of Messianic Judaism:

> Inasmuch as a segment of the modern movement of Messianic Judaism publicly declares itself to be a fourth branch of Judaism, we

of the Fellowship of Christian Testimonies to the Jews, at our annual meeting held October 16-19, 1975, feel constrained to make the following statement:

Whereas a segment of Messianic Judaism strives to be a denomination within Judaism alongside of orthodox, conservative, and reform Judaism, thus confusing law and grace, we of the FCTJ affirm that the New Testament teaches that the Christian faith is consistent with, but not a continuation of biblical Judaism, and is distinct from rabbinical Judaism.

Whereas a segment of Messianic Judaism claims to be a synagogue, and not a church, we of the FCTJ affirm that the New Testament clearly distinguishes between the synagogue and the church; therefore, Bible-believing Hebrew Christians should be aligned with the local church in fellowship with Gentile believers.

Whereas a segment of Messianic Judaism encourages Gentile Christians to undergo a conversion to Judaism, we of the FCTJ affirm that this violates the tenor of the New Testament in general and the Books of Galatians and Hebrews in particular for it involves converting to a religion that clearly denies the messiahship of Jesus.

Whereas a segment of Messianic Judaism adopts the practices of rabbinic Judaism (instituted by Jewish leadership who rejected the Person and work of Jesus Christ), e.g., kosher laws, wearing skull caps and prayer shawls, et al., we of the FCTJ affirm that any practice of culture, Jewish or non-Jewish, must be brought into conformity with New Testament theology.

Whereas a segment of Messianic Judaism isolates itself from the local church, rebuilding the "middle wall of partition," thus establishing a pseudo-cultural pride, we of the FCTJ affirm the necessity of the Hebrew Christian expressing his culture and his spiritual gifts in the context of the local church thus edifying the Body of Christ as a whole and not an isolated pseudo-culture.

Whereas a segment of Messianic Judaism opposes the usage of terms such as "Jesus," "Christ," "Christian," "cross," et al., and insists on using the Hebrew terms *exclusively*, we of the FCTJ affirm that, though we endorse tactfulness in witness, we reject a presentation of the Gospel which is a subtle attempt to veil and camouflage the Person and work of our Lord Jesus Christ.

Whereas segments of Messianic Judaism, by portraying themselves to be synagogues with rabbis for the purpose of attracting unsuspecting Jews, employ methods which are unethical, we of the FCTJ affirm that Jewish missions must be honest and biblical in their message and approach and reject the concept that "the end justifies the means."

Be it resolved, therefore, that we of the FCTJ stand apart from and in opposition to Messianic Judaism as it is evolving today.

Responding to this hostile action, a group of Messianic Jewish leaders issued the following statement:

In recent months, there has been some controversy as to what the Messianic Jews believe. Due to this controversy, Messianic Jewish leaders and others associated with the movement have purposed to issue the following statement which is to outline in a concise way the belief of Messianic Jews. We pray this statement will clear up any misunderstanding in this area.
As Messianic Jews we believe:

1. That the Holy Scriptures, Old Covenant and New Covenant, were given by God, are divinely inspired, and are infallible.
2. That the nature of God is plural, consisting of the Father, Son, and the Holy Spirit.
3. That no man can obtain salvation or eternal reconciliation with God unless they repent of their sins and accept by faith the atoning work of the Blood of the Messiah Yeshua (Jesus) and believe that He died and was resurrected in triumph over sin to sit at the right hand of God forevermore.
4. Because of this work of atonement, the middle wall of partition between Jew and Gentile has been broken down, and by God's Spirit are now one in the body of the Jewish Messiah, Yeshua.

To obtain financial support from the fundamentalist Christian community, the Messianic Jewish Alliance listed the following aims in the Fall 1975 issue of its quarterly publication:

The Messianic Jewish Alliance of America aims:

1. To continue to bring to the attention of the Christian churches of America their inescapable biblical obligation to present the message of the gospel to the Jew as well as to the Gentile.
2. To develop and promote a program designed to acquaint the Jews of America with the Messiahsip of the Lord Jesus (Yeshua the Messiah).
3. To maintain a vital relationship with Messianic Jewish people in Israel.
. . . To help finance this program the Alliance appeals for regular contributions from the members and friends of the Alliance.
. . . Gifts to the Messianic Jewish Alliance of America are deductible in computing your income tax.

What does this all add up to? The leopard has changed his spots; but he is still the same leopard. Hebrew Christians or Messianic Jews, the goal of both is the same, to convert Jews to Christianity. The approach of the Messianic Jewish Alliance certainly is new. There will be many who will agree with the Fellowship of Christian Testimonies to the Jews that it is also unethical, because the leopard is now attempting to enchant many spiritually depressed and Jewishly naïve and ignorant young of our people in the guise of a Lion of Judah.

There is, as yet, little reason for assuming that, in the long run, this new tactic will be any more successful or enduring than the many others which have preceded it. The Messianic Jewish leaders would love to have the Jewish press and the Jewish self-defense agencies utter shrill cries of alarm. The perceptive Jewish public relations experts learned long ago that the best way to handle such far-out folks as these is to wait patiently for their steam to run out and their engines to run down. In short, they should not be given valuable publicity by open hostility. But this external precaution must be accompanied by a major internal effort, educational and cultural, to instil in as large a proportion of our people as possible such a knowledge of and a pride in our religious heritage that they will readily and realistically assess the message and the intent of the leopard, no matter what the size or the color of its spots.

Chapter Thirteen

Conclusion

This account of Christian attempts to convert the Jews of the United States and Canada will be concluded with a number of general comments. Practically all of these attempts have been made by Protestant fundamentalists. Judged by the effort expended, the money spent, and the overall results, these attempts have failed. The only American religious groups that have had a fairly substantial number of Jews join their ranks are Christian Science, Unitarianism-Universalism, and Ethical Culture. None of these has made any very special effort to attract Jews. It is just that, for one reason or another, each has had something to offer that some Jews found to their liking, something that filled an important physical or spiritual need for a particular individual. It would seem that, if a non-Jewish religion desires to gain members from the Jewish community, the best plan to follow is to build up a religious mystique and then present it to the general public in such a way that some Jews will learn about it and be attracted to it, as seems to be the case at this writing with the way-out teachings of the paper-tiger Korean Reverend Mr. Moon.

There was a time when the small number of Jews who converted to Fundamental Christianity came almost exclusively from Orthodox backgrounds. Missionaries conceded that it was practically impossible to convert a person born as a Reform Jew. That time is past. The number of

193

Jews who are being converted to Fundamental Christianity is still small, but such converts no longer come just from Orthodox Judaism. Now they are mostly alienated young people who have been neglected by their parents and who feel unloved, abandoned. They hunger for love, for spiritual peace. They turn to sex, to drugs, to way-out religions, to anything which seems to offer a cure for their overwhelming sense of loneliness. Moishe Rosen, who works with such Jewish young people in San Francisco, estimates that about half of them come from Orthodox homes and the rest, about equally divided, from Conservative and Reform homes.

How many people born as Jews are now practicing Christians in the United States and Canada? This is a difficult statistic to determine accurately. The figure used currently by leading American Hebrew Christians is fifty thousand.

How does this compare with the number of persons born as Christians who are now practicing Jews in the United States and Canada? This, too, is a figure which cannot be calculated with absolute accuracy. In 1953 I sent a questionnaire on this subject to all Conservative and Reform rabbis in the United States. Sixty-eight percent of the Conservative rabbis and 91 percent of the Reform rabbis responded. At that time each Conservative rabbi was converting an average of one non-Jew a year and each Reform rabbi two non-Jews. On the basis of these findings, I estimated that about three thousand non-Jews were then being converted to Judaism annually in the United States. Using the 1953 rabbinic average as a guide (although the present rabbinic averages are probably higher), the present annual number of converts to Judaism in the United States and Canada would be at least forty-five hundred. Non-Jews who become Jews maintain no separate identity within the Jewish community; but, if the figure just given is valid, it would mean that the number of persons born as non-Jews who are now identified religiously with the American Jewish community is far in excess of fifty thousand. And this is so despite the fact that until very recently organized efforts by American Jews to convert American non-Jews have been non-existent.

May the American Jewish community hope that, at any time in the foreseeable future, all fundamentalist Christians will cease their attempts to convert Jews? No, it may not. To try to save the souls of "God's chosen people" is as natural to many of these backward religionists as breathing.

And will such future efforts be any more successful than they have been in the past? A direct answer to this question would be purely theoretical and therefore of dubious value. But perhaps there is a way to answer the question obliquely through the telling of a story that was popular among West European Jews during the last century:

Three men were traveling in the same railway carriage from Berlin to Potsdam. As they talked, it developed that all three were baptized Jews. They began to discuss the reasons for their conversions. One candidly asserted that he had embraced Christianity in order to advance himself politically. The second stated that his sweetheart, a devout Christian, had refused to marry him if he remained a Jew. The third turned his eyes heavenward and piously exclaimed, "I became a Christian after I was firmly convinced that Christianity is greatly superior to Judaism." Without a moment's hesitation, the other two retorted, "Reden Sie das den Goyim," which means, "Save that speech for the Gentiles."

Footnotes

CHAPTER TWO

[1] Anita Lebeson, *Jewish Pioneers in America*, p. 68.
[2] George Foote Moore, *Judah Monis*, p. 20.
[3] George A. Kohut, *Ezra Stiles and the Jews*, p. 42.
[4] *American Jewish Historical Society Publications*, Vol. XXVI, pp. 201-210.
[5] Lee M. Friedman, *Early American Jews*, p. 6.
[6] Kohut, *op. cit.*, p. 38.
[7] Lebeson, *op. cit.*, p. 96.
[8] Kohut, *op. cit.*, p. 46.
[9] *American Jewish Historical Society Publications*, Vol. IV, p. 198.
[10] Louis Meyer, *Jewish Era*, April, 1912, p. 49.

CHAPTER THREE

[1] *Jewish Intelligencer*, Vol. I, pp. 40-42.
[2] *Loc. cit.*
[3] *Loc. cit.*
[4] See Frey's *Narrative*, 9th ed., New York, 1832.
[5] H. H. Norris, *The Origin, Progress, and Existing Circumstances of the London Society for Promoting Christianity Amongst the Jews: An Historical Inquiry*, London, 1825, p. 22.
[6] *Jewish Repository*, May, 1813, p. 69.
[7] Sixth report, London Jews Society, p. 10.
[8] Seventh report, London Jews Society, p. 12.
[9] For full documentation, see article by G. J. Miller in publications of Bibliographical Society of America, Vol. XXX, 1936, pp. 1-56.

CHAPTER FOUR

[1] *Memoir of Miss Hannah Adams, Boston*, 1832, pp. 49-50.
[2] *Christian Herald*, August 1, 1818, pp. 272-275.

3 *Panoplist and Missionary Herald,* July, 1819, pp. 328-329.
4 Twenty-first report, American Society for Meliorating the Condition of the Jews, 1844, p. 24.
5 *Dictionary of American Biography,* Vol. XX, p. 341.
6 *Ibid.*
7 Twenty-first report, American Society for Meliorating the Condition of the Jews, p. 24.
8 Lee M. Friedman, *Early American Jews,* p. 101.
9 *Christian Herald,* March 1, 1817.
10 This letter is in the *Christian Herald,* November 4, 1820, pp. 392-397, and the *Virginia Evangelical and Literary Magazine,* January 1823, pp. 43-49.
11 *Hebrew Messenger,* January 1846, pp. 19-21.
12 *Loc. cit.*

CHAPTER FIVE

1 *Hebrew Messenger,* January, 1846, pp. 19-21.
2 George Houston, *Israel Vindicated . . . .,* December, 1820, p. 5.
3 Copy in archives of American Jewish Historical Society.
4 *Christian Herald,* July 5, 1823.
5 *Memoirs of John Quincy Adams,* Vol. X, pp. 90-91.
6 *Jewish Chronicle,* March, 1846, p. 282.
7 *Virginia Evangelical and Literary Magazine,* September, 1823, p. 496.
8 Sixteenth report, London Jews Society, 1824, p. 13.
9 Simon's report in *Israel's Advocate,* October, 1824, pp. 146-147.
10 *Loc. cit.*
11 *Israel's Advocate,* April, 1824, pp. 50-51.
12 *Israel's Advocate,* March, 1824.
13 *Israel's Advocate,* April 1824, pp. 51-53.
14 Second report, American Society for Meliorating the Condition of the Jews, p. 35.
15 *Israel's Advocate,* July, 1824, pp. 106-110.
16 *Israel's Advocate,* April, 1825, p. 49.
17 *Israel's Advocate,* May, 1825, pp. 69-70.
18 *Ibid.,* pp. 65-66.
19 *Israel's Advocate,* August, 1825, pp. 113-125.
20 *Israel's Advocate,* August, 1825.
21 Fifth report, American Society for Meliorating the Condition of the Jews, 1827, Appendix.
22 *Ibid.,* pp. 10-11.
23 Seventh report, American Society for Meliorating the Condition of the Jews, 1829, pp. 25-38.
24 Eighth report, American Society for Meliorating the Condition of the Jews, 1830.
25 Frey's *Narrative,* 9th ed., 1832.
26 Quoted in Frey's *Judah and Israel,* 3rd ed., New York, 1840.
27 Frey, *Report of the late Agency,* New York, 1839, p. 1.
28 *Jewish Chronicle,* June, 1854, p. 251.
29 Frey, *Report of the late Agency,* p. 21.
30 *Ibid.,* p. 6.
31 *Jewish Chronicle,* February, 1846, p. 248.

CHAPTER SIX

1 *Christian Herald,* July 1, 1820, p. 153.
2 *Jewish Era,* April, 1912, pp. 49-57.

CHAPTER SEVEN

[1] *Jewish Chronicle*, January, 1843.
[2] *Ibid.*, May, 1854.
[3] *Ibid.*, January, 1843.
[4] *Ibid.*
[5] Twenty-first report, American Society for Meliorating the Condition of the Jews, 1844, pp. 22-23.
[6] *Occident*, April, 1843, p. 47.
[7] *Jewish Chronicle*, Vol. II, p. 49.
[8] *Occident*, January, 1844, pp. 511-512.
[9] Twenty-first report, American Society for Meliorating the Condition of the Jews, 1844.
[10] *American Israelite*, January 12, 1855, p. 214.
[11] *Missionary Review of the World*, December, 1904, pp. 902-908.
[12] Letter in *Occident*, October, 1848, p. 348.
[13] *Jewish Chronicle*, June, 1854, p. 251.
[14] *Jewish Era*, January, 1908, p. 11.
[15] *Jewish Chronicle*, June, 1851.
[16] I. M. Wise, *Reminiscences*, p. 65.
[17] *Ibid.*, pp. 65-68.
[18] *Jewish Chronicle*, January, 1854, pp. 177-179.
[19] Quoted from Lee M. Friedman's *Early American Jews*, p. 111.
[20] *American Israelite*, August 17, 1855, p. 47.
[21] *Ibid.*, August 31, 1855, p. 58.
[22] *Ibid.*, November 14, 1855, p. 147.
[23] Quoted in *Jewish Messenger*, April, 1859, p. 100.
[24] *Israelite Indeed*, September, 1859, p. 153.
[25] Forty-first Anniversary report, American Society for Meliorating the Condition of the Jews, p. 5.
[26] *Israelite Indeed*, May, 1870, p. 246.

CHAPTER EIGHT

[1] *Jewish Messenger*, May 17, 1867, p. 5.
[2] *Hebrew Messenger*, January, 1846.
[3] *Ibid.*
[4] *Ibid.*, p. 22.
[5] *Hebrew Messenger*, November, 1846, p. 258.
[6] Friedman, *Early American Jews*, p. 111.
[7] Sprague, *Annals of the American Pulpit*, Vol. VI, p. 761.
[8] From preface of Jaeger's *Mind and Heart in Religion*.
[9] *American Israelite*, July 12, 1872, p. 8.
[10] Henry Einspruch in *Hebrew Christian Alliance Quarterly*, July, 1932, p. 1.
[11] *Missionary Review of the World*, August, 1891.
[12] Published minutes of the Conference, p. 11.
[13] *Israelite Indeed*, July, 1864, pp. 14-15.
[14] *Jewish Messenger*, March 5, 1875, p. 6.
[15] Philadelphia *Sunday Mercury* as quoted in *Jewish Messenger*, August 12, 1870, p. 5.
[16] *Occident*, May, 1862, p. 95.
[17] Quoted in *American Israelite*, May 2, 1873, p. 1.
[18] Tractate Sanhedrin 106a.

[19] Pp. 11-12.
[20] *Occident*, October, 1843, p. 352.
[21] *Ibid.*, January, 1844, p. 511.
[22] *American Israelite*, January 16, 1857, p. 222.
[23] *Israelite Indeed*, August, 1866, p. 25.
[24] *Loc. cit.*
[25] *Ibid.*, February, 1860, p. 190.
[26] *Ibid.*, August, 1866, p. 27.
[27] *Ibid.*, July, 1866, p. 22.
[28] *American Israelite*, May 12, 1876.
[29] *Ibid.*, May 26, 1876.
[30] *Ibid.*, June 20, 1879.
[31] Quoted in *Israelite Indeed*, May, 1869.
[32] *Jewish Messenger*, April 7, 1876, p. 4.
[33] *American Israelite*, August 20, 1875, p. 5.
[34] *American Hebrew*, September 30, 1887, p. 116.
[35] New York *Sun*, March 12, 1876.

CHAPTER NINE

[1] *American Hebrew*, October 2, 1891, p. 208.
[2] *Hebrew Standard*, January 18, 1894, p. 1.
[3] Letter to author.
[4] Letter to author.
[5] *The Friend of Zion*, December, 1945, p. 85.
[6] *Fifty Years*, pp. 29-30.
[7] *Missionary Review of the World*, August, 1923, pp. 635ff.
[8] New York *Times*, July 2, 1967, p. 12.

CHAPTER TEN

[1] *American Hebrew*, November 18, 1887, p. 28.
[2] Emma Felsenthal, *Bernard Felsenthal*, p. 72.
[3] *Glory of Israel*, June, 1903, p. 134.
[4] *The Chosen People*, November, 1952, pp. 4-6; Joseph H. Cohn, *I Have Fought a Good Fight*, 1953, p. 178.

CHAPTER ELEVEN

[1] *American Hebrew*, December 5, 1902, p. 65.
[2] *The Chosen People*, March, 1952, pp. 5-6.
[3] From second edition, titled *My Return to Judaism*, 1922, pp. 61-62.
[4] *Ibid.*, pp. 109-110.
[5] *Hebrew Standard*, June 3, 1910, p. 9.
[6] *Brooklyn Jewish Examiner*, March 8, 1946.
[7] New York *Times*, January 31, 1947, p. 18.

CHAPTER TWELVE

[1] *Jewish Post and Opinion*, January 4, 1974.

Index